READING GEORGE SZIRTES

JOHN SEARS

Reading
George Szirtes

BLOODAXE BOOKS

ISBN: 978 1 85224 814 7

First published 2008 by
Bloodaxe Books Ltd,
Highgreen,
Tarset,
Northumberland NE48 1RP.

www.bloodaxebooks.com
For further information about Bloodaxe titles
please visit our website or write to
the above address for a catalogue.

Bloodaxe Books Ltd acknowledges
the financial assistance of
Arts Council England, North East.

Cover design: Neil Astley & Pamela Robertson-Pearce.

Printed in Great Britain by
Bell & Bain Limited, Glasgow, Scotland.

Patricianak, and i.m. Marion Sears, 1934-2002

ACKNOWLEDGEMENTS

All quotations of George Szirtes' poetry are taken from his *New & Collected Poems* (Bloodaxe Books, 2008). Early versions of parts of Chapter 6 were published in *The Anachronist*, Volume 11, 2005, and in the Scapes issue of *Cahiers Charles V*, 2006. Thanks are due to the editors and the anonymous readers of both journals for their comments. Shorter versions of other chapters were delivered between 2004 and 2007 at conferences in London (at The British Library), and at universities in Debrecen, Warwick, Paris, Nantes, Stirling, Oxford, Manchester and Bergen. I'm grateful to the organisers of all these events, and to the panels and audiences for their comments and suggestions. Thanks are also due to George Szirtes for his support for and help with this book, and to Raphaël Costambeys-Kempczynski, Ann Hoff, Michael Murphy and Berthold Schoene. My thanks and love go to Patricia Allmer, who has supported me throughout.

The writing of this book was made possible by a sabbatical term granted by Manchester Metropolitan University's English Research Institute.

Quotations from 'Translating Zsuzsa Rakovsky' and 'Fables of Home' are taken from the online versions of the essays, available at http://www.hungarianquarterly.com/no150/031.html.

Quotations from George Szirtes' interview with Lidia Vianu are taken from the online version available at http://lidiavianu.scriptmania.com/george_szirtes.htm

CONTENTS

1

Introduction: Reading George Szirtes

To read is to translate

W.H. AUDEN, 'Reading'

George Szirtes' poetry is formed by the act of reading. His poems often perform kinds of reading, engaging in scrutinising and interpreting the world or representations of it in paintings, photographs, or other poems. Many of his poems are informed by the works of other writers, acknowledging and responding to contemporaries and to specific traditions, constructing and contributing to a shared community of the written and the read. Increasingly frequently they have been actively engaged in the specific demands of transforming, by translation, the works of other, Hungarian, writers into English, an engagement that expresses Szirtes' own double, Hungarian and English, identity. Reading is the mechanism through which art's encounter with the world and the reader's encounter with the poem become manifest, available for interpretation within the formal structure of the poem. It provides a recurrent metaphor for the ways in which Szirtes' poetry tries to make sense of what it addresses, the experiences and histories it encounters – sometimes his own, sometimes those of other members of his family, sometimes those that describe a culture or a group identity. Poetry's reading and the reading of poetry, understood in relation to the activities of performing, informing and transforming, involve a comprehension of poetry as *formed*, a response to the world that uses formed, organised structures and patterns of words to try to make sense of reality.

Reading and cognate activities like interpreting, scrutinising, analysing, and decoding, as well as opposing terms suggesting the obscurity, illegibility and incomprehensibility of the world, offer images and metaphors that thread their way through Szirtes' poetry, constructing realities comprised of signs demanding (and sometimes resisting) different kinds of interpretation. A poem in *The Slant Door*, 'In the Classroom', describes '*M. Le Professeur*' 'Scribbling important illegible words / To a bunch of idiots'; 'The Courtyards', a key sequence of poems in *The Photographer in Winter*, notes 'little dingy signs', a graffitied 'message in rough capitals' and a 'blind woman' who reads the world as she 'feels her way along'; *Blind Field* opens with the act of reading that 'begins' as 'You turn the page'. Throughout the *œuvre*, reading offers a multitude of metaphors for the poet's scrutiny of the world, and the poem's effort to make the world, a space both 'important' and 'illegible', make sense; the title poem of *Reel* offers the world as 'Extended clauses of a broken sentence / of which you recognise the odd stray word', a world encoded in a language both legible and opaque, susceptible to analysis but also unyielding, withholding the meanings it seems to contain. Translation itself offers the definitive figure for this double offering and retaining of meaning; the increasing prominence of translations in Szirtes' work indicates his developing sense of the work's fluid, shifting position in relation to Hungarian literature and language, and to Hungarian versions of the historical experiences Szirtes analyses in his own poetry. Hungary both contains and withholds meanings and potential solutions to the questions Szirtes' poetry asks; in collections like *Metro* and *Bridge Passages* it occupies an enigmatic position, a territory open to and resistant to scrutiny.

His poetry, a product above all of the history it struggles to represent and understand, explores, through these interpretive processes, some of the most difficult questions facing European cultures in the aftermath of the Second World War. At its most powerful, in expressing a deep emotional and intellectual engagement with profoundly personal and often traumatic experiences, it sustains an intensity of reference and intellectual comprehension that remains, as it's put in a poem called 'Turquoise' in his late collection *Reel*, 'perfectly aware / of its mortality as part of the design'; it casts a cool gaze across landscapes of historical destruction and suffering, and finds in them redeeming details and images, fragments of compassion and connection that sustain the work and the reader. It is always overtly concerned with the difficulties of how to "speak" appropriately of unspeakable events, of using language to express complex, personally felt but socially experienced ideas, emotions and perceptions; its constant struggle is with what, in another late poem, 'The Looking-Glass Dictionary', are referred to as 'blank languages whose words refuse to mean'. The poetry explores the possibilities of literary forms as a set of devices enabling poetry to do certain things, but is also haunted by the underlying anxiety that poetry may not be able, in the end, actually to do these things at all, that what poetry can do with 'blank languages' may be very different from what poets and readers demand of it. The desire that poetry be effective within the world of action, and that it have some kind of effect upon its readers rather than simply 'refusing to mean', is central to Szirtes' understanding of how poetry works, and of what kinds of work it might do. This desire is however always tempered by uncertainty; he frequently refers in essays and reviews to Auden's comprehension of poetry as 'a way of happening, a voice', a space in which the 'happening' of the world can be meditated upon and understood.

Szirtes' work sees this exploration the possibilities offered by poetry as a formal mode of expression in terms of a kind of artistic duty, a way of fulfilling the requirement that art should say complex things within structural limits and frameworks, and do so with the authority of intellect and perception. Conspicuous, sometimes elaborate, formal construction is often a defining element of a Szirtes poem, and he has written frequently of his preoccupation with form. His poems work within what he calls, in an essay on 'Translating Zsuzsa Rakovszky', the 'whispers' and 'ghosts' of form. They consistently locate themselves in-between the formal (the structural consistencies and regularities aspired to by the poem itself) and the informal or formless (the chaos of the world, what Louis MacNeice calls, in a phrase that reverberates through Szirtes' early poetry, 'the drunkenness of things being various'), into which the poem inserts itself, and which it seeks to represent, contain, engage with or respond to. This deliberately ambiguous location allows the poems to generate fluidity out of their aesthetic architecture, to demonstrate the mobility of form that allows an intellectual (formed, organised), as well as an emotional, response to the world. In his poems, syntax and enjambment run counter to Szirtes' preferred metres in a typical movement that he understands as 'counterpoint': 'For me,' he writes in key statement of credo, 'Formal Wear: Notes on Rhyme, Meter, Stanza & Pattern', 'the music of poetry lies in what I think of as counterpoint: the counterpoint between the line and the sentence', where the line measures formal requirements against the rhythms of grammatical rule, regulating the poem's distilling of sense. Discussing the translator's relation to poetic form in 'Translating Zsuzsa Rakovszky', Szirtes writes: 'I listen to Frost's description of the basic unit of verse being the sentence, which I take to be the point, and I pin this out against the complex patterns of stanza structure – counterpoint.' The allusion here is to classical music, but the associations are with the oppositional or dialectical structures familiar to literary theories. He describes this as 'a flexible poetics...capable of surprising through its narrative sequence via the sentence, while offering reassurance through rhyme, metre and stanza'.[1]

Sometimes Szirtes' 'surprising' sentences are fractured, abbre-
viated, almost list-like in their paratactic co-ordination, their attempt
to include as much as possible, but organised by metre and rhyme;
elsewhere, end-stopping serves as a structuring element, a closure
that works to control the line, and allow the fragments to come
into alignment with the formal structure, allowing different units
– the stanza, the rhyme-scheme or the line itself – to determine
the spacing of the poem's argument and the information it con-
tains. Many of Szirtes' poems utilise forms that are left deliberately
incomplete (like the thirteen-line pseudo-sonnets that make up the
sequence 'Metro'), or are shattered (like the seemingly fragmented
sonnet sequence that constitutes the collection *Bridge Passages*), or
are ambitiously, splendidly over-ornate (like the Hungarian sonnet
sequences that conclude *Portrait of My Father in an English Land-
scape*). Many incorporate conventionally European forms (like the
Italian *terza rima* which Szirtes increasingly seems to prefer), forc-
ing another perspective on the consideration of the Englishness of
his work.

Peter McDonald has argued that 'form is the serious heart of a
poem – an amused or amusing poem as much as a troubled or
perplexed one – where such "authority" as poetry bears must
reside'.[2] Szirtes' complex use of form, his reliance upon form as
the mechanism through which difficult, demanding questions of
history and aesthetics can (however inadequately or incompletely)
be addressed, testifies to the location of the seriousness of the
poem within the form of the poem itself. Szirtes' poems often
exploit the confluences and indeterminate spaces between lyric
and narrative; they sometimes veer towards symbolist and mod-
ernist styles and forms, and frequently return to a compromised,
problematic lyricism via vestigial or transformed pastoral and
Romantic traditions. They engage, across the *œuvre*, with a signifi-
cant selection of the range of forms available to the contemporary
poet writing in English, and do so with a creative zeal that sug-
gests that formal experimentation is an important marker of the
poet's personal sense of difference, as well as a signifier of the aes-
thetic and political seriousness of the particular poetic project.

His poems, often haunted by 'ghosts' of private memory and of
the public past, are also deeply indebted to the formal variety that
constitutes the wider, European poetic tradition. Form enables
community, he has argued, in a passage that seeks to account for
the poet's place in relation to tradition:

> The community is, by its nature, a community of ghosts. One of my
> favourite images of the artistic act is from Emily Dickinson, who said

that art was a house that tried to be haunted. Each artist – but since we are talking of poetry here, let us say each poet – builds some kind of house, the point of the house being to entice the ghost in. My own house is what I am inclined by history and instinct to build, but the ghost it is trying to attract is related to those of other writers of similar predicaments and temperaments. I think I can vaguely see my house as a series of rooms arranged in the form of a tenement block of the kind that seems almost to sing to me in Budapest. I do very much suspect that I am, in some sense, erecting the buildings my own lost selves might have inhabited.[3]

Szirtes' poetry is overpopulated with these ghosts or 'lost selves', verbal traces of figures haunting the poet's consciousness and the worlds he constructs. As early as *November and May* his poetry is working through images and experiences that evoke ghostly memories of his mother. Ghosts, furthermore, appear as formal emanations, elements of a larger, deeper pattern implicit within each poem and sometimes detectable across whole groups or sequences, and frequently (as in the quote above) connected to images and metaphors deriving from architecture – the haunted house, the 'tenement block', the 'buildings' erected to house 'lost selves'. Form, an integral manifestation of the 'spectral' histories and ghostly doubles and alternate selves that Szirtes' poetry often addresses, is both internal to the individual poem and imposed upon it, intrinsic and extrinsic; its double position corresponds in indirect, sometimes indeterminate ways to the 'inner cartography'[4] mapped out by Szirtes' earlier work, a mapping of internalised experiences onto the external form of the poem which is also a transformation of those experiences into the poem's form, a reworking of the internal into the external.

In this reworking, the internal world – the raw material of lyrical experience, the poet's subjective encounter with the world – returns as the external world, itself unknowable in anything other than its external lineaments, the world Szirtes describes in a short poem, 'Soil' (published in *Blind Field* and later reprinted, significantly, as the final poem in each of the retrospective selections *Selected Poems 1976-1996* and *The Budapest File*), as

home, which is nowhere to be found
and yet
is here, unlost, solid, the very ground
on which you stand but cannot visit
or know.

This palpable sense of banishment from the knowable world and, importantly, from 'visiting' that world (with all the connotations of exile and exclusion that such a ban implies) underpins all Szirtes' poetry and is integral to the uncertain province of 'home' and 'ground' within this poem and, implicitly, throughout the *œuvre*. The curtailed line 'and yet' expresses the residual hope in 'Soil' for presence in absence, which is subverted by the poem's succeeding elaboration, in which the unknowably absent is reasserted as the ultimate feature of an experience of belonging irretrievably past – a metaphor for the poet's experience of returning to a place from which he has been exiled. It is an 'and yet' which silently appends itself to all Szirtes' poetic assertions, haunting their authority with an implicit alternative narrative, the 'ghost' of another form and another argument, a proviso that tempers and undermines, qualifying the very possibility of statement within such an unreliable medium as poetry.

A kind of ambivalence lurks within this residual 'and yet', the ambivalence of an intellectual engagement with the world that situates its seriousness within multiple perspectives. Ambivalence is a correlate of seriousness, of a refusal of the simple; it manifests itself, in the poetry, in the particular set of difficulties presented to readers by Szirtes' work. His *œuvre* can conveniently be divided into three rough 'periods' – an early period, up to and including *Short Wave* (1983); a middle period, extending roughly from 1984 to the publication in 1994 of *Blind Field*; and a late period stretching from the mid-1990s up to the present. These periods, as we shall see, map onto significant personal and historical events in significant ways. Difficulty, in different ways, is integral to each period. In a review of *Portrait of My Father in an English Landscape* (1998), the central collection of Szirtes' late period, John Greening observes that 'Szirtes uses "pre-ordained" formal difficulties to confront the challenge of coherency'.[5] Coherency, here, is what the poems both aspire to (in terms of ethical and thematic consistency) and, the reviewer suggests, what is also imposed upon them externally (by the poet's allegiance to traditions and conventions), creating poems which are pre-bound by formal determinants, rigidly entrapped in formal expectations. My contention throughout this book is that Szirtes' poetry constantly resists such pre-determination – form, far from being established before the poem, exists as a template which comes into being through the poem's specific counterpoint between the pre-existing formal pattern and the specific transformation of that pattern by the given poem.

Reviewing *Metro*, a key text in the middle period, Sean O'Brien comments that 'Szirtes has accepted some major problems for which lyric equipment is likely to prove insufficient'.[6] O'Brien's comment pinpoints the initial problem that Szirtes encounters, the

necessity of moving from the conventional lyric voice available to
contemporary poets (what McDonald calls 'the stereotypical short
lyric poem', which, among other things, 'will cultivate a knowing
irony in relation to everything but its own control of language'
and with which the reader 'will be able to identify')[7] into a poetic
space which eschews the comforts afforded by such a voice in order
to explore other material, material that is sometimes so 'other' that
the (English) lyric voice has neglected or failed, historically, to
accommodate it. The 'insufficiency' of lyric equipment to provide
the requisite seriousness, the necessary combination of emotional
distance and ethical proximity to the subject-matter, becomes the
ground of the formal problem Szirtes sets himself in poems like
'Metro', and in that collection and others in this period. The
founding tension is between his sense that selfhood springs from
the world in these poems, and that, at the same time, that self-
hood is destroyed (as the absence of selfhood, the failure of the
lyric 'I', testifies) in the poem's act of recuperating that world, and
the version of the self that the poem constructs is, anyway, inade-
quate to the demands faced by the poem itself. Seamus Heaney
characterises this as 'the poet's need to get beyond ego in order to
become the voice of more than autobiography'.[8] Lyric, in Szirtes'
grappling with this 'need', comes into critical and constructive
conflict with narrative, and generates 'difficulty', that density of
language, form and symbolism that presents its readers with deep,
sometimes irresolvable problems of interpretation – ambiguity,
indeterminacy, the uncertain but palpable sense of the massiveness
of events that lie beyond the borders of the poem.

Language is stretched in such poems. Form works hard to con-
tain what language constructs, and the tensions (the counterpoints)
between the two provide moments of crisis that in each poem, each
foray into the terrifying histories Szirtes addresses, threaten by
their scope to drain, flatten, oppress the reader. For O'Brien this
is ultimately an effect of the poet's 'own imagination', 'a zone in
which all periods co-exist'.[9] But this collapses the historical into
the personal, seeing, in the archaeologies the poetry performs,
another form of the self-psychoanalysis of the poet (O'Brien com-
pares Szirtes' verbal layering and density to 'Freud's image of the
mind as Rome at the opening of *Civilisation and its Discontents*').[10]
Szirtes constantly resists this collapsing, and his poetry (particu-
larly in the work of the 'difficult' middle period which O'Brien is
reviewing), while inviting (and always aware of the possibilities of)
a psychoanalytical reading, does so without falling into a conven-
tional lyric-confessional mode; it tries always to sustain Heaney's

requirement that it be 'more than autobiography'. Reviewing Szirtes' next collection, *Bridge Passages*, Sylvia Kantaris comments that 'The main content of the book is, in fact, intensely – but not heavily – serious', and notes that the poet 'is only too uncomfortably aware that he can't find his own identity'. So much for self-psychoanalysis – the intense 'seriousness', Kantaris suggests, lies in form itself, in the poet's willingness to be 'committed' (another word laden with ethical and political import) 'to putting proper words in their proper places in order to record things that suggest but resist full exposure'.[11] Such a commitment, with its echo of Coleridge's definition of poetry as 'the right words in the right order', brings us back to formal constraints as embodiments of ethical duties.

Another way of thinking about Szirtes' use of form and its relation to difficulty is to consider Antony Rowland's concept of 'awkward poetics', as outlined in his book *Holocaust Poetry*. Rowland refers in his discussion to Szirtes' introduction to a translation of the Hungarian poet Miklós Radnóti's *Camp Notebook* (a collection of poems written by Rádnoti about his internment and forced march during the Second World War; he was eventually murdered by the Nazis in 1944), but does not address Szirtes' poetry. Nevertheless the concept of 'awkward poetics' as Rowland uses it in discussing Ted Hughes, Sylvia Plath, Geoffrey Hill and others, is useful for examining Szirtes' own poetics. Rowland examines Tony Harrison's subversion of conventional poetics by his 'inserting irregular metrics into mellifluous pentameters', and by 'discussing how the advent of the Holocaust challenges the concept of classical humanism'. 'Awkward poetics' thus operates, for Rowland, at two levels: the formal subversion of rhythmic and metrical conventions, and the (connected, even consequent) discursive challenge to ideological orthodoxies. Rowland goes on to cite Emmanuel Levinas: 'In Levinasian terms, awkward poetics enable the poet to "adopt a position of interpretative responsibility towards the victims they are representing", which includes the rigorous examination of inherited structures.'[12] 'Irregularities' – the recognition that 'perfect metre' is banal and predictable ('doggerel', says Rowland), and that its distortion through variation, counterpoint, breakage, or resistance, provides the engine of poetic creativity at any given historical moment – is central to the possibility of 'awkward poetics'.

One is reminded of Seamus Heaney's determination, in an interview with Harriet Cooke in *The Irish Times* in 1973, 'to take the English lyric and make it eat stuff that it has never eaten before'.[13] Szirtes' poetry seeks, at its most powerful, a similar transformative effect, without the urgent, contemporary, political imperative that

motivated Heaney's anger at the height of the 'Troubles'. Szirtes'
own imperative is more retrospective, more a need to adapt the
existing frames of poetry – the formal tradition – to come to terms
with burdens and inheritances that poetry itself can barely support,
including his complex response to the Holocaust (the historical
event to which, Rowland argues, awkward poetics offers a provi-
sional, ethically sustainable response, alert to 'the specific difficul-
ties of engaging with an event so resistant to artistic representa-
tion').[14] Szirtes' poetry, furthermore, seeks responses to a compound
of historical and private events and atrocities – the Holocaust, the
Hungarian revolution of 1956, his own and his family's migration
and relocation in England, his mother's suicide, the Eastern and
Central European revolutions of 1989 – events that demand, in
different ways and to different degrees, careful, measured treatment
within the confines of the poem. His poetry seeks to respond to
these events with a care and degree of measured distance that is
ultimately, of course, impossible; nevertheless, the poetry resides
partly in the seeking, the responding, the distance, the measure.

One aspect of Szirtes' difficulty, then (and there are others,
thematic and contextual, that will be explored below), manifests
itself throughout his career, and concerns questions of form and
structure and their relation to the world of the poem and the act
of its reading. His earliest poems establish these concerns. 'Black-
birds', the first poem in the pamphlet *The Iron Clouds*, published
in 1975, exemplifies some of the ways Szirtes' work responds to
other poetry, inserting itself into and engaging with traditions and
conventions.

Blackbirds hover in the classroom:
Their panic rams ceilings down our throats
with wings scampering against the
exiled bushes. Stuck behind the windows
an excited child runs up and down
gesticulating to a horde of invisible headmistresses.

Where is the real headmistress? Where is
    the real headmistress?

Squatting on the chimney stack
dictating lethal memoranda
to the trees. She has worked
herself into mythologies:
Librarians take her out and clean her
but find no date to stamp on her.
    No fines are paid.

Blackbirds dash themselves against the glass
unwilling to accept my help.

They hate my fat fingers
and shit on the floor repeatedly.
The room is filled with blackbirds.
Open the window. Someone must open the window
    and let them out.
Vocative. Imperative. Accusative.
O good headmistress, free the black bird!
Subjunctive, subjunctive, subjunctive.[15]

The poem's title echoes Wallace Stevens' 'Thirteen Ways of
Looking at a Blackbird', inviting a reading in terms of a response
to or extension of modernist experiments in perception and repre-
sentation. Much later, Szirtes will open *Portrait of My Father in
an English Landscape* with 'Rabbits', a poem that echoes Stevens'
'A Rabbit as King of the Ghosts'; one of the poems in *Reel* des-
cribes the poet's father as being 'Like a black bird'. 'Blackbirds'
might also evoke, more distantly, other poetic blackbirds: the 'black-
bird' Edward Thomas hears in 'Adlestrop', or R.S. Thomas listening
to another blackbird in 'A Blackbird Singing' (Thomas also replied
to Wallace Stevens in his 'Thirteen Blackbirds Looking at a Man').
These poems respond to and develop the modern and postmodern
pastoral tradition to which Szirtes' work has, as we shall see, such
a complex relationship. Szirtes' poem both fits into, and extends
into a particular direction, this tradition.

The poem narrates, in unrhymed, semi-free verse, the invasion
of a school classroom by a flock of blackbirds. Demanding to be
read as a kind of narrative but also as an allegory or a generator of
free associations, it deals with the perceptions of a child, who seems
to meld with the poet's memories of his own childhood ('They
hate my fat fingers'), of the excitement of a sudden change in the
conditions of reality, the world's resistance to the child's desired
intervention ('unwilling to accept my help'), and its confusion and
consternation within the hierarchical institutional structure of the
school, with its formal demands of reading and writing, symbolised
in the 'headmistress' 'dictating lethal memoranda' and transmuting
into a library book. The poem, like the blackbirds, seems both lit-
eral and metaphorical – it hovers, like the blackbirds themselves,
in a space between a movement towards allegory (what the events
described might actually stand for) and metaphorical conceit – the
extended metaphor of the headmistress as a library book – and a
reliance upon simple language and familiar cliché ('Their panic
rams ceilings down our throats', they 'shit on the floor repeatedly')
which conveys in adult language the excited, spontaneous response

of the child to the new event. The poem's form, furthermore, is free, loose and irregular, but contains within it lines fulfilling or approximating the requirements of conventional English rhythms (like the mixture of dactyls and spondees in 'Open the window. Someone must open the window'), shadows of the formal regularity that Szirtes' poetry will develop and against which it is, at this early stage, clearly straining.

The poem's surreally comic atmosphere (reminiscent of the world of Mortmere created by Edward Upward, or that of a Donald Barthelme short story), in which the description of events relies upon incongruity and mis-placed-ness, doesn't so much develop towards a resolution as degenerate into repetition, and establishes as a central concern the complexity of reality and the poem's efforts to encapsulate it, issues which will preoccupy in different ways all Szirtes' later poetry. Language and form are here harnessed to the representation of the bizarre, an absurd situation laden with Freudian symbolism, yet sustaining a hint of the sublime in the explicit disruption of the implicitly regimented routine of the school. At the same time 'Blackbirds' sustains a Hitchcockian aura of menace (the lines 'Blackbirds hover in the classroom' and 'Blackbirds dash themselves against the glass' evoke *The Birds*, in which the central female character is a schoolteacher and one major scene involves an attack by a flock of birds on a school; the absent headmistress suggests elements of that film's paranoid, patriarchal anxiety about feminine authority).

The poem's location in a school classroom implies, perhaps, a concern with conventional structures of authority (and with experience; Szirtes was working in a school when the poem was published), but also establishes a provisional concern with the child's ways of perceiving and responding to the world; its concluding, comical renditions of the child's rote learning of grammatical moods and cases – 'Vocative. Imperative. Accusative. …/ Subjunctive, subjunctive, subjunctive' – gesture towards the recurrent concern with the structures and effects of language that will organise and direct much of Szirtes' later work. That last line faintly echoes, and parodies, the prayer-like conclusion of T.S. Eliot's *The Waste Land* ('Shantih. Shantih. Shantih.'), and the image of the headmistress 'squatting on the chimney stack' might also echo Eliot's unpleasant image of the Jewish landlord who 'squats on the windowsill' in 'Gerontion'. We might also note the repeated anxiety about the reality of the headmistress: 'Where is the real headmistress? Where is / the real headmistress?', which suggests a symbolic concern both with feminine authority within institutional structures (for 'classroom' we might read 'family'; for 'real head-mistress' we might read 'mother'), and with the nature of reality itself, a concern extending to the reality of nature, symbolised not only by the disruptive blackbirds but also by the significantly 'exiled bushes', the world outside the classroom.

Finally, we might consider what the 'blackbirds' signify. They change from the plural 'blackbirds', mentioned three times in the poem, to the singular and separated adjective and noun 'black bird' in the penultimate line, which the narrating voice, in a moment of apostrophe, calls to be 'freed'. 'Free the black bird' suggests a symbolic dimension, setting up an opposition between nature and culture, or freedom and constraint, suggesting that the 'blackbirds' may symbolise (as birds conventionally do) liberation, specifically the types of liberation afforded by art. Such a symbolic reading might draw together Szirtes' blackbirds with the pastoral blackbirds of earlier blackbird poems, the modernist blackbird of Wallace Stevens, the birds of Hitchcock and of Keats, Shelley, Hopkins and the Romantic tradition, and allow us to read the poem as a fantasy about the liberating potential of poetry in conflict with the sonorous, regulating structures of language, signified by the final assertion of grammatical authority. Such a reading relies on the work of the reader and on the experiences of reading that make up the reader's, the poem's, and the poet's histories; as Szirtes has noted of Georges Braque, 'We can read these shapes most of the time, because we have learned to read them. Our readings have, of course, a history, and history breeds expectation: we expect to find things, and therefore we do'.[16]

Contrasting 'Blackbirds', as one point of origin for Szirtes' poetic output, with the final poem of the later collection *Reel*, offers some instructive insights into his development, and conveniently frames his *œuvre*. 'Winter Wings' is a short example of concrete poetry, the two stanzas typographically arranged to represent two pairs of wings, in the manner of George Herbert's 'Easter Wings', to which Szirtes' title clearly alludes.

> How brilliantly the sun
> for a moment strides
> through the glass
> then hides
> in deep
> recesses
> in the very aisles
> it so briefly caresses,
>
> so the heart stops and restarts
> without noticing

it has stopped:
a swing
lurching,
an eye lost
in mid-blink, dark birds
in full flight, swimming though dust.

'Winter Wings' offers a moment of profound perception encoded in a form that expresses, in condensed, compressed language, its intensity. Consisting of a single sentence carefully punctuated in five places to emphasise moments of pause and suspense, it articulates the simple experience of seeing sunlight through a glass window, finds a symbolic correspondence for it in 'the heart' which 'stops and restarts', and extends the correspondence back into the world in which the perception originated, in which all beauty will end as the poem ends, in 'dust'. The poem revolves around the comparison 'so' which balances the two stanzas, allowing the switch from description and assertion to simile. The second stanza hinges on the word 'swing', the child's experience of dizzying play (like the dizzy experience of blackbirds in the classroom) momentarily returning to repeat in anagrammatical form the 'Wings' of the poem's title, before 'lurching' like a heartbeat back into a final confusion of perceptions and movements, 'an eye lost / in mid-blink, dark birds / in full flight, swimming through dust.' The 'dark birds' could be the 'Blackbirds' of the first poem in *The Iron Clouds*, returning here as embodiments of the symbolic 'Wings' of the poem itself, content and form momentarily united in the sublime perception the poem seeks to represent.

This perception is both pastoral – a flash of sunlight seen in a village church – and implicitly religious (the poem's subheading locates the event in 'Wymondham Abbey'), drawing further connections with Herbert's religious poetry and reinforcing the 'expectations' of (formal) history. Above all, however, it tries to express in lyric verse the beauty of the visual experience of a shaft of sunlight, expanding a moment of perception into a lasting form that finds a location within a tradition. In doing so, and in its position as the final poem of *Reel*, it echoes another contemporary poem of the sublime, Seamus Heaney's 'Postscript', a Meredithian or sixteen-line sonnet which concludes his collection *The Spirit Level* with a moment of profound perception of light and movement that 'catch[es] the heart off guard and blow[s] it open'.[17] As with Heaney's powerful, emotional concluding poem, reading Szirtes' poem is also the experience of entering into the poem's form and, through that, into the tradition to which the poem alludes. We

experience the poem as form laid out on the page and bound to-
gether by internal structures and patterns, following the 'swing'
and 'lurch' of the poem between its thematic and emotional co-
ordinates of inside and outside, perception and representation, and
between the words and the world to which the words refer. In
doing so, the poem 'swings' beyond itself, exceeds the limits of
the momentary lyric experience and enters, 'lurching', the perma-
nence of the tradition on which it draws.

'Winter Wings' is, on one level, an exercise in form, and demon-
strates a key direction in Szirtes' development that will be explored
in much more detail below. It shows how Szirtes' poetry develops
from the loosely structured, sometimes bizarre lyrical and narra-
tive experiences related and described in poems like 'Blackbirds',
towards a formal dexterity that allows detailed, condensed emotion
to be expressed within a restricted but highly organised space, a
space that re-invigorates and extends the limits of lyrical conven-
tions. The routes that this development takes include expansion
from short lyrical poems into long, complex sequences, various
experiments with different forms, and the oscillation between
lyric, pastoral-Romantic, modernist-fragmentary and other poetic
traditions which come into focus at different moments in Szirtes'
career, which, seen in this way, takes on elements of a remarkable
consistency and regularity of progression and development. We
might note here, for example, that the surrealistic concerns of
'Blackbirds' indicated above are re-enacted in a slightly later
poem, 'In the Classroom', published in Szirtes' first full collec-
tion, *The Slant Door*; that poem concludes, as does 'Winter
Wings', with the word 'dust' ('They patch the holes / With litera-
ture and cough up dust').

The early lyric dimension of Szirtes' work is, as he develops as
a poet, increasingly tempered by his turn towards a lyricised form
of narrative achieved through the deployment of modernist devices
of objectivity and distancing, such as montage and the juxtaposition
of fragmentary memories and perceptions. Likewise the surrealistic
elements evident in his early poetry develop into politically laden
images and symbols of the confusion and chaos of the postmodern
world. Such devices never quite lose their basis in a dream-logic
that is both personal to the poet (these are, after all, his memories
and perceptions, his imagined collocations and juxtapositions, and
the self, however fragile or elusive, always remains the position of
enunciation, and cannot be wholly 'unselved') and achieves a gen-
eral significance in proportion to its efforts to respond to general
situations, so that in a long poem like 'Metro' Szirtes can present

deeply personal images and imaginings and mesh them together into a profoundly complex and disturbing meditation on the nature of memory as a form of history. The reader of poems like 'Blackbirds' and 'Winter Wings' encounters flexible aesthetic constructions, forms in which images, memories, perceptions, emotions and assertions intermingle to produce powerful aesthetic effects, which develop and deepen on re-reading. Szirtes, writing of Joseph Brodsky, offers a description that might equally apply to his own poetry: 'The verse appears to be thrown off with a casual, almost slangy harshness, but the structures are cast iron, and the diction is extremely supple.'[18] The aesthetic effects his poetry achieves, in turn, encapsulate a series of themes central to the movement of a certain kind of Western literature in the late twentieth century. These include the increasingly problematic status of historical truth and, with it, of authority; the difficulty of sustaining (within this crisis of truth) the importance of art; the effects on both truth and art of traumatic experiences of genocide, exile, migration, and deprivation; and the possibilities of different kinds of art and different conceptions of historical truth as palliatives to these experiences.

Another very early poem, 'Babies on a Train', describes this reality in stark terms: 'The world is splintered into painful glass / and forms a savage bed on which to lie.'[19] The ambiguities here ('to lie' resonates in the fictions of the poetry, an ambiguity that returns throughout Szirtes' work; does 'the world' form 'a savage bed', or are 'forms' also, like 'the world', 'a savage bed'?) are central to the functions of form in Szirtes' work. Upon this 'savage bed' of crucial concerns – a 'splintered' world, the act of 'lying' – Szirtes' poetry maps out another territory of questions specific to its own projects: the role of individual memory in constructing the past; the role of the poet's perceptions and conceptions in understanding the real world; the relations between poetry and other – particularly visual – forms of artistic representation; the usefulness of poetic traditions in formulating and framing responses to contemporary anxieties; and an underlying uncertainty about the efficacy of language itself as the medium through which all such concerns need to be addressed.

Such a range of themes clearly maps onto the issues addressed by contemporary literary and cultural theory, and Szirtes is profoundly aware of the relations between his poetry and the positions and assumptions of the work of contemporary theorists. He shares with many of them a fundamental scepticism about the workings of language, which is tempered by a willingness to rely nevertheless upon its potentials. He is prepared to engage, within his poetry, in precisely the kinds of active reading that his poetry demands of its readers, and, when necessary, he is able to take advantage of the poetry implicit in modern theoretical writings, to exploit the verbal proximity between theory and its objects of analysis. His central concerns have political resonances in precisely the ways celebrated by contemporary theoretical arguments – they touch on issues of personal, cultural and national identity, fictions of selfhood, experiences of division and difference, the workings of memory and its various forms and technologies, questions of representation and mediation in image and language, problems of translation and transliteration, and on issues of intertextuality and canonicity – the relations between artists and artworks, and between periods and styles of artistic production. Ultimately Szirtes' work engages via this range of concerns with deep ethical questions of duty, responsibility, expectation and demand. A reader of his poetry will encounter in many forms these central concerns.

Likewise, he shares with much contemporary theory a deep scepticism about the supposed effectiveness or transparency of verbal communication, and has written (in 'Formal Wear') of how elements of this scepticism relate to his background:

> My personal sense of language probably has its roots in my family's transplantation to England and our complete, abrupt switchover to English in 1956. I cannot help feeling that what language theorists tell us must be true, that language is a very thin integument or skin stretched over a mass of inchoate impressions, desires, and anxieties. I cannot help feeling that the gap between signifier and signified is potentially enormous, and that the whole structure of grammar and syntax is a kind of illusion that hides this unpleasant fact from us.[20]

This sense of the fragility and unreliability of language, and particularly of the forms into which language is organised in poetry, words and grammar straining to contain 'a mass of inchoate impressions, desires and anxieties', imbues much of Szirtes' poetry, and lends a specific urgency to his own exploration of the possibilities of particular forms as verbal containers of meanings. It lends his own use of English (his second language) with a particular set of qualities which, at times, has been noted by reviewers. Sean O'Brien, reviewing *Reel*, comments on Szirtes' 'idiosyncratic' ear, and notes that 'There are points...when the reader may ask if English is really the medium for what comes next.'[21]

Such comments pinpoint one aspect of the 'thin integument' of language and its fragile concealing of the complex, unstructured memories and emotions that constitute the self, its potential always to slip into the private or the obscure in its efforts to be specific in the performance of its functions (T.S. Eliot called this 'the intolerable wrestle with words and meanings'); they also draw attention to the cosmopolitanism of Szirtes' formal borrowings (in this case, O'Brien is commenting specifically on his use of the Italian form of *terza rima*). They do, however, neglect the potential spaces opened up by the immigrant's relation to English, the sense of operating aslant to or looking awry at the language, the degree of flexibility and subtlety that an 'idiosyncratic ear' can achieve in the face of more commonplace deformations of the language. They also ignore the necessity (historical, contemporary and increasingly politically urgent) of importing elements of the European tradition into English (Boyd Tonkin, reviewing the anthology of Hungarian writing Szirtes edited, *Leopard V*, argues that the writings it contains will help English readers 'resist our home-grown form of mind-control by means of the screaming headline and the squirming soundbite').[22]

The writer Eva Hoffman, herself a Polish exile, expresses something of Szirtes' situation when she describes her own sense of the frustration of linguistic displacement, culminating in the general observation that 'we want to be at home in our own tongue. We want to be able to give voice accurately and fully to ourselves and our sense of the world.'[23] Szirtes' deliberate choice to write solely in English (perhaps an extension, as Michael Murphy notes, of the family decision to embrace the necessity of speaking English at home on arriving in England)[24] expresses Hoffman's desire to 'give voice' to the self within the language available to it, and is also an identification, a striving both to accommodate and be accommodated within a language and a literary tradition, and an assertion of the possibilities and freedoms that that tradition must signify to the exiled refugee displaced into it. For Szirtes, Hungarian too is a territory unfamiliar in difficult ways, a language returned to in 1984 in some bafflement, and within which he has embraced the rigorous discipline of translating Hungarian works into English.

Szirtes' historical location between cultures is thus also the experience of being situated in-between languages, fully native in neither, constantly aware of his specific position in relation to each. As his comments above on theories of language suggest, his poetry is motivated by the effort to understand and represent through these languages the specific historical situations in which he has lived. As it develops, it draws with increasing urgency on the different traditions to which these historical contexts give him access. He was born in a middle-class district of Budapest in 1948, to a father who worked in plumbing and eventually in the Communist Ministry of Works, and a mother who worked as a photographer for an evening newspaper. These parental occupations offer important histories for Szirtes' poetry to explore, from the 'bridges' and 'architectures' of the poems in *Bridge Passages* (1991) to the persistent presence of photography as an art form and medium of representation, evident most clearly in collections like *Blind Field* (1994) and *The Photographer in Winter* (1986). A major dimension of Szirtes' work since the mid-1980s is devoted to recording and interpreting his parents' lives and experiences via the different but related media of photography and family narratives and memories, suggesting that we can read these aspects of his poetry through frameworks afforded by recent theories of 'postmemory' which try to account for how contemporary artists seek to make sense of histories which they experience second-hand, through the memories and narratives of parents and grandparents. Szirtes' poetry, in this context, clearly affords a space within which certain kinds of reconciliation can be performed to limited, provisional degrees, a momentary ordering of the past and of its effects via the potential 'redress' of poetry.

He notes in 'Fables of Home' that his family origins are, in keeping with the complex historical and territorial changes affecting Hungary in the twentieth century, 'confused': 'My father's grandparents came out of Moravia and Bohemia, and my mother's family came from Transylvania.' Both parents were Jewish (although Szirtes' mother sustained until her death in 1975 the myth that she 'came from a Lutheran background').[25] They had both survived the Holocaust (Szirtes' father was sent to a labour camp in 1944; his mother survived three months in Ravensbrück concentration camp) and returned to Budapest at the end of the War. The family left Hungary in 1956 to escape the arrival of the Russian army to quell the Hungarian uprising. Walking with two suitcases across the border into Austria, they reached Vienna with the intention of emigrating to Australia. Instead, they were transported to England on 2 December 1956, and were housed at Tidworth army camp and at Westgate in Kent, before settling near Wembley in north London.

Szirtes' English education began at Kingsbury County Grammar School in Brent, moving to Harrow School of Art in 1968. Subsequently he studied fine art at Leeds College of Art and Design (where he met and was taught by the poet Martin Bell, an important influence on his development as a writer) and at Goldsmiths' College. In 1970 he married the artist Clarissa Upchurch, whose work features on the covers of many of his books. In 1971 Szirtes underwent a religious conversion and Baptism, an experience that has a significant effect on his conceptions of poetry and art, as will be discussed below. The suicide of his mother in 1974 is perhaps the major event of this period in terms of the development of his poetry; his mother's life, her memory and her ghost haunt much of his work until the late 1990s. Since 1973 he has held teaching posts in schools in Cheshunt, Hitchin, and Letchworth, at Norwich School of Art and Design, and at the University of East Anglia where he currently works. In 1984 he returned to Hungary on an Arts Council travelling scholarship, and he has subsequently spent extended periods there, including a nine-month residency in 1989, which fortuitously coincided with the revolutions in Eastern and Central Europe that precipitated the collapse of communism. Szirtes provided radio reports from Budapest for the BBC during late 1989, and published in *Poetry Review* a series of written commentaries on events. In 2002 he was awarded a PhD from Anglia Polytechnic University (now the Anglia Ruskin University).

Szirtes was thus educated in English, the language of all his poetry and most of his prose writings, but has received no formal literary training. 'We spoke English at home, and so I largely forgot what Hungarian I had known', he has commented; 'when I began to write, it did not occur to me to write in Hungarian.'[26] Nevertheless his origins are Hungarian, and the central productive tension in all his poetry rests on the difficult, fluid relation between these two national, cultural and linguistic identities, a condition he has often described as 'in-between' and as 'uncommon...; it makes you a strange being, and sometimes it is hard to accept being regarded by English readers as an ambiguous phenomenon of that sort.'[27] This 'uncommon', 'strange', 'ambiguous' or in-between experience is important for understanding the tone and effects of much of Szirtes' poetry; such words could equally describe a poem like 'Blackbirds', and certainly resonate with many of his major poems.

The 'triangular relationship between Hungary, myself and England'[28] is explored throughout his poetry on the various terrains of the self and its personal memories. It exists in family histories and memories, which occupy a shady border territory between the personal and the historical; in literary traditions (both English and Hungarian) as repositories of linguistic resources through which memories can be encoded as representations; and in languages themselves, insistent markers of territorial experience, as properties and kinds of knowledge differentiating people in terms of levels of

belonging, worked at by Szirtes in translations and versions of
Hungarian poetry and fiction. Again, his earliest poetry displays
an awareness of this 'in-between-ness' and of its influence: *The
Iron Clouds* features a poem called 'Budapest 1951', an evocation
of childhood memories of 'evenings cold as catacombs' which is
nevertheless tempered by the adult's awareness of the frailty of
memory: 'That these images persist does not bring grace / Nor the
right to dwell...'. More recently he has commented, during a read-
ing in Poland (and in terms that echo the confluence of poetry with
architectural imagery noted earlier), that 'In retrospect now, it seems
to me sometimes, that I think of my poetry as a kind of Budapest
tenement block, being built somewhere outside London.'[29]

His poetry begins within this situation or condition of 'in-between-
ness', as a questioning of the 'right to dwell'. Szirtes started writing
in the 1970s, under the immediate but slightly historically distant
influence of major Western literary figures like T.S. Eliot and W.H.
Auden, as well as more contemporary voices like those of Martin
Bell, Peter Porter and the 'Group' and 'Movement' poets of the
1950s and 1960s, contemporary American voices like Robert Lowell
and Anthony Hecht, and major contemporary poets from Ireland
like Derek Mahon, Seamus Heaney and Michael Longley. The
tangible influence of Hungarian literature comes much later, after
his first return to Budapest in 1984. In a review of Martin Bell's
Complete Poems (a book for which he provided the etching of Bell
used as a frontispiece, and which was edited by Porter) Szirtes
observes, in a description equally applicable to his own work, that
'There are faint echoes of Eliot and Auden, and the odd genuflec-
tion to Wallace Stevens'.[30] As the critic Lidia Vianu puts it in a
perceptive interview with Szirtes, his poetry 'swims in many people's
works'.

In the same interview Szirtes cites Eliot as his 'first great literary
experience', and allusions to or echoes of Eliot's poetry (like those
detectable in 'Blackbirds') pepper Szirtes' work. Jonathan Raban
wrote, in 1971, of the 'long shadow over contemporary poetry' cast
by Eliot;[31] if Eliot can be construed, as he was by so many younger
twentieth-century writers (like Martin Bell), as a kind of intimi-
dating role-model for poets in the 1970s, these echoes can perhaps
also be read in Szirtes' context as expressive of the migrant's resi-
dual urge towards an Eliot-like self-assimilation into official English
culture, a desire to disappear into the 'crowd flowing over London
Bridge'. At the same time, they signify the burden of a powerful
poetic tradition (and a powerful theorisation of that tradition and its
relation to the 'individual talent' of the poet) to which the young

poet feels bound to respond. Eliot is both a profoundly influential resource and a vital constraint, and a significant aspect of Szirtes' development as a poet has involved an implicit dialogue with the monolith of Eliot.

Likewise, and more problematically so, Auden, 'a great hero of mine', Szirtes has said, 'because of his gift of phrase and his lyric gift, not so much because of his Goethean wisdom'. Szirtes' later work returns insistently to Auden's tones and imagery; his own extraordinary formal and metrical range is prefigured in Auden's pre-eminent metrical versatility, and his central concerns overlap in significant ways with those of Auden. His troubled pastorals, his concern with the frozen, the chilled, the static forms of memory and frustrated desire, and his conviction that poetry remains important in a world increasingly deprived of it, all have their precursors in one or other moment of Auden's *œuvre*. In his weblog entry for 23 July 2005, Szirtes addresses (not for the first time) Auden's notorious assertion, in 'In Memory of W.B. Yeats', that 'poetry makes nothing happen' but is instead 'a way of happening, a mouth'. Szirtes registers his own understanding of Auden's assertion as seeking to express how poetry responds to the world: he's interested in 'the way it made things happen, the way it would redress the world'. This echo, in discussing Auden, of Seamus Heaney's conception of poetry as 'redress', gestures towards a complex understanding of Auden's statements in the light of contemporary attempts, in different political contexts and for different purposes, to comprehend poetry's persistence, an understanding towards which Szirtes' own poetry constantly strives in seeking to encapsulate what he's called 'the complex polyphonic music of what happens'.[32] 'I am', he notes in 'Fables of Home', 'like all poets, fascinated and seduced by the music of what happens'.[33]

A significant element of Szirtes' task as a poet has been to negotiate the presence – the 'constant shadow' – of both these towering figures, and this element constitutes, in a sense, an ever-present undercurrent in his work. Eliot and Auden, like Szirtes, were both migrant poets, relocating in new cultures (but not, significantly, new languages) in order to continue their own developments. So too, it should be noted, are Peter Porter (from Australia to England) and Seamus Heaney (from the North to the South of Ireland). As Michael Murphy has shown in his analysis of Szirtes alongside Auden and another major migrant poet, Joseph Brodsky, the experiences of displacement, exile and return and their impact upon poetic creativity have been profound for all three poets.

Szirtes' poetry explores a deep concern with the condition of

exile, which he experiences in a form that changes as his relation-
ships to England and to Hungary develop. The politics of his par-
ents' migration in 1956 are complex and contingent upon an aware-
ness of Hungarian history; their escape from Budapest was, they
felt, an escape from the possibility of a return to Nazism as well
as an immediate response to the arrival of the Russians (which,
many believed, would herald a right-wing reaction, an upsurge in
fascist sympathies in protest at Communist rule). The urgency of
their escape is palpable; leaving along with 250,000 other Hungarians,
they were forced to leave behind virtually everything, and the actual
experience of escape is remembered as a traumatic moment of dis-
ruption, both foundational and dislocating, by the older Szirtes in
poems like 'Border Crossing' (in *Metro*) and 'My father carries me
across a field' (in *Reel*). As a child accompanying a migrant family,
there is furthermore a degree of disempowerment in Szirtes' expe-
rience of the movements of the exile; he is, as Marianne Hirsch
phrases it in her description of the postmemorial experience, 'marked
by [his] parents' experiences' as well as by his own partial memories
of movement.[34]

His displacement consequently manifests itself in his poetry as
triple, a displacement in geography (from Hungary to England), in
language (from Hungarian to English) and in time, from the past
(which is constructed in his poems in peculiarly distinctive ways)
into the present. These modes of manifestation are specific to Szirtes
and to the particularity of his experience: they both define and
make impossible a conventional definition of his identity, and cul-
minate in what Hirsch calls a 'condition of exile from the space of
identity',[35] the condition that Szirtes describes as 'in-between'. At
the same time, as Murphy observes, Szirtes sustains the conviction
that exile is a defining feature of modernity shared by millions of
people: 'We live in a world which is full of people in transit',
Szirtes comments in a newspaper article in 2000 that Murphy
cites.[36] For Murphy, the experience of exile manifests itself most
overtly in Szirtes' poetry in its preoccupation with 'resolving the
different ways we experience the past';[37] consequently Szirtes' use
of photography, as a process of recording the past, comes under
careful scrutiny in Murphy's analysis of his work.

Szirtes sustains in his early poetry a curious observational dis-
tance from the objects, artworks, scenes and people he describes, a
distance that contributes to the 'making-strange' of the world that
seems, at certain points, to be the initial project of the poetry, as
if the poem itself were performing the kind of distancing that the
photograph performs – capturing and sealing off a moment of

perception, re-writing it as image of a moment of the past made present. Photography itself, as the profession of Szirtes' mother and as both a practice and a medium, a labour and an aesthetic, the creating, framing and fixing of the 'frozen moment' of time in an image, provides powerful instances of this in Szirtes' poetry, and (as he is aware in collections like *Blind Field*) much recent photography theory has explored the relations between the photographic image, remembrance, mortality and resurrection, and the construction of identity and difference. One of the most significant theorisations of photography, Roland Barthes' *Camera Lucida*, is also an extended elegy for its author's mother, an overlap of theme that resonates powerfully with some of the functions of photography in Szirtes' work.

Photography is highly significant for Szirtes, and will be discussed in detail in chapter 5 below. The frozenness of the photograph, however, extends as a system of images and metaphors beyond the limits of its frame, and is manifest in his preoccupation with the 'frozen' elements of experience, the Keatsian 'cold pastoral' that recurs in many forms in his early volumes – the 'evenings cold as catacombs' in 'Budapest 1951' (in *The Iron Clouds*), the poet's hands 'so cold I can hardly write' in 'The Town Flattened' (the second poem in *The Slant Door*), the church floor 'like black ice' in 'The Swimmers' (in *The Photographer in Winter*). Frozenness is a form of distancing, of 'freezing off' the immediate and fixing it motionless so that the poet's gaze can examine it more closely. It's also a symbolic form of preservation, slowing the past down until it stops in an endlessly frozen moment that the poem then presents. It's tangentially present in poems like 'Blackbirds', with their underlying sense of an analytical, objective 'eye' scrutinising events from one remove – the adult looking back upon the child, or the bystander commenting on events merely overseen rather than participated in.

This distance is also the distance of the outsider from the solidity of the immediate culture (which, of course, questions the very basis of that apparent solidity), the migrant's unavoidable sense of not-belonging in the world in which they find themselves, a sense which the poetry seeks, through the 'redress' of art, to alleviate. Furthermore this distance is a product of displacement from the familiar (and, by implication, from the "family" of the mother-nation and the mother-tongue). Distance from home is of course the defining emotional experience of the exile, and Szirtes' early explorations of the possibilities of modernist objectivism and lyric separation from the world are formal expressions of this emotional condition, objective correlatives for a psychological state that remains implicit in the verse itself, and which, of course, provides the metaphor of the 'Cold War' to describe the wider historical period in which these poems were written.

With his return to Hungary in 1984 everything changed, but not in ways that we might expect. Szirtes rediscovered a language, a mythology and a geography – specifically the urban geography and mythology of Budapest but also the wider spaces of the country and its cultures and histories – only to find himself equally distanced from this new 'home' (he notes in his weblog in 2005 that he still finds speaking Hungarian for much more than half an hour 'exhausting'). Eva Hoffman, seeking to account for precisely this condition of rediscovery, cites Mary Antin: 'It is painful to be consciously of two worlds'.[38] For Szirtes, the two worlds are multiply double – past and present, here and there, frozen and moving. In seeking to account for this doubling and redoubling of the distance of exile his poetry becomes, immediately after his return to Hungary, deeply introspective, and develops and expands its former concerns with careful, detailed observation into a condensed and sustained effort to retrieve, in poetic forms, the sensations of a past that simultaneously presents itself to the poet for reclamation and resists that reclamation, remaining, as the poetry gradually reveals, the province of experiences that belong to the previous, parental, generation. This is the internal dynamic of Szirtes' long sequences of the late 1980s, 'Metro' (1988) and 'The Photographer in Winter' (1986), major poems of post-war European experience inserted into English traditions, which are, in one important sense, narratives of the rediscovered, newly significant histories that he has partially imbibed. In another, however, they represent the need continually to struggle to make formal sense of contradictory, potentially terrible discoveries.

The tensions of these long poems reach a crisis point in the fractured sequences of *Bridge Passages* (1991), the collection which marks Szirtes' most immediate encounter with historical and political forces. This collection also explores a potential resolution to the issues outlined above in the incorporation of translations, specifically of poems by the Hungarian poets Ottó Orbán and Zsuzsa Rakovszky. The liberatory potential of translation, its affording of a combination of escape (from the burdens of conforming solely to an English literary heritage into which the migrant poet has to insert himself) and a new rigorous discipline, as well as the canonical spaces it opens up and the bridges it establishes between languages and cultures, are crucial to understanding Szirtes' development subsequent to the revolutions of 1989. From the wary, hesitant stasis of *Bridge Passages* he turns to photography (in 1994's *Blind Field*) and family and other histories (in 1998's *Portrait of My Father in an English Landscape*) as frameworks through which to conduct a reassessment of his own position in relation to myths of Englishness (a project that develops in the new poems added to *An English Apocalypse* in 2001, and is elaborated in a multitude of ways through the poems in *Reel* [2004]). This is always, for Szirtes, a multi-faceted, almost circular process; in order to scrutinise Englishness, a major element of his own identity necessarily also comes under scrutiny; in order to scrutinise himself, his own family presents contexts and traditions that demand attention; and in order to analyse these traditions and contexts, the Hungarian element of his identity demands analysis.

Such a summary reduces the complexity of the *œuvre* to a manageable narrative, picking out salient features to emphasise their significance, and neglecting other currents and developments. It takes little account, for example, of the influence of an entirely different context on Szirtes' development – that involving the poets and artists he encountered while beginning the process of learning his art. Szirtes' early development as a poet working in English, if not an "English poet", took place within a complex and lively, and very English, cultural milieu based in the Hertfordshire market town of Hitchin, where he lived and worked in the early 1970s (Hitchin's central church, St Mary's, is the setting of the early poem 'The Swimmers'). The group of writers, artists and printers working in Hitchin at this time included the poet and publisher Peter Scupham (dedicatee of the important sequence 'Backwaters: Norfolk Fields') and the printer and schoolteacher Roger Burford Mason, both of whom published early poems by Szirtes printed in limited runs on their home presses.

Connected to this group was another poet and publisher, John Cotton, whose Priapus Press was based in nearby Berkhamsted and published work by Brian Aldiss, Wendy Cope and many others. Scupham's Mandeville Press was responsible for publishing work by several well-known poets including Seamus Heaney, C.H. Sisson, Michael Schmidt, Andrew Waterman, Freda Downie and Bernard Bergonzi (for whose *Years* Szirtes provided an illustration as a frontispiece); Scupham also, with John Mole, ran the Cellar Press, which published work by Anthony Thwaite (later Szirtes' editor at Secker and Warburg), John Fuller and others. Burford Mason's Dodman Press published Szirtes' *The Iron Clouds*, work by John Gohorry (who ran his own End House Press in Hitchin until 1981 and had his poetry published by the Kit-Cat Press based in Hunton Bridge), John Cotton, John Lucas and Jeff Cloves (who ran Ourside Publications in nearby St Albans).

This thriving and highly productive, locally based small-publishing scene was profoundly influential in promoting and stimulating Szirtes as both artist and poet. With Clarissa Upchurch he established The Starwheel Press in 1978, publishing mainly artists' work along with work by each of the press's founders. His early poetry was presented in high quality, limited edition print runs alongside work by many older, more established poets. *A Mandeville Fifteen*, published by the Mandeville Press in 1976, features Szirtes' 'Children' (later collected in *The Slant Door*) alongside poems by John Fuller, Lawrence Sail, Andrew Waterman, Katharine Middleton, C.H. Sisson and Peter Scupham himself. Such enterprises involved Szirtes in writing, printing, publishing, illustrating and editing his own and others' work, and allowed him to develop early a sense of productivity across a range of media and genres.

Perhaps partly as a result of this early period of publishing, Szirtes is a prolific writer in a variety of genres. His work spans poetry and prose, novels, reviews of literature and art, translations of Hungarian poetry and fiction, an ever-expanding daily weblog, work in radio, painting and illustrating, and publishing. His earliest poems were privately printed, and the first selection of this early work was published in 1978 in Faber's *Poetry Introduction 4*, alongside work by, among others, Alistair Elliot, Alan Hollinghurst and Craig Raine. Szirtes' first collection, *The Slant Door*, was published in 1979 by Secker and Warburg, who also published the next four volumes up to *The Photographer in Winter* (1986). Szirtes then moved publishers to Oxford, who issued his next five volumes, including *Selected Poems 1976-96* (1996). Subsequent collections, including the two retrospective selections *The Budapest File* (2000) and *An English Apocalypse* (2001), along with *Reel* (2004) and *New & Collected Poems* (2008), have been published by Bloodaxe Books. In addition Szirtes has published in England and Hungary a large number of translations of works by major Hungarian poets and novelists, and edited the significant anthologies *The Colonnade of Teeth: Modern Hungarian Poetry* (with George Gömöri, 1996) and *Leopard V: An Island of Sound* (with Miklós Vajda, 2004).

The project of this book is to read these collections in sequence in order to trace some of the trajectories of the qualities of Szirtes' poetry argued above – seriousness, difficulty, awkwardness – and to resituate them continually as the poetry develops, in relation to its shifting historical and cultural contexts. In one of *Reel*'s major poems, 'Meeting Austerlitz' (discussed in Chapter 7), Szirtes elegises his friend, the writer W.G. Sebald, who died in a car crash in 2001. Apart from commenting on their shared experience of migration – Sebald left Germany in the 1960s to work in England – the poem also seeks a common understanding based in words and their interpretation, in the two writers' essays into the territories of language and form in order to try to make sense of experience: 'The attempt to impose / order was a perilous task, all but beyond words / while the alternative universe of flux / offered no sympathy and kept no records'. 'The attempt to impose order' is, of course, the intention of all writing and reading, a human effort to understand and to record; Szirtes' poetry seeks its own forms and ideas of order, and, within them, finds particular kinds of beauty.

2

'Cold pastorals': *The Slant Door*, *November and May*, *Short Wave*

Art meets the world at an awkward
Angle...

PETER PORTER, 'The Orchid on the Rock'

Szirtes' first collection, *The Slant Door*, was published in 1979 by Secker and Warburg, who also published his next three books, *November and May* (1981), *Short Wave* (1983) and *The Photographer in Winter* (1986). Secker's list in the late 1970s included George MacBeth and Alan Brownjohn (both influential in different ways on Szirtes), John Mole (who had been published with Szirtes by the Mandeville Press), Peter Reading, Anne Sexton, Erica Jong and Freda Downie (whose *Collected Poems*, published posthumously by Bloodaxe in 1995, is edited by Szirtes), as well as translated work by Miroslav Holub. Szirtes had already published several poems in Hutchinson's annual *New Poetry* anthologies and in various magazines through the 1970s, as well as in pamphlets and small chapbooks published by private presses in Hitchin, Letchworth and elsewhere. The context in which *The Slant Door* was published offers some insights into the specific qualities and features of the work the collection contains. Even a cursory survey of poetry published in 1978 and 1979 suggests that Szirtes emerged as a poet contributing to a vibrant and highly diversified English poetry scene, characterised by a wide range of significant collections and works from a number of previously "marginal" or at least "non-mainstream" sources.

Neil Corcoran (writing in 1993) lists the major poetry collections of 1978 as Tony Harrison's *The School of Eloquence*, Geoffrey Hill's *Tenebrae*, Ted Hughes' *Cave Birds* and Peter Porter's *The Cost of Seriousness*; these are followed, in 1979, by Seamus Heaney's *Field Work*, Hughes' *Moortown* and Craig Raine's *A Martian Sends a Postcard Home*.[39] With the exception of Raine's first volume (Raine and Szirtes were both included in Faber's *Poetry Introduction 4* in 1978), these are all works by major established poets with origins in the 1950s and 1960s. To this list of key texts we might add

Denise Riley and Wendy Mulford's *No Fee*, Ken Smith's *Tristan Crazy*, Roy Fisher's *The Thing About Joe Sullivan*, Tony Harrison's *From 'The School of Eloquence'*, Jeffrey Wainwright's *Heart's Desire* and Barry MacSweeney's *Odes* (all 1978), and, in 1979, Douglas Dunn's *Barbarians*, Fleur Adcock's *Below Loughrigg*, James Berry's *Fractured Circles*, Edwin Morgan's *Star Gate: Science Fiction Poems*, Hugo Williams' *Love-Life*, Michael Longley's *The Echo Gate*, Derek Mahon's *Poems 1972-78* and Derek Walcott's *The Star-Apple Kingdom*. Such a list represents some of the peaks of a period of extraordinary creativity for poetry in English (Bloodaxe Books, Szirtes' current publisher, was established in 1978), a diversity evident in styles and allegiances as well as in authorial origins.

Szirtes differs from all these writers in that he writes in a language not his own. This linguistic separation distinguishes him from almost all contemporary British and English poetry and is a defining feature of his identity. His self-consciousness concerning the 'location' of his work in relation to a perceived 'mainstream' of English poetry is a recurring preoccupation of his essays and interviews. 'I have never actually tried to be a foreign writer', he told Lidia Vianu in 2001; 'I wanted to be an English one. The success might lie in the failure'. Later in the same interview, Szirtes uses an architectural metaphor to describe his position: 'I sometimes think of my poems as buildings...somewhat to the side of the mainstream of English verse'. In the 'Preface' to *The Budapest File* (2000) he describes his own range of reading in the 1960s (Szirtes was initially largely self-taught as an artist and a writer, having studied sciences up to 'A' level) as 'an eclectic mixture that nowhere included the mainstream'.[40]

This self-construction as marginal in terms of both the production and the consumption of poetry is crucial for understanding the motivations and allegiances forged, in Szirtes' early collections, with an English poetic tradition undergoing rapid and dramatic transformation, as well as for grasping Szirtes' 'marginal', partially excluded relation to the language and traditions of English verse. Such a positioning of the poet can be a strength as well as a hindrance. His sense, as he tells Lidia Vianu, that he 'cannot write the songs of the tribe' because he feels 'excluded from it' begs a series of questions about what, in the 1970s and 1980s, constituted 'the tribe'. Several reviewers of his early work saw his relation to the English language as potentially positive, a freedom rather than a constraint: D.A.N. Jones noted that Szirtes 'brings some energetic new blood into English poetry', while Robert Welch, reviewing *November and May*, writes that 'Szirtes' is an open language' and Shirley Toulson comments on *The Slant Door*'s 'surprisingly fresh, spontaneous way with English cadences'.[41]

Corcoran's authoritative but conventional analysis of post-war English poetry lists increasing regionalism, the external influences of American and other foreign poetries in translation, and the increasing importance in the academy of foreign literary theory, as determinants on much 1970s English poetry that, he argues, 'is written as in some sense oppositional or antagonistic to an idea of a dominant cultural or political or linguistic system'.[42] As much recent criticism has argued, the contested territory here is Englishness, and Szirtes' relation to conventions and traditions of English poetry and, by extension, English cultural identities, is a useful place from which to begin reading his poetry. Raphaël Ingelbien has recently suggested that 'In their eagerness to identify writers with certain ideas of England and Englishness, some commentators have been insensitive to the aesthetic complexity of many a poem'.[43] Szirtes' early conceptions of 'England and Englishness', emphasised by his recycling and revisiting these ideas in his 2001 retrospective and collection *An English Apocalypse*, are evident in his responses to and negotiations of spaces within English poetic forms and traditions. The most tangible traces of 'English' poetic traditions and their influences in his work are found in the 'aesthetic complexities' of his poems, in their use of quotations and allusions; in formal and structural imitations, borrowings and adaptations; and in thematic echoes and recurrences deriving from reading other poets' work, which they approach, as they approach reality, from an awkward or 'slant' angle.

These connections and echoes are also, of course, a way of subtly undermining or challenging those perceived traditions. A recurrent thread of images in these early poems, for example, is Szirtes' insistent concern with the 'frozen'. As a resonating motif, this can be traced back through modern Irish, rather than English, poetry; it can be seen in Derek Mahon's preoccupations with the imagery of snow, his 'favourite element' according to Sean O'Brien,[44] as indicated in the title of his 1975 collection *The Snow Party*, and finds its source in Louis MacNeice's poem 'Snow', which provides the epigraph for *November and May* and is effectively acknowledged by Szirtes in the short poem 'Snow' in *The Slant Door*. John Lucas, reviewing the former collection, cites MacNeice in noting its 'almost numinous sense of variousness of things'.[45] MacNeice's poem offers a standard of economy, formal precision and imagistic density (to the extent of semantic conflict in 'snow and pink roses') towards which Szirtes' poetry constantly strives, and embodies the 'shock' of perception typical of Szirtes' early lyrics as the light of the external world is internalised and domesticated. The poem uses the light of the snow to figure difference through the transformation of the internal (domestic) world, illuminating the inside and producing an aesthetic experience grounded in an intoxicating, deranging excess of perception ('World is crazier and more of it than we think'; 'The drunkenness of things being various').

Szirtes' own poem 'Snow' re-experiences MacNeice's encounter with difference in the shared moment of seeing the world: 'Look, it has snowed in the night / And the roads are bright as skin / Lit by the moon.' The poem extends its own exploration of difference by imitating the imagistic density of Chinese verse in its seamless extension from image of beauty to sinister conceit: 'the snow is moonlight / And there will be no morning ever again.' Its meaning extends through a mode of description that internalises perception, locating in the 'moonlight' of the snow a darkness of desire ('We shall live in white like brides'), presenting an implicitly corrupted purity both sexual and coldly chaste, reminiscent of death : 'nor shall night be over'. The poem achieves a deeper, more sinister historical resonance in its faint echo of Sylvia Plath's 'Daddy' and that poem's allusions to the death camps, implicit here in the menacing collocation of 'skin' and 'Lit'. The notion that poetry 'captures' and makes present, within the formal structure of the poem, the external, perceived world and its tainted history, is fundamental to Szirtes' aesthetic, and, at this stage in his development, involves the concomitant realisation that art 'fixes' or 'freezes' reality by representing it in formal structures; his version of the 'more than glass between the snow and the huge roses' includes language, form, and tradition – all that intervenes between 'world' and its perception by the reader of a poem. His poem both acknowledges MacNeice's and repositions its insights in relation to the demands of a different, contemporary aesthetic, offering what Peter Porter might call an 'epiphany of a poor light';[46] not the intoxication or derangement of the world, but a slightly poised and self-consciously surreal slippage between perception and expectation, between word and thing.

Szirtes' early poems address this slippage, this incommensurability of word and thing, by focusing on the problem of visual perception and its encoding in language, drawing in order to do so on recent developments in English, Irish, European and American poetry and, in particular, on poetry's relations to the visual arts. In 'Children' (*The Slant Door*) he asks, 'Tell me what you see?', and the poem lists a world of images and framed photographs, 'the outdated frippery of a photographer's studio'. The collection closes with 'An Illustrated Alphabet', which enacts in miniature a range of possible relations between word and image. *November and May* opens with 'A Girl Visits Rembrandt's House', which condenses the artist's costumed self-portraits into its own portrayal of alienation and apparent blindness as 'Her hand moves on his hand and his face'; the poem moves out into the city, concluding with 'dim eyes, stub hands, smooth outrageous breasts', visual and tactile metonymies of desire inculcated by the 'red lights and tourists' of Amsterdam. One of the few critics to address Szirtes' work in the 1980s, Anthony Thwaite, comments on his 'acute visual perception in his shaping of a seen world, juxtaposing details with both clarity and mystery'.[47] At the same time, these early volumes were recognised by reviewers as being indebted to European traditions of the visual arts, specifically those of surrealism and the gothic. Rodney Pybus, reviewing *Short Wave*, comments that Szirtes' poems are 'scarcely ever Vermeer, more likely to be closer to the macabre side of Goya or the troubling paradoxes of Ernst', and notes that 'Szirtes' own brand of surrealism seems [in his second collection] to be changing'.[48]

A substantial proportion of Szirtes' poetry is concerned with representing in words the visible world. It provides an objective space for words to engage with and verbally reconstruct, and, at the same time, it offers something profoundly unreliable, the subjective encounter with external reality, which Szirtes' early experiments with the co-ordination and combination of images explore. 'The poet', writes Iain Sinclair, 'begins in observation. And ends in dissolution.'[49] Szirtes has written of the early importance of 'learning a craft, of the importance of observation and distance'.[50] His poetry typically begins in the detailed observation of a world of objects thrown into sharp relief by the perspectives of history, and by the added perceptions available to a man trained as an artist; it then extrapolates from this an argument, or a series of conceits and analogies, that are sometimes tangential to the original observation but that elucidate or elaborate a meaning or series of meanings based in that observation. Szirtes' work (like that of Derek Mahon, a significant early influence) draws on pictorial art as a frame of reference and as a theme, providing subject material for poetic analysis, as is implied in titles like 'Group Portrait with Pets', 'Posthumous Portrait' and 'Nativity Scene' (all from *The Slant Door*).

The 'dissolution' towards which Szirtes' poetry moves – its collapsing of forms, its "unfreezing" of the frigid spaces of tradition – is embedded within his earliest work, which emphasises poetry as a distinct use of language, reliant on formal and grammatical devices uncommon elsewhere in linguistic usage. In mixing detailed description of objects and landscapes, verbal representations of paintings and photographs and the recollection and, eventually, the analysis of memories and histories, Szirtes' early poetry combines features common in English poetry of the 1960s and 1970s – on occasion, as with *Short Wave*'s engagement with Peter Porter's poetry discussed below, Szirtes responds directly to his contemporaries – and it is against this historical context that his work needs initially to be considered. If detailed observation is one origin of his work, this includes careful observation – reading – of the work of other poets.

One major influence on Szirtes' poetic development was his meeting Martin Bell, his tutor at Leeds Art College in the early 1970s. Bell (who died in 1978; *The Slant Door* is dedicated 'For Clarissa and to the memory of Martin Bell') was an established poet, included in the third volume of Penguin's Modern Poets series, and senior member of Philip Hobsbaum's 'Group' of writers (including Peter Redgrove, Brownjohn, MacBeth, Porter and Edward Lucie-Smith, later meeting as 'The Poet's Workshop', which ran from 1966 to 1972) who met weekly at Hobsbaum's flat to read and criticise each other's work. Influenced by the 'Movement' poets of the 1950s, 'The Group' represents a gathering of largely mainstream poets working together but not subscribing to any shared or consistent aesthetic agenda. Their now legendary meetings were seen by many as a strict disciplinary experience for many younger poets, a firebranding that equipped them for venturing forth into the world. Bell's *Complete Poems* (published in 1988 by Bloodaxe, with an introduction by Peter Porter and a frontispiece etching of Bell by Szirtes) displays a dense, allusive style combined with sometimes terse, condensed epithets. His major influences derived from T.S. Eliot and French symbolism (he was an accomplished translator of French surrealist verse); Porter notes that his first published work condensed several different allusive frames and narratives 'in Auden's manner', and that Bell was 'a fine delineator of versification and verbal troping'.[51]

Bell also writes self-consciously in the shadow of William Empson's cryptic, difficult poems. His poetry is often, consequently, eclectic, and sometimes obscure; it provides Szirtes with a model for how images can fit within the twists and turns of condensed argument and description. Bell's satire on early Group sessions, 'Mr Hobsbaum's Monday Evening Meeting', echoes in its title and form Eliot's quatrain poem 'Mr Eliot's Sunday Morning Service';

its allusion to 'Mrs Porter's favourite son' condenses Peter Porter
with Eliot's appropriation of 'Mrs Porter' in *The Waste Land*; 'Dr
Leavis' as 'guardian of the Grail' invites further comparison with
The Waste Land.[52] The poem's overall effect is pointedly humorous,
adding social comment to literary allusion and sinuous dexterity; its
influence can be traced in certain elements of the form, tone and
poetic manner of early Szirtes, in poems like 'The Cosmo Guide to
Culture' (in *The Slant Door*) and 'Skeleton Crew' (in *Short Wave*),
and in some of the poems in *Short Wave* discussed below.

Szirtes derives from Bell an awareness of form as limitation or
constraint, within which the dynamics of the poem's language – its
words, word-orders, rhetorical devices and patternings – are forced
to work to full effect. Bell's awareness of the utility of rhyme as a
conveyor of meaning at semantic and grammatical levels and of
rhyme's complex relations to rhythm, his fluency in exploiting
balances between end-stopped and enjambed lines, and his broader
matching of form to content in terms of appropriateness, provided
important models for Szirtes. Above all, Bell's ability to incorporate
his reading into his poetry productively in the form of allusion,
citation and translation, indicated ways in which the contemporary
poet could both respond to and adapt the materials offered by tra-
dition. Szirtes' poetry, likewise, seeks ways of responding to and
adapting literary and painterly traditions. His traditionalism is for-
mal and ideological, incorporating a strong sense of the poet's duty
to the past, which is also an awareness that the poet should not be
enthralled by that past. The poems in *The Slant Door* initiate the
process of discovering ways in which these sometimes conflicting
impetuses can be transformed into forces that help to generate
effective poetry.

The Slant Door

The title poem of Szirtes' first collection offers a vignette of dom-
estic pastoral, a scenery with which much of his early work is
concerned, marked in its very beginning by the warning 'red light'
of evening and approaching darkness. The 'door' of the title bears
the marks of natural erosion: the 'small grooves' worn by the rain
suggest age and transience in contrast to the prevailing imagery,
offered in the first and third stanzas, of the youthful family. In
another poem, 'Group Portrait with Pets', Szirtes writes of the
'arranged embrace' of the family as the 'small space' available to
the artist; 'The Slant Door' probes deep into 'this tiny circle'. The

second and fourth stanzas deal with another space entirely, that of the 'greater forces' and 'greater power' of the natural world, imminently destructive. The poem's overriding metaphor is of silence, the silence appropriate for a sense of the sublime to intrude into the 'fragile' and 'flawed' domestic world: 'But we must be quiet if we want to hear / The rain's approach'. 'The greater power', it argues, 'lies in quiet', in the refusal of the 'prattle' and 'squabbling' that mark everyday human and natural discourse. In the final stanza the silence collapses the force of the impending storm and the power of poetry; both can transform the world, 'blot out gardens and our slanting door'. Silence becomes the silence of form, its menacing presence a version of the power of poetry to transform the world (the 'squabbling' of the birds as a contemporary parliament of fowls) into 'metaphors'.

The 'quiet' of 'The Slant Door' becomes the central motif of 'Background Noises', a small allegory of the power of art to supplant subjectivity, which explores its theme as 'our surrogate music', initially a metaphor for the presence of the self in the world. In an assertion of the primacy of perception over its ordering by thought, the poem instructs us to 'Hold off the intelligence and listen'; what we hear are the traces of others, fragments of what the poem calls 'the survivors': 'an ear, a hand, a bum / On a chair'. This is 'solid, untearful matter', a solidity that the poems in *The Slant Door* find increasingly elusive. Its descent into 'Quiet' is also the self's disappearance into reality, the erasure of its difference through its merging with 'the same world', another version of the trope of death that concerns the collection. 'The quietest music', more extreme in its near-silence than 'our surrogate music', leads to the dissolution of subjectivities: 'you and I / Fade in accompaniment, pronouncing names / That once had power'. The loss of the power of the name, intimately linked to the loss of selfhood, leads to the endless 'dancing' or oscillation of identities 'on thin air', the medium of the transmission of music and noise. 'Background Noises' offers art as the potential erasure of difference, its 'irregular cadences' products of 'friction between noise and sense'. The 'Noises' remain as noise until poetry (or music) codifies them, organising them into formal coherence; but art also threatens their functions as guarantors of perception and therefore of subjective existence. The contingency of 'solid, untearful matter' contrasts with the 'thin air' of the 'quietest music', just as the dialogues implicit in 'you and I' and 'I to you' emphasise the poem's oppositional logic, which, in turn, threatens to collapse amid the tension between formalism and formlessness that is embodied in the poem's irregular but intermittent metre, its lack of rhyme, its status as an incomplete sonnet.

In 'The Speaking Likeness', 'Noises are precise', each with its linguistic counterpart – 'just count the words / Describing all particularities'. Furthermore, noises are 'rarely...incoherent, / They always tell us something'. Noise, then, is information, linguistically coded and with its own rhetorical tag ('onomatopoeia'). But noises of 'scraping' and 'grating' modulate in the poem into symbolic 'saxophones and horns' – the random thingness of 'buckets' and 'lifts' becomes a 'dance' in which 'we make a noise, among noises, in the world'. Human presence, marked by music and language, intervenes in the randomness of 'noise'; finally it becomes 'the queer far tumult of children', the noise of childhood itself, that concerns this poem, a noise both distant and intimate, reducing the adults who perceive it to 'Talking heads, speaking likenesses'. Becoming a 'speaking likeness' involves the disappearance of identity into noise, where 'noise' symbolises the non-differentiation of otherness, the 'tumult' of others. Self-erasure is again the repressed desire and anxiety of this poem, in its final recognition that the resemblance of words, music and noise implies a similarity between them that the poem exploits in its own use of the sounds and music available to the poetic use of the word.

The poems in *The Slant Door* are haunted by this sense of the potentially destructive power of representation, its ability to turn reality into something other, its 'freezing' of the world of things into the world of language. 'Silver Age' laments the sadness that 'an age, whatever age, should pass'. 'But no use, no cure', it decides. The passage of time becomes the freezing of the past and also, importantly, its silencing: 'It's the cold turns them numb / And prevents them from talking, / Mud in mouths for every lengthening year'. In response to this silencing, the poem's function becomes that of representation, allowing and constructing a space for the articulation of the experience of the past. 'Silver Age' echoes Auden's 'In Memory of W.B. Yeats' in its image of the 'mercury falling', and offers an elegy for all lost time, its hardening into history: 'Earth turns steel / And bone powders like Napoleon's buttons'. This perception of temporal transience and the irredeemable 'pastness' of the past imbues many of the poems in *The Slant Door* with elegiac qualities; the final stanza of 'Nils' combines the characteristic images into a sequence:

I spin away from time and house,
Freezing silver spreads my veins:

> Below me disappear the lanes
> Of childhood – Faster goose!

Elsewhere temporal consciousness and its accompanying pastoral nostalgia modulate into the awareness of mortality and its pervasive presence. 'Facelift' (echoing Eliot's 'Whispers of Immortality') symbolises the transformations of ageing as the stripping away of surfaces to reveal death and violence: 'beneath the skin the skeleton shows through / damp and crumbling, smelling of decay, / reminding us of sickness, murder too.' 'The Village Politicians' describes a photograph in which 'The fireplace is threatened / By encroaching darkness. Time fixes them like glue'. And in 'H' of 'An Illustrated Alphabet', it is 'the frost' that remains, 'hidden and durable'.

This preoccupation with the traditional poetic themes of temporality and mortality (the 'compound reminder / Of minutes and fragments of minutes' in 'Homecoming') within the perception of everyday objects and events is also the initial source of the 'surreal' dimension of Szirtes' work noted by reviewers. It extends the symbolic force of his careful observation of the potential othernesses that reside within everyday events and phenomena. His attention to the thingness of things involves a recognition that their persistence depends upon art's rendering of them, just as art's effectiveness depends on its ability to capture reality, its attention to 'what is left when mythologies disappear' ('At Colwick Park'). In 'Summer Landscape', this tension between the real and its poetic rendering finds a level of irresolvability – the poem argues for the persistence of the world 'long after you move', and asserts that 'Houses remain far longer than your gaze / Can hold them'. The real world comprises a sequence of images: 'the gardens now / Push hedges out all bristling in a blaze / Of withered sticks. Roads grow steep and white...', which crumbles, in the poem's centre, to the 'dust' of cliché: 'Here descriptions bite / The dust.' The next assertion cements mortality within the world of the poem, its words undermining the 'presence' of the world: 'We end at nothing'.

Szirtes' preferred metaphor for this process, and one that haunts his entire career, is that of freezing, here emphasised in an internal rhyme worthy of Martin Bell: 'You, the trees, / The houses, freeze before oncoming night'. At the poem's end, a new series of images, lacking the semantic links present in the opening stanzas, continue this rhyme and mark a potentially destructive closure (the bees 'bombard the pane'; 'Summer dies by degrees' towards the impending cold of winter). The solidity of the world, the poem suggests, is also the certainty of its death, and art's attempt to capture it is similarly doomed; summer offers a metaphor of transience that renders the artist / poet momentarily impotent ('My hands drop down') in the face of the 'oncoming night', which, like the storm in 'The Slant Door', threatens to obliterate this pastoral landscape.

Other sources of destruction also concern *The Slant Door*. Its pointedly placed opening poem, 'Virius and Generalic', consists of unrhymed quatrains dealing with names and histories sufficiently unfamiliar to English readers to require an explanatory note, informing us that the characters of the title 'were twentieth-century Yugoslav naïve artists. Virius died in a concentration camp at Yemin during the war. Sixteen years later Generalic painted a *homage* to Virius'. The poem combines this history with a description of Generalic's painted homage, an image of death and mourning. The space of the image is carefully delineated in the second stanza: the painting depicts

> a tomb of grass
> in a field by the church
> ringed with space only,
> the pronged wire distant.

Such a space symbolises a compromised pastoral, the naïve artistry mimicked by the limpid language (another version of Antony Rowland's 'awkward poetics')[53] and marking history's presence through metonymic compression – 'the pronged wire' standing for the camps and the experiences they contain – and by its distance (itself another feature of post-Holocaust writing, a form of writerly defence against the real). Szirtes' compressed, 'awkward' elegiac lament also offers, from its own historical distance (which doubles that of the painting from the death it commemorates), a gesture of solidarity, the artist appealed to in his lamenting of his friend. Its concluding sequence of images summarises a history of extreme suffering indicated by the 'thirst' of the water and the 'Byzantium of worms' that establishes death's kingdom. The poem's overtly Christian symbolism ('a cock of hope') seeks an ameliorative function refused by the simplicity of the description.

The poem merely renders, in economical language, the contents and form of the painting, but in doing so it transforms the painting into a verbal parable of mourning and of the function of the work of art in performing the act of mourning, its content a version of the burden of history inherited by post-Holocaust artists. Poem and painting merge into a single figure of loss, the image lost to words, the world lost to the image, and the horror of the Holocaust. Other

Holocaust writing echoes in this poem; the 'Byzantium of worms', for example, alludes to Miklós Rádnoti's 'Root', in which (in Wilmer and Gömöri's translation) 'The world begins to teem with worms'. In using Yugoslav naïve artists as vehicles for his parable, and in echoing the Hungarian of Rádnoti (who died on a forced march in 1944, after imprisonment in a camp in Serbia, and whose poem 'Forced March' Szirtes will translate in *The Photographer in Winter*), Szirtes indirectly asserts a major location of the politics of his poetry in Eastern Europe. This location lends the figuring of loss unavoidable personal and general political significances concerned with the experience of Szirtes' mother and, through her, his understanding of the functions of poetry in relation to traumatic historical experiences.

These significances emerge in later poetry as major concerns. In *The Slant Door* they remain largely embedded, surfacing in momentary images – the 'unpalatable dream / Of fighting and twisted muscles, escape and pursuit' that interrupts the 'suppressed excitement' of 'Nativity Scene', or 'a body hanging with showered age, / The skin glistening' in 'Dwellings'. 'At the Dressing-table Mirror' returns to personal memory, narrating in detail a remembered incident and its persistence as a signifier of identification and love. The mirror functions as the container of an image in which memory resides; in its reflection the boy and his mother are joined, 'surprised by the net in which they find / Themselves doing what their image shows them doing.' The momentary enjambed emphasis on 'Themselves' draws attention to the mirror's role in the 'finding' of the self; mirrors, like windows, occupy important positions in Szirtes' poetry as signifiers of the potential otherness of the world, in which 'surprise' accompanies self-recognition. The mirror also offers a memento mori, a symbolic event to which the poet is momentarily returned in memory by 'throwing out old books or turning up a card / In her writing, or noticing a look in his daughter's eye'. Memory returns in reading or a 'look'; the traces of a life remain as writing or as other forms of inscription available to be read.

The poems in *The Slant Door* touch on themes which remain nascent, pitching the world and the perceptions of the adult poet against the desire to record what Derek Mahon calls 'the landscape of a childhood / only he can recapture'.[54] Their attention to the detailed observation of the world, and its relation in turn to the recording and representation of that world in poetry, suggest a poet in the process of learning his 'craft'. Szirtes experiments throughout his early poetry with a variety of strict and loose forms, giving some indication of the variety to come ('Summer Landscape', 'Recovering', 'Sleeping' and 'Bones' use *terza rima*; many poems are structured in stanzas of various lengths; 'Silver Age' and 'The Swimming Pool in the House' are varieties of sonnet). His next collection, *November and May*, sustains this formal diversity but also represents both a consolidation of aesthetic themes and concerns and a subtle shift of direction.

November and May

Szirtes' second collection was published in 1981. Dedicated 'To Mandeville and Dodman', the Hitchin-based presses that published his earliest poetry in the 1970s, it formalises several of the themes of *The Slant Door*, not least the importance to Szirtes' poetic of a particular reworking of the English pastoral tradition that is described, in 'The Silver Tree' (the first of a sequence of poems titled 'Misericords'), as 'cold pastoral'. This borrowing from Keats' 'Ode on a Grecian Urn' perfectly encapsulates the dominant genre and mood of Szirtes' early poetry; his scrutiny of perception and memory through aesthetic fixity elaborates a coded version of the world as divided between movement and stasis, the living and the dead, the fluid and the fixed. Drawing on the Romantic conception of art as stasis laden with potential that is elaborated in Keats' poem, 'The Silver Tree' explores this dialectic, offering other oppositions to figure the transformative effect of representation upon the world. The poem narrates the making of a silver tree (its version of the 'Grecian Urn') by 'five girls' in 'a hot steamed up room'. The 'tree made of silver paper' which they build is artificial, a figure of unrefined artistry, 'growing / from a trunk so clumsy only a child / could be taken in by it'.

Art's ability to 'take us in' is here questioned; the tree, as symbol of the aesthetic, is palpably unreal. Its fakeness, however, is transformed in the series of conceits that constitutes the poem. As the words elaborate its appearance it becomes both the world of the poem and the girls themselves: 'lovelier than hair', it is transformed into 'a genuine silver tree they seem to spin / out of themselves'. The mythic transformation of girl into tree derives from Ovid's *Metamorphoses* and is a key motif of modernist poetry – Ezra Pound, following Gautier, writes in 'Hugh Selwyn Mauberley' of 'Daphne with her thighs in bark',[55] an image returned to and adapted by Szirtes in 'The Ghost in the Tree': 'Tarred and feathered in leaves, with her haunches / Scraped raw on bark'. In Szirtes' poem the image of girl 'transformed' into tree figures the transformation of the world in and by poetry: 'the triumph of Aluminium' is the poem's version of the power of artifice to recreate, making the world anew but also rendering it artificially. It refers forward in the collection to the images of creative modernity in the 'Romance' poem 'The Rocket': 'A rocket made of aluminium, / Children wrapped in baking foil'.

'The Silver Tree' pushes this conceit further through recognising the doubleness of this transformation in the figure of 'ambiguity' – 'And just as they become the tree, the tree / becomes them'. World, art and artist are intertwined in the process of 'freezing' the 'hot steamed up room' into a metaphor, marked by the pun on 'frieze':

> As the tree grows they grow, although
> infinitely more slowly, and enter into
> the frieze where mothers and smart daughters dance
> in a cold pastoral. Ice is eating them.

The vowel sounds of 'grows – grow – although – slowly' culminate in 'cold', emphasising the slowing-down of the poem's action into the 'frieze', which returns us to the created object by echoing 'tree'. The homonymic pair 'frieze' / 'freeze' establishes the intimate connection between representation and frozenness as central to this poem. Artistic creation, the poem asserts, involves an 'infinitely' slow progression, the Keatsian freezing of life into the 'cold pastoral' of art (later, in 'The Outhouse', the cold is described as 'an effacement / of all that promised warmth'). The interdependence of art and the real is the last source of dynamism, a constant dialectic which becomes, in the final verse paragraph, 'the film re-running'. 'Desire for perpetuity' is desire for life and for art; the poem's argument extends, finally, into a surreal vision of a patriarchal and mythical future in which 'mothers and smart daughters' 'hang like fruit, sucked out, perfect'.

The image of 'freezing' pervades the early poems of *November and May*, particularly noticeable in the context of enclosed, private or domestic, spaces. Snow falling in 'The Car' 'had risen up / The windscreen and had reached the top, / Freezing it as steady as a crystal'. 'The Icy Neighbour' presents 'the permanent chamber of frost', the neighbour's house with its 'very dust frozen on the tables and sills'. Later, in 'The Museum', it is 'Midsummer' but the museum is 'cold'. The chill in *November and May* is closely connected another prominent thread of images to do with light, which stands for the experience of the sublime. 'Of Grass' attempts to

render the colour of the grass, 'so soft, so bright, / No metaphor
could touch it or scumble it'; 'The Car' starts with 'light skedad-
dling across the bars'; 'House in Sunlight' maps the domestic
world of 'Custom' as a 'guiding light', with 'mirrors and photo-
graphs' in which 'forms suddenly appear'; the 'terrifying head
thrust in at the window' in 'The Outhouse' is 'made blue by light
that had crossed continents, tundra and ice'; and 'Half Light' des-
cribes the appearance of a ghost in 'darkness that is luminous'. In
the latter case light is clearly connected to its opposite, suggesting
that the function of light is to symbolise the machinery of percep-
tion in the visual field.

'Half Light' demonstrates how this symbolic thread is harnessed
to the ideological and formal project of these poems, which is to
offer a meditative extension of the difficult process of mourning.
It provides a ground of argument and experience, and a tone and
modality of expression, from and through which the poems in
November and May constitute an extended, sometimes indirect
elegy for Szirtes' mother. Their concern with light, dark and cold
weaves these image-threads into a long meditation on the potential
of poetry as a medium of mourning. 'Cold pastoral' and the asso-
ciated ideologies of nostalgia that come with such a generic allu-
sion provide a literary precursor for the elegiac mode into which
Szirtes' poetry is now moving. In 'Half Light' this elegiac func-
tion, a mode of severe poetic difficulty, is asserted through the
representation of perception melded with memory. The rational
dimension of thought encounters the irrational, and the poem rep-
resents the negotiated outcome of the contradictory, impossible
perception with which it opens: 'She is standing in a darkness
that is luminous'. This statement is immediately contradicted by
an alternative assertion attributed to the cat: 'That is a lie, dark-
ness cannot / be luminous unless I choose to make it so'. What is
contested here is the logic of the simile 'darkness that is luminous',
rather than the logic of the apprehension of a ghost (the reader is
not yet aware of this possibility; the figure of the woman is simply
a woman, as this stage) – not the perception, but its appropriate
rendering in words and rhetorical forms, is under scrutiny.

The poem negotiates this contestation by temporarily abandon-
ing the simile, stating instead that 'she who is standing there inhabits
darkness'. This transforms the opening assertion into a simple,
logically consistent statement. 'That argument is appropriate', the
poem asserts, as if pleased with its momentary foray into logic.
We then shift to the question, not of perception, but of knowledge
and its loss: 'I no longer know / who that woman might be'. The

real world is evoked through its noise and solidity, constituting its 'physical and mental space', but 'Half Light' inhabits another space, that of memory and mourning. The 'someone' who 'is standing, waiting quietly' is, the poem asserts again, 'making that darkness luminous'. The darkness is, by now, no quality of the material world but a symbolic space, the darkness of death, inhabited by 'A mother / dead too early' who 'burned brightly enough'. Her ghostly presence is both desired and resisted by the poem. While she 'would scarcely deign to blow such a thin flame / that darkness itself was the more noticeable', 'Half Light' can only conclude with a tormented, uncertain rhetorical question: 'Whose fingers if not hers then scratch away / behind the lids, causing the sensation of light?'

In *November and May* a 'more noticeable' darkness of mourning and loss begins to permeate Szirtes' work. 'The Ghost in the Tree' offers the tree as a memorial, a 'transfigured' monument (just as the poem 'transfigures' the tree into words) to a dead woman, allowing the poet to 'find comfort in her darkness'. 'Necromancy', a kind of companion poem to 'Half Light', offers another ghostly visitation, a mother's 'kiss' felt by 'the daughter-in-law not the son'. The bedroom mutates, under the aegis of this ghostly kiss, into a gothic chamber with 'Blood coloured curtains, blankets rucked like tombs' and 'Sheets wound as sheets will'. The 'sleep' of death permeates the world of the domestic in the second half of the poem, balancing the ghost itself, which becomes, in the poem's centre, 'A live thing'. This reversal parodies art's freezing of reality; the ghost (art, product of 'necromancy') becomes real and the real becomes ghostly. The poet's 'hand' is the agency of this analogy, a 'hand' that 'moved in a slime of known events / Intangible as dreams'. The world of 'known events' is transformed, in poetry, into a space of words, 'intangible as dreams', that replaces even dreams ('He never could remember dreams'). Mourning, here, is integral to the process of representation; it involves memory (the mother 'had been dead three years') and imagination, here figured as 'Necromancy', a word that literally means 'corpse-divination', but has been etymologically confused by the medieval elision 'necro-' with 'nigro-', meaning 'black', to mean 'black magic'. The ghost of the mother, obeying 'her [i.e. the daughter-in-law's], though not his, necromancy', becomes the object of the poem's concluding complex of emotions, 'an affection without hope like desire'. 'Desire' signifies the condition of mourning, the sense of loss that accompanies grief. The poem performs its act of mourning through a symbolic displacement from the dead to the living, who become (in a metaphor that prefigures *Short Wave*) 'waves', moving things in contrast with the 'frozen' world of the past and the dead.

'Half Light' and 'Necromancy', both poems about ghosts, exemplify a dimension of uncanniness increasingly characteristic of Szirtes' poetry. The uncanny has been described by Nicholas Royle as embodying 'a crisis of the proper' and 'a crisis of the natural'; it is a contradictory psychological and aesthetic mode, collapsing the familiar (the bedroom in 'Necromancy') into the unfamiliar (the 'darkness that is luminous' of 'Half Light'). The uncanny, Royle suggests, affords a means of 'thinking about so-called "real life", the ordinary, the familiar, the everyday'.[56] Szirtes' poems, grounded in the careful observation of the familiar and the everyday ('Brimstone Yellow', in the short sequence 'The Dissecting Table', describes 'an itch / on the eye that tries to follow' the 'toss and passage' of two butterflies'), push through the surfaces of the mundane world into spaces of sometimes sinister uncanniness, lending his early work its surrealist edge. 'Floating' begins with the 'splash' of 'children', but quickly shifts focus onto 'a comical underworld that is / Fringed with horror', in which specific, personal memories and fears emerge: 'At night the sea eats away mother's face / Till she is thin and polished'. Swimming and diving become metaphors of watery 'resurrection', and the swimming pool itself becomes a bizarre space of conflicting lights and colours: 'They burn in lime / And rise raw red to dazzling surfaces'.

'Homage to Postman Cheval', a distinctly late-Audenesque sequence of four sonnets, expresses most clearly the importance of surrealism to Szirtes' early work and establishes in its description of its subject an allegory of its own reading that summarises Szirtes' concern at this stage in his career with the aesthetics of poetry. Ferdinand Cheval (1836-1924) worked as a postman and spent 33 years building, in his spare time, an 'ideal castle' in his home town of Châteauneuf-de-Galaure, a monument of naïve art constructed out of stones, found objects and seemingly random detritus of the everyday, described in Szirtes' poem as 'A labyrinth, an ornamental grotto'. Cheval was fêted by the surrealists – Max Ernst made a postcard collage titled *Le Facteur Cheval* in 1932, and André Breton's poem 'Facteur Cheval' shadows Szirtes' 'Homage', the opening line of which – 'An architrave of breasts' – echoes Breton's description '*Sans se retourner tu saisissais la truelle dont on fait les seins*'.[57] The careful formalism of Szirtes' rhymed iambics contrasts markedly with the uncanniness of its subject, which comes, as the poem progresses, to figure the poem itself. The poem describes Cheval's palace in terms invoking the uncanny – 'Grim Freudian corridors', 'a multiplicity of doors' – and cementing the spaces of the building as analogous to the 'ornamental' forms of poetry; Cheval, the poem asserts, 'built' his 'rhymes of moon and spoon and June'. 'What of this, pray, is not ornamental?' it asks in a rhetorical aside addressed, implicitly, to itself as well as to the viewer of the building. The poem extends through this analogy, asking 'By what trick, what mad juxtaposition / Could White House, Pyramid be linked in vision?' The 'vain ambition' of Cheval's work is compared to other eccentric moments of art and literary history – 'Dadd before his Masterstroke' and 'Pope with his pet Toad' – and the third sonnet elaborates the palace as a world in miniature, encompassing 'Kashmir, / The Vatican', 'Mount Athos' and 'Brasilia', 'Chih-li' and, eventually, 'Heaven'. The palace offers a figure of the demotic sublime, which one observer called 'A heap of bad taste' and the poem describes as 'doggerel' (the 'doggerel' of strict, consistent formalism, eschewed by Szirtes' poetry); but, it notes, Blake and Keats were 'not above doggerel', implying the elusive presence of the Romantic sublime in the background of Szirtes' evaluation of Cheval.

The poem's final sonnet opens with an assertion that prioritises the everyday as a suitable object of aesthetic scrutiny: 'The imagination feeds on what it gets'. The list of images and books that follows indicates the mundanity of sources of inspiration, but also extends the geographical range that the poem attributes to Cheval's project. The work of the imagination, it suggests, constructs a world in desire, just as the postman's letters allow another mapping of the world linked by systems of communication. Amid this expansive geographical meandering, the poem allows Cheval's assertion that 'Home is Best' (a point of closure that will reverberate throughout Szirtes' later work), before concluding with an allusion to Cheval's other great building work, the mausoleum where his body now rests.

Architecture (as we have seen) provides one of the metaphors Szirtes uses to describe his own poems. Cheval's palace becomes, in this poem, a monument to the creative vision shared by architecture and poetry, a celebration of the embedded theme of many of the poems in *November and May* – the ability of the poetic imagination to transform 'what it gets' into objects of aesthetic value. The recurrent themes of the collection – desire and memory, art and representation, the mundanity of the everyday and its potential to transform, momentarily, into the surreal and the uncanny, and art's 'freezing' of the world in the genre of 'cold pastoral – are presented in poems of increasing formal assuredness, in which a distinctive tone gradually emerges. Szirtes' next collection for Secker, *Short Wave*, plots a further phase in the development of these concerns, and their focusing into a coherent poetic project.

Short Wave

Szirtes' third collection comprises three sections, the third of which contains a sequence, *The Kissing Place*, first published by The Starwheel Press, the private press run by Szirtes and his partner Clarissa Upchurch during the 1980s. The central section provides the title's collection, while the first, 'The Sleepwalker', develops and establishes certain familiar themes and concerns. *Short Wave* extends the processes of observation and recording characteristic of the earlier volumes but adds to them a new level of literary awareness, a new sense of the poet's place in relation to contemporaries and traditions, and a new willingness to assert, rather than simply record, the effect of the poetic upon the world. This effect is recorded in a line in 'Slow Tango for Six Horses', the penultimate poem of the 'Short Wave' section. The fifth of the 'Six Horses' is 'Blankness', characterised as 'high class but likes the gutter'. The 'strange' company she keeps evokes 'danger', and, the quatrain concludes, 'That deep Blankness is the real thing stranger'. This line adapts and responds to the concluding sentence of Alan Brownjohn's 'William Empson at Aldermaston', published in Brownjohn's *Travellers Alone* (1954) and in the selection of his poems in *Penguin Modern Poets 14*.[58]

Brownjohn's poem considers Empson's presence on an anti-atomic weapons march at Aldermaston ('I generally do the first day of the Aldermaston march', Empson wrote in a letter to Robert Lowell in 1962).[59] It protests at 'death', symbolised by the atomic bomb developed at Aldermaston, described as a 'thing' separate from the reality of everyday life and human agency: typists.../ do not make the thing' and 'scientists.../ do not fire the thing'. It notes the way the carnival of protest mirrors the 'discreet pavilions of the State', and asks what the research establishment's workers and their families did during the protest: 'Many faces looked the way / Of the procession', it observes, 'speaking not a word / But merely watching'. It is the blankness of these faces that puzzles the poet: 'That deep blankness / Was the real thing strange'. The implication is that those who knowingly work to support such research are already complicit with death; the 'real thing' is the 'blankness' of death itself, 'strange' and yet 'real'. Szirtes' poem seizes on the line's potential as an encapsulation of his own aesthetic agenda in *Short Wave*: 'Slow Tango for Six Horses' exploits to the full the symbolic potentials of the line from Brownjohn's poem, opening up a space for an extended meditation on writing.

Szirtes' poem is densely allusive: its 'dream of horses' nods to Ted Hughes' 'A Dream of Horses',[60] famously described by Al Alvarez (in contrast with Larkin's 'At Grass') as 'unquestionably about something; it is a serious attempt', Alvarez goes on, 'to re-create and so clarify, unfalsified and in the strongest imaginative terms possible, a powerful complex of emotions and sensations'.[61] Hughes' horses 'whinnied and bit and cannoned the world from its place'; Szirtes, a radically different poet from Ted Hughes, nevertheless shares with him an underlying concern with 'the real thing strange' (the world 'cannoned' from its place). 'Slow Tango for Six Horses' traces this 'cannoning' through a series of allegorical stanzas exploring the whiteness of the page on which the poet inscribes the symbolic world of writing. The opening sestet condenses reference to Georgette Heyer's regency romance *The Grand Sophy* (1950) (with its self-consciously deceptive poet-suitor Augustus Fawnhope) and Tobias Smollett's *Peregrine Pickle* (1751), in which Mr Gauntlet, 'looked upon in the army as an expert swordsman', also has 'a passion' for a Miss Sophy. The names of the six white horses (perhaps itself an allusion to Tommy Cash's 1970 country song of the same title) evoke different aspects of the literary: Bernarda alludes to the last play of Federico García Lorca, *La Casa de Bernarda Alba* (1936; 'Alba' means 'white'); Arsenic, Foolscap, Snowdrop and Blankness represent different forms taken by the whiteness that has pervaded (in the form of 'Snow') so much of Szirtes' early poetry; and Catherick is the surname of the central character of Wilkie Collins' gothic novel *The Woman in White* (1859-60). The 'Slow Tango' of this poem is a movement through the various forms and versions of whiteness, the different blanknesses that confront the writer about to write.

A short, thirteen-line poem in the opening section exemplifies Szirtes' aesthetic strategy in this collection. 'A Girl Sewing' offers a small vignette that exemplifies the process of the poetic imagination. Its links with similar poems in his earlier collections are clear: it establishes familiar tensions between stillness and movement (reminiscent again of Keats' 'Ode on a Grecian Urn'), and between creation and destruction, and, in the balance between the 'perfection' of 'imagined girls' and the 'mass of mean forgotten things', between the imaginary and the real, and between forgetting as a form of negation and imagining as a form of creation. The underlying opposition is between watcher and watched, the girl's sewing offering a figure of the poetic imagination at work, quickly dissolving into different (visually based) activities of 'reading' or 'staring'. Observation quickly becomes allegory, description becomes deduction, and, in the centre of the poem, the aesthetic is presented as a profoundly specular and (despite the poem's grounding in a distinctly patriarchal world-view) uncertain experience, a consequence of the tendencies of light and shadow to erase 'littleness' (the 'mean forgotten things' that make up reality): 'Sometimes the light makes littleness too subtle / so it seems nothing: light so weak that shadows / become indiscernible on a flat surface'. Poetry thus both records and threatens reality – just as things 'fray or tear almost as soon as finished', so art 'freezes the creases of a finished garment'. Poetry here acts in a manner analogous to photography, the mode of representation with which much of Szirtes' subsequent writing will engage. The 'freezing' effect of artistic representation, and its further connection to sequences of imagery to do with light and dark, now takes on deeper personal resonances as Szirtes' work begins to search for ways of responding constructively to his mother's life and to her death, themes that begin to dominate his work from 1983 onwards.

The poems in *Short Wave* circulate round a perception of the world as a liberating 'plenitude' (in 'Abundance'), a further apprehension of MacNeice's 'drunkenness of things being various' as a threat to the order and meticulousness of poetic form, as in the closing four lines of 'Hand Dance':

> And think of all the kisses trapped and freed
> to catch again, again in the long night
> which is longer than their reach or grasp,
> which can't be caught by hands and casts no shadow.

Death, 'the long night', is also desire, the 'reach' of the hand and of the imagination. The 'Dance' of the hands, like that of art, is a formal patterning with its own conventions and traditions – 'What fine old dances can they twist and turn to' – which are also, like 'the long night', potential traps to be escaped from. 'Early Rising' uses the motif of the bedsheets as winding sheets from *November and May*'s 'Necromancy' to explore further the interrelations of body parts as metonymic signifiers of mortality. The poem's pastoral and Romantic insights (the blackbird as moral messenger, her 'sculptured fioratura [sic]', borrowed from Anthony Hecht's 'A Lot of Night Music',[62] signifying a melodic decoration, another symbol of art) are laden with the weight of mortality: the 'garden' is 'stone' and the protagonists 'move in stone between alive and dead', 'The window' is 'frozen with its motes of dust', the faint optimism of the poem's central and redemptive claim that 'Love may last as long / as life perhaps' undermined by the hesitant modality of its phrasing. The tone of such a poem (markedly different from the jaunty rhythms of 'Postscript: Reply to the Angel at Blythburgh', discussed below) suggests that Szirtes is working through the potentials of pastoral elegy in order to lay them to rest. And yet this is the prevailing tone of *Short Wave* – a slow-moving, carefully modulated and insistently focused sequence of images that provides the basis for aesthetic meditation.

Increasingly, observation develops significance from a primary aesthetic assertion, rather than the other way round. In 'A Pheasant' the bird emerges into view out of such a statement:

> The most beautiful things are not so much
> useless as startling: waves that rise in a throat,
> the brushed mouths of a pheasant's abdomen,
> his blue head lolling on a kitchen table.

The initial assertion about 'beautiful things' here concerns a switch from function to effect, suggesting that Szirtes' motivation in such imagery as the stanza's third line is to 'startle'. In its symbolic function as art, the dead bird, the poem argues, 'cannot exactly said to be dead / because his brilliance is undiminished'. The 'brilliance' of the work of art ('more than half his life') establishes its potential to illuminate the darkness that pervades other poems in the collection.

Szirtes then offers, in this poem's penultimate stanza, a sequence of allusions reminiscent in its complexity of Eliot's quatrain poems in its metaphorical density, and displaying how much his poetry has learnt from Eliot, Martin Bell and other modernist precursors. The stanza alludes firstly to II Chronicles 9.21, which documents the sources of Solomon's wealth: 'For the King's ships went to Tarshish with the servants of Huram: every three years once came the ships of Tarshish bringing gold, and silver, ivory, and apes, and peacocks'. This allusion elides into a reference to John Masefield's 'Cargoes', which reworks the Biblical verse into 'Quinquiremes of Nineveh from distant Ophir' carrying 'a cargo of ivory / And apes and peacocks'. The 'peacocks' stimulate the phrase from Tennyson's 'Now Sleeps the Crimson Petal' – 'Now droops the milk-white peacock like a ghost / And like a ghost she glimmers on to me', lines which resonate in the ghostly mourning-world constructed in many of Szirtes' poems.

This series of religious and literary associations invokes wealth, beauty, poetry, nature and, emphasised at the end of the stanza, 'melancholy', with all its Keatsian resonances as well as its Hungarian ones. Szirtes writes, in the 'Introduction' to *Leopard V: An Island of Sound*, of the importance in Hungarian literature of the noun *bú* (pronounced like a long 'boo'), and its adjective *bús* (booosh)'; 'you can never make that "oo" sound quite long or closed enough',[63] he adds – hence the emphasis on the same vowel sound in the phrase 'drooping moonily' in 'A Pheasant'. The poem concludes with a paraphrase of Feste's apothegm to Maria in *Twelfth Night*: 'He that is well hanged in this world needs to fear no colours',[64] a statement which may work back to the 'dead soldier in full dress uniform' of the third stanza (Shakespeare's Maria interprets 'colours' to refer to military flags of identity). It finishes with a hesitant qualification: 'The living we are not so sure about', suggesting again that life may need to 'fear' the symbolic power of art. Such dense allusion is unusual in Szirtes' work, and suggests that the poem itself constitutes the product of a struggle to render in words an increasingly complex apprehension of the relations between symbolic and representational functions, between words and things, and between the formal demands of poetry and the tendency for ideas and ideologies to lack formal precision.

The collection closes with its longest poem, 'Postscript: A Reply to the Angel at Blythburgh', which offers Szirtes' fullest dialogic engagement with the work of another poet, a dialogue which mobilises his most focused and significant commentary yet on his conception of poetry and its possibilities. The poem responds to the work of Peter Porter, and in particular to Porter's combined attack on the efficacy of poetry and, by extension, of other forms of faith and commitment, in the face of deep human suffering. Its form, consisting of seventeen "Burns stanzas", sestets rhyming AAABAB with 'B' rhymes ending shortened, two-stressed lines, lends it a rolling, ballad-like rhythm that counterpoints its high literary seriousness. The poem is modelled on James Fenton's 'Letter to John Fuller' (1972) which uses the same form for a similar purpose; it alludes also to Fuller's own verse letters collected in *Epistles to Several Persons* (1973), all written in "Burns stanzas".[65] Its title responds initially to Porter's poem 'An Angel in Blythburgh Church', published in the collection *The Cost of Seriousness*[66] which deals with the death, in 1974, of Porter's wife (Szirtes' opening lines engage with the title poem of Porter's collection). 'An Angel in Blythburgh Church' attacks the 'wooden' certainties of 'faith': Porter (who elsewhere calls himself a 'Residual Christian':[67] Szirtes' poem describes 'Residual Christianity' as 'ineffective') echoes the nostalgic, agnostic turn of Larkin's 'Church Going' in asking 'What is it / Turns an atheist's mind to prayer in almost / Any church on a country visit?' Its conclusion resists religious certainties: 'death', it asserts, is 'the only angel'.[68]

Szirtes is also responding here to Porter's poem 'The Cost of Seriousness', which, also sceptical of religious faith, meditates on 'the white page of art' (reminiscent of the 'blankness' of 'Slow Tango for Six Horses') and offers an expression of aesthetic despair ('life or art won't work') in which 'words, Mallarmé-like, / undefine themselves and say / things out of the New Physics: self-destruct!' 'The cost of seriousness,' the poem asserts, 'will be death': 'we stand,' it laments, Beckett-like, 'by a grave and mourn'. The power of Porter's poem lies in its implicit repudiation of its own nihilism by the very fact of its existence; formally complex, lyrically effective and beautifully articulated, it constitutes a summary of a particular apprehension of and response to what Porter elsewhere calls (in 'An Exequy') 'the pointlessness of poetry'.

Szirtes' response initially agrees with Porter's poem, but quickly counters his atheistic nihilism with its own expression of religious faith. Where Porter sees only death, Szirtes sees 'Not death so much then, but the pain'; 'hurt fades to classic pain', his poem asserts. It is, the poem argues, 'religion's task' to 'explain / What suffering means', and it proceeds to consider relations between religion and art. In doing so it asserts the significance of religion as a guarantor of value, and, at the same time, offers important insights into Szirtes' understanding of poetry in relation to religious faith. 'Art', it asserts, 'comprises *grazie*, / That neat Italianate way / Of making ugly things obey / The rules of dance'. This relationship between the 'ugliness' of things and the 'rules of dance', the formal structures of the artwork, has been integral to Szirtes' early poetry, and here becomes its organising argument ('the dance' will be an important motif in a later collection, *Portrait of My Father in an English Landscape*). Art's ability 'to fabricate or to omit, / To make the hazy definite' assumes a central position in what is effectively a declaration of credo linking religious faith to aesthetic conviction. Porter's 'Scream and Variations'[69] is invoked in art's ability to 'round a shape to flatter it / Or hear it scream'; art, Szirtes asserts, can make the 'scream' 'learn / A civilised and formal turn / Of speech'. As an embodiment of art, the Blythburgh angel finally offers shelter from 'despair': 'The eyes that stare / Down into the empty aisles / Shield from despair'. The poem expresses in a final direct address (reminiscent in tone of Auden) to Porter its version of hope in art's salvationary potential, its redemptive force:

> Peter, if one verse we write
> Shields anyone, however slight
> The shelter or how foul the night,
> Let's think of her,
> And bless the angel's loss of sight
> At Blythburgh.

Poetry's role, for Szirtes, is redemption, rather than the 'point-lessness' with which Porter condemns it. In arguing with Porter, Szirtes also implicitly challenges, from a religious perspective, the agnostic or atheistic tradition that extends back to Auden's despair at poetry's ineffectiveness (discussed in the introduction). For Szirtes, poetry (like religion) 'saves', in its application of the 'rules of dance' to the 'ugly' world; its redemptive value is, simultane-ously, its aesthetic force, residing in its formal integrity and in its transformation of reality into art. The allusion in 'Reply to the Angel at Blythburgh' to Orpheus' descent into hell to 'fetch his bride', and the assertion that he 'failed', assume crucial significance in this context (as well as alluding forward to Szirtes' own poetic 'descents into hell' in his next two collections). Orpheus symbolises art's failure, its inability to capture that which it seeks (which Porter refers to, in a poem called 'To Make it Real', as 'a piece of the real').[70] Orpheus' presence in Szirtes' poem is an implicit recogni-tion that faith in art is always faith in the final failure of art to 'capture' the real, an anxiety that this chapter has traced though Szirtes' early collections, and which functions within each poem analysed here as a guarantee that the poem itself works. The poems in *Short Wave* engage in dialogues with Szirtes' contemporaries and with the poetic tradition. They summarise provisionally the ways in which this comprehension of poetry as the creation of art out of the learning of the failure of language, and the anxiety that accompanies it, will now be put into practice in Szirtes' writing.

2

The Photographer in Winter and Metro

Could it have been her – young woman
in this rolled up photograph,
one summer more than fifty years back...?
Were stories told about her all the truth?

PETER ROBINSON, 'The Woman in the Photograph'

In 1985, Martin Booth published a polemical intervention into debates about contemporary poetry, *British Poetry 1964-84: Driving through the barricades*. As its deliberately aggressive, avant-gardiste title suggests, the book's argument, pursued through a detailed and comprehensive survey of the contemporary scene, is uncompromising: 'In Britain, poetry has gone from being largely sterile to immensely virile and has returned to sterility within a decade and a half.' 'British poetry is in a mess,' Booth asserts at the outset, and he proceeds to diagnose the causes of this mess. Among the dozens of targets singled out for attack is George Szirtes, whose first three collections are characterised as 'withdrawn and laid back'. Booth quotes six lines from 'The Artichoke' (in *November and May*), and suggests (as a constructive criticism) that Szirtes 'should not be looking at vegetables', for he is 'an accomplished wordsmith'. 'He should,' Booth suggests, 'be writing about his childhood, using what he heard from Bell in Leeds'.[71]

In 1984, the year before Booth's book was published, Szirtes returned to Hungary for the first time since 1956, on a British Council travelling fellowship. The two collections he published in 1986 and 1988 (which, with *Bridge Passages*, discussed in the next chapter, form a kind of 'Hungarian trilogy') respond directly to this experience; it could be argued that they also respond (consciously or not) to Booth's critique. Both focus on geographical and temporal returns, to the places and times surrounding and predating the poet's childhood. Childhood memories and experiences saturate the worlds of these books, and constitute a major part of their significant narrative elements; they are mediated through an increasingly assured visual consciousness (despite Booth's criticism of 'The Artichoke', a criticism not geared to accommodate such a possibility, Szirtes' poetry is always grounded on meticulous and considered observation) and through a language increasingly willing to take verbal and formal risks, but also bolstered by the author's re-acquaintance with Hungary and with the potential resources offered by a second language and literary tradition.

The new material provided by Hungary – images, memories, emotions, words – immediately intensifies and extends the potential range of Szirtes' poetry. In turn, the poetry explores ways of responding to this new complexity, these new and enriching levels of memory and experience. New geographies of emotion are established in *The Photographer in Winter* (1986), which maps new experiences of Budapest onto the poet's memories of his own past and his speculations about the history preceding him. These are extended deeper in *Metro* (1988), into an ambitious three-dimensional, archaeological reconstruction of the city and the different times it contains. In many ways, *Metro* elaborates on and refines themes and possibilities established first in the earlier collection; while each book is distinct, they are closely connected in that both mark progressive stages in a development of the experience- and observation-based poetry of the earlier volumes, towards a deeper and more problematic preoccupation with the nature of the past. Childhood constitutes one element of this; the narratives associated with Szirtes' mother ('Metro' offers 'my words for what she meant') and her family, offer, along with those found by the adult Szirtes, further threads. Movement (implicit in the title *Metro*) is central to each volume; each conceives of the past and its relations to the present in terms of temporal and geographical displacements and in terms of the movement of desire, 'the undersong' of 'Metro'.

Psychoanalysis understands desire as a movement through a "network" of psychic relays and interchanges that can be understood in terms not unlike a railway system. Szirtes offers, in these poems, a meditation on the relations between memory and desire that exploits the potentials of this psychoanalytic conception. Trains are, of course, familiar symbols of technological modernity and (more sinisterly) of a connected Europe; they are spaces of double intimacy, both private and public, enclosed and exposed, in which public figures can be encountered in private, intimate moments. Szirtes exploits such double potentials throughout these collections – for example, the Italian poet Cesare Pavese is seen, in the poem 'Ghost Train', sitting 'alone with a woman who smokes' – that is, alone and not alone. Szirtes' analysis of desire most fully exploits the metaphorical potential of railways in a short but central sequence in *The Photographer in Winter* entitled 'Trains', providing an initial template for the reading of both collections.

The first poem in 'Trains', 'Level Crossing', meditates on the possibility that sensory experience – 'hearing' and 'seeing', the modes of apprehension of voices and images ('voices', in 'Metro', are 'not heard but seen') that will dominate these collections – can allow us to 'reassemble time and hold it still'. 'There's no turning back', the poem concludes, from the metaphorical force of the train hurtling through the level crossing, a figure of the irresistible movement of history. Its 'vague murmuring', as it passes into the future, will only 'breed memories like rain'. In the next poem, 'North China', this sense of existing in a present precariously balanced between past and future is made more solid: the poem situates us in a time 'neither past / Nor future', but instead 'a lost / Continent of moments' (where 'moments' carries the meaning of movements as well as instants of time). This poem succumbs to a Keatsian 'drowsy numbness', an anaesthetic torpor contrasting with the sensory world of 'Level Crossing', and returns us to the 'frozen' territories familiar from Szirtes' earlier work and integral to the emotional landscape of *The Photographer in Winter*: 'We're on the edge of all that's frozen, formal, / Furious and unattainable' (the adjective 'furious' will later be used, in *Bridge Passages*, to describe the events of 1989). The 'frozen' city of North China symbolises an exoticised past, its frigid 'opulence' inculcating the illusions of desire, concluding in the final image-laden word, 'mirage'.

These symbolic functions are, like a railway network, all interlinked in the "confessional/autobiographical" nexus of meanings that Szirtes constructs. The historical significance of trains, railway carriages and stations is deeply structured in the experiences of European Jews, as well as in the Freudian mythology of desire (as film directors like Alfred Hitchcock well knew). The movement they offer is, at one level, a version or repetition of the displacements, exiles and final journeys enforced upon Hungarian and other Jews during the Holocaust ('They put me on a train,' the mother's voice recounts in 'Metro'). Trains offer a public solitude symbolising the double (personal and public) significance of 'The unfinished business of old Europe', a business which constitutes the burden of history. This potential doubleness, and its comprehension, concerns each collection; the external world of social and political action and events is scrutinised for its correspondence to the interiority of perceptions and emotions, memories and experiences. *The Photographer in Winter* and *Metro* address history's 'unfinished business' in ways argued over in contemporary debates about postmemory, the persistence of traumatic historical experiences across generations. Szirtes' poetry, after all, addresses a history

which 'belongs' to him in a direct sense, but to which he has not
been privy – he encounters it at one remove, a child of the imme-
diate post-War years seeking a logic to account for the residues in
his own life of the near but immensely distant past. 'Metro', in
particular, is a postmemorial text, exploring the ripples and traces
of a history of experience outside the immediate frames of reference
of its author and meditating, in the process, on how time and
memory seem to operate at unconscious levels across generations.

The final 'Trains' poem, 'Windows, Shadows', meditates on
the nature of the perception of historical time and its spatialisation
in images of inside and outside, before and behind, the external
world of public spaces and its mirroring or otherwise in the inter-
nal, psychological spaces of subjective perception. The poem returns
to a collocation used in a brief lyric in *Short Wave*, 'The Design of
Windows', the concluding stanza of which echoes Larkin's 'High
Windows':

> Better are the black and unadorned
> rectangles of glass, new windows
> like negatives, that flaunt their recklessness
> in blocks whose shadows leap across the ground.

The form of 'Windows, Shadows', its title words repeated as rhyme
words on the third and sixth lines of each sextet, insists upon the
significance of these words as metaphors of desire, returning insis-
tently through lexical repetition but shifting, mutating in import
as their significances progress through the poem, and as the poem
moves from light to dark and from the still towards the moving
image (foreshadowing Szirtes' later explorations of photography
and film in *Blind Field* and *Reel*). The 'single carriage' is populated
by a 'quartet of ghosts', figures of a social world divided but shared,
split at the level of possible communication – 'Can we speak with
the same voice / despite the windows?' – but sharing the oxymoronic
'darker light' in which it might be possible to 'exchange / a life for
shadows'. The flickering gloom of 'Windows, Shadows' offers the
train journey as an allegory of the passage through life, revealing a
Matissean vision of darkness within the light, of 'black windows /
making fiction out of fiction' (Matisse's *Open Window, Collioure 1914*,
painted on the threshold of the First World War and looking out
onto a dark, threatening emptiness, seems to be implied here).
The world outside, 'a gallery of portraits', exists only in represen-
tation, mediated through the shared specularity of windows and
shadows; it is a 'fiction' of a 'fiction' in the images that circulate
in the poem. The doubling of this 'fiction' of the real lies at the

core of this poem – its version of the frozen history through which the train travels ('It's freezing here') is the illusory world of images constructed by windows and shadows, a 'landscape' of trickery across which the poem moves 'like a fake / legation'. The poem finally asserts the primacy of the illusion, the disappearance of reality into the circular, imagistic spaces of the poem itself: 'Some windows may be touched / only by shadows'.

A corresponding poem in the 'En Route' sequence in *Metro*, 'The Love of Windows', turns the metaphorical force of the window in a different direction. Echoing the abandonment of language for 'the thought of high windows' in Larkin's poem, Szirtes' poem declares a 'love' for 'the height of windows', which are 'blinding truths or lies', 'silent studies / in deception'. 'Words' in this poem register a 'life too small and faint to read'. Windows, as constructed in the words of the poem, are both mediations of the real and barriers to it; they offer views which are always only views, requiring verbal elaboration, and their metaphorical function in these poems suggests that *Metro* and *The Photographer in Winter* will be much concerned with the problem of how to negotiate, in the 'fictions' of words, the deceptive visions, the 'mirror' worlds, offered by 'windows' and 'shadows'.

The Photographer in Winter develops the 'cold pastoral' of Szirtes' earlier collections into a systematic metaphor of near-allegorical import. Frozenness, snow, ice and the cold wind are recurrent emotional features and qualities of the spaces and times represented in these poems; they constitute a symbolic climate of betrayal, deception and intransigence in which the past is immersed and preserved. The cold fixes and renders static; it removes life from the past (most clearly in 'The Swimmers', which asserts a symbolic connection between the 'black ice' floor of an English church and the 'icy Danube' of Budapest); and it fogs or obscures the poet's vision of that past, like the metaphorical 'snow / Which breaks my picture up' in 'The Photographer in Winter'. It establishes a prevailing mood of oppressive stillness comparable to a kind of death; the poems in *The Photographer in Winter* are much possessed by death, by 'the bone beneath the swing / and softness of the hair', as it's put in 'Cruse'.

Metro, in contrast, opens with images of fluidity. Its initial medium is water and the sea, the 'swimmers' in 'The Lukács Baths' establishing an amphibian world of 'green efflorescence' 'at the bottom of deep pools' which develops, in subsequent poems, into a new, more mobile or fluid metaphorical system. In 'The House Dream', the dead man's 'hands were minnows'; 'A Card

Skull in Atlantis' sinks, in the end, into 'silt, / washed down by rivers'. 'Grandfather in Green' presents the dead grandfather as 'a pebble on a beach / of softness across which swept the pale green tide', and 'Siren Voices' ('Their voices might have been / the sea sprayed up') deals overtly with the mythical lure of the sea. Oceanic metaphors abound in these poems, suggesting a deeper Freudian resonance – or, in 'On a Winding Staircase', 'a debt to history' – in a collection dealing with the poet's relationship to his mother and her past. *Metro* is, after all, a near-anagram of 'mother'.

The symbolic movement between these collections is, then, from the frozen to the thawed, from the immobile and rigid to the fluid and flexible, a progression from the deathlike stillness of the past towards a kind of life or life-in-art, or at least the potential life-likeness that the world of the aesthetic offers. Each condition represents a way of conceptualising the past as it is re-encountered on returning to Budapest. The past in *The Photographer in Winter* appears fixed, waiting for the poet's return, and constitutes an entity – a space, a trace, a historical reality, 'a simple world' (in 'Meeting, 1944') – to which he can only respond, noting its 'pattern' ('Level Crossing') but (in 'Windows, Shadows') lamenting the necessity of 'making fiction out of fiction, and a body / out of nothing' (that 'body' becomes the destroyed terrain of 'Metro'). It's a past constituted in memories, and in narratives of other people's memories, but also in architecture and in the public and private spaces of the city, 'geometries' and 'symmetries' saturated in meanings that evade full capture in words. Poetry, encountering this world, seeks, in the metaphor of the image provided by photography, a way of fixing it without freezing it, a way of representing it as dynamic and present or alive. 'The Photographer in Winter' makes explicit the role of art in this process: 'as I click the shutter / I feel the cold blood thawing in my veins'.

In *Metro* this thawing becomes fluidity, the dynamic of new experience measured, responded to and re-structured by poetry. 'I love the city', 'Undersongs' begins, 'the way it eats you up / And melts you into walls along with stone / And stucco.' Becoming part of the architectural fabric of the city, the poet 'melts' into its specific chronotopic functions, the networks of intersections and interactions between time and space that lend meaning and historical significance to places. The prevailing metaphor of the title poem 'Metro' exploits these functions through the device of the Budapest Metro system, a symbol of urban interconnection as well as of the underworld, the repressed or buried past (the unconscious of repressed desire) that the collection seeks to excavate.

The collection concludes with 'Burns Night by the Danube', its epigraph – 'In Memoriam 1956' – locating it historically in the October revolution, 'funeral and feast', and the poem asserts with grim authority that the history of which it writes is public property: 'But everyone gets walk-on parts / In history'. The collection's meticulous detailing of the private dimensions of the past has not, the poem suggests, been in vain (again, the emphasis on observation and recording needs to be noted): '*Specifics and particulars / Are everything*'. *Metro* adds a new kind of poetic intensity to Szirtes' *œuvre*, and develops a poetry determined to confront and work to unravel the obscurities of its own origins.

'When I went back to Hungary for the first time,' Szirtes commented in a radio interview, 'Budapest was the most intense experience I'd had in my life I think, and it was going to have to filter back. And when it began to filter back, it began to filter out in these longer poems, because the material was more narrative in some ways, and because there were shadows behind shadows and levels behind levels.'[72] This double process of 'filtering back' and 'filtering out' (further liquid metaphors) took place during the four years that separated this initial experience of return from the publication of *Metro*, suggesting that the poetry produced in this period offers an extended engagement with the logics and consequences of what Szirtes has elsewhere called the 'marvellous and disorientating experience' of returning.[73]

The Budapest that Szirtes re-encountered in 1984 seems a space saturated initially by parental, rather than immediately personal, memories, and specifically with the ghosts of memories that predate the poet's birth in 1948. Furthermore, the parental experience distils, in the crucial sequences of these collections, into imagined and recollected versions of the life of the poet's mother – 'My first return to Hungary was driven by curiosity about my mother's past', Szirtes has written in 'Fables of Home'[74] – a life made manifest in narrative versions offered by an imagistic, highly formalised poetry in which fragmentary, contingent realities and fantasies are corralled, reconstructed and pieced together. Form is crucial in these volumes; it structures experience at moments when experience threatens to overwhelm, and, in true modernist style, it provides a necessary brake on the emotional dimension of the work, lending it the trappings of tradition and convention that serve partially to objectify and 'make strange' experiences over-familiar or potentially overwhelming to the poet (and therefore requiring 'filtering through and back').

Modernist allusions abound in these collections, from the frequent echoes of T.S. Eliot's poetry (discussed further below) to specific citations of important motifs like 'Proust's madeleines' (in 'Burns Night by the Danube'), or Ezra Pound's 'few thousand battered books' (in *Hugh Selwyn Mauberley*) alluded to by 'A few thousand books gathering dust and amber' in 'A Greek Musée' (also in *Metro*). If 'Windows, Shadows' echoes Matisse, modern painting structures a central, surrealistic poem in *The Photographer in Winter*, 'The Green Mare's Advice to the Cows' (dedicated 'i.m. Marc Chagall died 1985': Szirtes describes himself, in his interview with John Tusa, as 'a Chagallian painter').[75] In drawing on modernist traditions Szirtes extends his poetry's debts to visual as well as poetic experimentation, and simultaneously extends the range of these traditions, investing them with new resonances.

Form also constitutes one aspect of what is referred to, in 'The Photographer in Winter', by the character of Szirtes' mother as 'art..., the difficult'. The 'difficulty' of art, and Szirtes' explorations of modernist experiments with and responses to it, constitute significant subtexts in these collections, and account in part for the problems that these poems present to the reader expecting the simpler lyric experiences and poems of observation that had characterised Szirtes' earlier work. One reviewer of *Metro* notes the form of the title sequence, and asks 'whether these forms are suited to a poetry that relies so heavily on *images*'.[76] What becomes clear from considering *Metro* alongside its predecessor it that is precisely the tension between poetic image and an increasing awareness of the place, even the necessity, of narrative in counterpoint to image that concerns Szirtes at this point in his development. Narrative constitutes the context and backdrop against which images develop new levels of significance and assume new degrees of relief; images, meanwhile, invest narratives with momentary but intense points of focus and punctuation, pause and stasis. The two collections meditate on image and narrative as exclusive but complementary modes of aesthetic recording. Importantly, they also ponder the status and fate of reality within this tension.

Szirtes' poetry in this period adapts the early modernist effort to transcend the simple 'fixing' of the frozen moment in poetry and invest the image, instead, with active aesthetic and political force. Peter Nicholls has noted the tendency of Ezra Pound's imagism to move away from the 'passivity' of aesthetic impressionism, effecting 'a subtle shift of attention away from the object itself towards something else which allows desire to be mediated by a tradition or a set of conventions'.[77] Similarly, in Szirtes' use of the image, traditions and conventions mediate desire by allowing the images contiguous connections with each other (hence the importance of the 'Trains' sequence), as might be demanded in poems of lengths conventionally associated with narrative. The epigraph to 'Metro', taken from Derek Mahon's 'A Disused Shed in Co. Wexford', reads: 'What could they do there but desire?', and the poem itself explores 'desire, pulled like a tooth', as an emotional and political experience inculcated by fragments, an urge to connect, complete and fill in the absences, the spaces in what the poem calls 'the lost history'. Mahon's poem is invoked for its historical empathy, its remarkable symbolisation of the desire for justice, its learning of the virtues of 'patience and silence' as registers of the orders of suffering.

Silence, in particular, resides at the heart of Szirtes' poetic project to remember his parents and his past. The life of his mother, which the long sequences here seek to comprehend, is framed by her profession of photography, her unspoken experience of the concentration camps, and by the underlying drive or desire, on the part of the poet, to know the past and its contribution to the reasons for her suicide in 1975. Silence is the auditory mode of the image, a momentary perception frozen in time; it is the tragic miracle of the photograph to fix movement and life as silence and stasis. In Szirtes' reworking of it, the early modernist conception of the poetic image becomes an element in a notional (but incomplete and unrealised) narrative constituted by assemblage, comprising a 'collage' of apparently sequentially organised fragments, lines, descriptions, memories, citations and notations, held together (momentarily frozen) by the demands of form, and constructing a 'version' or 'analogon' of the reality to which it alludes. Szirtes elaborates this point in the interview with John Tusa, where he describes his comprehension of the past constructed in these poems 'not so much as a series of conscious principles, but as a kind of a rather incoherent bunch of apprehensions, desires. That's why I like these words, apprehensions and desires, because they're vague, and they don't have very very clear objects.'[78]

The 'incoherence' to which Szirtes alludes here, the lack of 'clear objects' of reference, suggests also that a specific and evasive kind of indeterminacy resides in the tension between image and narrative; the readerly desire to glean a structured, ordered narrative from the poem is resisted by the poem's drift of images, so that narrative coherence is elusive, and the reader is left instead with a sensory apprehension of mood. Movement, in this poetic mode, is uncertain but also perpetual, a drift or migration (a displacement) of meaning from one image to the next, each lacking final resolution. 'The Photographer in Winter' asks us to 'Imagine trying to focus though this swirl / And cascade of snow', suggesting that (in the recurrent photographic metaphor) narrative direction as well as the image is as blurred as the city itself. Images ('Imagine' demands the internalised construction of an image) combine within but also set themselves off against narrative to enable constituent elements of the world the poem represents to coalesce momentarily, and then disperse, within the verbal space of the poem and within the specific, brief image, presenting a world strenuously and continuously becoming (the unfulfilled condition of desire), rather than simply existing to be 'reflected' by words.

Sequences of images work, through collocation, repetition and incremental development, to build a verbal version of the moral and political experience of fragmentation with which the poem deals. At its simplest, this process occurs in what seem superficially to be lists; in 'Metro', for example, we read the following list of excavated objects:

> ...the tunnelling
> Begins, the earth gives up her worms and shards,
> Old coins, components, ordnance, bone and glass,
> Nails, muscle, hair, flesh, shrivelled bits of string,
> Shoe leather, buttons, jewels, instruments.

In the context of a postmemorial poem responding to inherited memories of the Holocaust such a list cannot sustain a neutral reading; the world it constructs is specific to a moment in European history, alluded to by each of its elements. Each element functions as testimony to human suffering and to the destructive forces of human agency; its increasingly corporeal constituency, accruing significance and force as each element adds its weight to the previous, asserts a relentless and punishing physical suffering as its theme – the words punch above their weight, assaulting the reader at moral as well as aesthetic levels. The final line (with the word 'Jew' firmly embedded in 'jewels') is terrifyingly reminiscent of the lists of property yielded up by new inmates in the camps, piles of objects (the "possessions" of the utterly dispossessed) like those now exhibited in the memorial museum at Auschwitz-Birkenau. This list is postmemorial in its function, the 'bare bones' of an 'account' that calls to account but necessarily fails to account *for*, bearing instead some notional witness to a past accessible only through its fragmentary persistence in the present.

A list like this constructs an historical incompleteness (it seeks to represent or epitomise an experience impossible to imagine or recuperate) through a sequence of complete objects – 'the specificity of the fragment', argues Simon Critchley, 'is that it is a form that is both complete and incomplete, both a whole and a part'.[79] This list allows a fragmentary insight into the shattering and shattered experience of the past, a history both complete and incomplete. It offers that past in and as traces of itself, fragments that gesture towards a potential redemption or completeness (can such a list ever be complete? What kind of completion or fullness does such a list aspire to?), even as they signify death and dissolution, the impossibility of redemption, as the consequences of history. Excavation here is also exhumation, the exposure of the materiality of death within the remains of the past, and the implicit connection between the two worries the rest of the collection.

Elsewhere, lists function in different ways. In 'The Photographer in Winter' we read of the winter that

Sometimes it is water
Creeping down a window, a sharpened pen
Above the lintel, a white screen which men
Must penetrate like knives, a curious shriek
Which cuts the eye.

The sequence of images here relies not so much on metonymic increments but on developing levels (hence offering the implication of a narrative progression) that allow the conception of a meaning – the penetration of surfaces as an analogy for the writing (or, more broadly, the representational) process. Grammatical repetition – the caesura in each line followed by the indefinite article, each subsequent noun qualified by one adjective – reinforces the repetitive element. Connections are established across and between the different elements through the echoing of the 'sharpened pen' ('pen' repeated from shar*pen*ed') in 'penetrate', the semantic or metonymic links between 'window', 'lintel', 'screen' and 'eye', the movement from 'pen' to 'eye' which embodies the poem's exploration of links between poetry and photography, and from visual to auditory experience (the 'shriek') and back to the 'eye'; there's also a further cinematic dimension in the intertextual connection to the famous razor blade image in Buñuel and Dalí's *Un Chien Andalou* (1929), an image latent in the collocation of 'penetrate', 'knives', 'cuts' and 'eye'.

Further levels of verbal coherence accrue through initial and internal alliteration ('water', 'window', 'white'; 'creeping', 'sharpened', 'pen', 'penetrate') and through assonance ('creeping', 'screen', 'shriek'). The 'sense' of such a passage depends upon this cascade of carefully organised verbal effects (a quality of this collection described by one reviewer as 'a genuine acoustic of fear'),[80] allowing the poetry to establish meanings beyond the sequential logic demanded by narrative desire, residing too in the logic of contiguously connected images, and offering instead the poem and its world as a space in which implicit significances resonate, rebounding and echoing across the page.

The Photographer in Winter

The sequence 'The Photographer in Winter' opens the first of these collections and immediately establishes tensions between apprehension and desire, and between the real and its the verbal representation. Its epigraph, taken from late in Orwell's *Nineteen Eighty-Four* (Szirtes, born in 1948, returned to Budapest in 1984) after Winston has been apprehended and subjected to Room 101, locates the poem in a tragic-dystopic no-time; Winston's 'frozen hands' imply his impotence, Julia's 'ill-defined' change suggests the frustration of desire and emphasises the transformation of conventional word-thing relations that Orwell diagnoses as at the heart of authoritarianism. The relations between words and things come under close scrutiny in Szirtes' reworking of this initial scenario, which might be subtitled 'Betrayal'; the first words that Julia and Winston speak to each other in this part of Orwell's novel are 'I betrayed you'.[81]

Everything in Szirtes' collection falls back into the 'Winter' of this opening sequence, 'A winter of betrayals' (of both individuals, including the poet's mother, and nations: the Hungarian sense of betrayal by the West during the events of 1956 is also evoked by the word), a time imbued with complex aesthetic and moral significance. The book concludes with three translations of Hungarian poems, the last of which, Dezsö Kosztolányi's 'Pieties for September', describes a 'September morning' tempered by seasonal awareness: 'I know what cold is coming'. The 'cold coming' (echoing Eliot's 'Journey of the Magi') haunts both Kosztolányi's reworking of Keatsian autumnal motifs and his poem's central recognition – that the luxury of the present, tempered by awareness of the future, is strangely reminiscent of the past: 'It's exactly as it was in childhood, / the adults talking incomprehensibly / among themselves...'. The poems in Szirtes' collection locate themselves within the ontological orbit of this assertion. They inaugurate his extended poetic enquiry into the possibility of an accurate apprehension of the past as a kind of truth to which the necessary 'fictions' of poetry must defer, but a truth always contested, ambiguous, mobile and uncertain.

Photography, as one version or expression of this kind of truth, is of course crucial in 'The Photographer in Winter'. The poem's initial experiences are overwhelmingly specular and defamiliarising: Winston, in the epigraph, 'saw' Julia, just as the poem's narrator, in stanza 2, 'can see' the addressee, the imagined/remembered figure of the mother. 'We look and listen', she is told, and the statement combines the actions of photographer and attentive, recording poet. Szirtes' poem offers the quote from Orwell as a clue to understanding both its setting (Budapest, under the rule of various authoritarian governments during and after the War) and the ways language, in such historical circumstances, reveals by distorting and concealing. After an initial three-stanza unrhymed section the poem settles into eight sets of four six-line stanzas rhyming ABBCCA, comprising a total of 210 lines. It opens with an imagined job interview, in a frozen past ('*The whole era has been sealed in ice*') in which language, too, is frozen, '*consonants of ice*' and '*a draught of vowels*' signifying a stultified newspeak; 'What seems and is has never been less certain', it elaborates. The figure addressed in the opening stanzas, we learn, is frozen in a different way: '*It's snowing in the crematorium / where you are named*'. Death permeates this frozen world, '*white as a dead face*'.

'The Photographer in Winter' can be summarised as a metropolitan elegy, a reworked, postmodern *Waste Land* seeking to make sense of Hungarian experience through the effort of comprehending the events of the poets' mother's life. It imagines shadowing the mother's movements, an act both of homage and of slightly sinister surveillance, reminiscent of the activities of the AVH (Hungary's secret police force between 1945 and 1956): 'I'm watching you. / You cannot get away. ... / I see your every move.' This chilling paranoia, redoubled in the final line of section 3 – 'Hold it right there. Freeze', contributes powerfully to the sense of unease that pervades the poem, and suggests an underlying ideological uncertainty, at this stage in Szirtes' career, about motivation and direction (answered in part by the reworking of this poem's themes and ideology in the later 'Metro').

Its debts to Eliot's city poems are manifold. Echoing Prufrock's 'time / To prepare a face to meet the faces that we meet', it instructs the mother to 'Wake up, wake up. The faces disappear. / Your own must be put on.' Drawing on his 'Preludes', the poem notes the 'private smells' of 'flights of stairs'. It eschews, however, the

solution of the Eliotesque objective correlative as a means of im-
porting emotional significance into impersonal poetry, seeking
instead a means of short-circuiting the loop of desire through art.
The fifth section addresses this problem directly, relating the child's
memory of the artist-mother at work, and realising that art trans-
forms memory, just as memory transforms experience: 'memory
would fail / to keep the living and the dead apart'. This suggests
that memory (as a function of photography and, implicitly, of
poetry) is understood here as fixing the past, allowing the dead to
live on in illusion just as the image does. 'The process of embalm-
ment' described here thus refers to three distinct activities, all en-
gaged in simultaneously at this moment in the poem: the mother's
hand-tinting of her monochrome photographs, the poet's memory
of watching her do this, and his reworking of this image into words.
Art and artifice intervene at each level, a form of preservation
constructing 'the redeemed / perfection of the unbelievable', a
world which 'art must somehow fit together'.

The poem proceeds through figures of fragmentation, 'tiny pieces'
of light mutating into 'pictures', 'whole rolls of film' (gesturing
forward to Szirtes' later concern with film) that seek to record 'the
world we see / Disintegrating at our fingers' ends'. Its argument
constructs an aesthetic of imperatives – 'The situation offers me
no choice' – in which the demand placed on the artist is balanced
by the recognition that art transforms what it represents, and, in
doing so, makes the world anew. The 'frozen' world of 'The Photo-
grapher in Winter' is at once the icy Budapest of winter and of
Cold War history, the world of the past imagined by the poet, and
a version of the aesthetic worlds created by photography and poetry.

Other key poems in this collection develop from or respond to
this frosty, troubled opening. The collection moves towards its
central sequence, 'The Courtyards', via the creative fable of 'The
Button Maker's Tale' (which centres on the artist's 'hunger / For
risk and failure') and the short sequence 'The Swimmers', a poem
of mortality and memory set in St Mary's church in Hitchin, where
Szirtes' mother is buried. The church's floor 'is like black ice',
beneath which 'The dead / Press water and each other down the
centuries / Of darkness'. 'The Swimmers' offers a contemporary
version of Thomas Gray's 'Elegy Written in a Country Churchyard'
(1750); its vision of mortality as dissolution consists in its meditat-
ing on time as a river 'dissolving everything', in which the dead
swim. The poet reads the gravestone of Venables Hind (now located
near the church entrance), no 'mute inglorious Milton' but 'a small
round passive cliché', a suitable representative of 'these verbose

and delicate people', the articulate dead whose voices clamour (like Mahon's mushrooms) to be heard by the living.

'The Swimmers' offers not muteness but this clamour of the dead to be heard, and the demand placed on the living to hear them: 'I've strained / To hear you speak coherent sentences', the poet laments, before inserting another delicate Eliotesque cadence, the voice of the poetic dead: 'A tongue as washed-out and as disinfected / As the water; full of hesitations / And precise declensions, but quite unaffected.' These 'deaths by water' are, the poem suggests, 'full of high sentence'; like Prufrock, however, we hear, in the end, 'no singing, nothing but sea'. Human voices will not wake us; like 'the rest', we will all 'go under', drown in the ice of the black church floor. The poem then switches from the fluid, drowning present of Hitchin church to a historical near-drowning in the 'dullish red' Danube in 'the last week of the Terror'. It presents 'a miracle', the survival of a girl with 'something of an angel's clarity', an event imbued with a spiritual significance seemingly lacking in the immediacy of the church. History, the poem implies, invests such moments, such impossible survivals, with deep significance.

'The Courtyards' condenses the tension between internal and external forms of experience. Budapest apartments are constructed around courtyards of sometimes astonishing architectural beauty, spaces both outside and yet within, connected to but separate from the city, 'as if a street had turned its stately back / on public matters'. 'The Courtyards' imagines these spaces as containers of sublime memory, a three-dimensional repository through which 'you rise through slices of pale light' towards 'a trancelike ring of silence at the top'. The poem's second section lists images of 'the inchoate' which is, it asserts, 'what gets lost'. History, for this poem, is disorder, momentarily redeemed in poetic form, but susceptible to 'such imprecision' which inculcates 'fear'. Sections three and four counterpoint 'outside' and 'inside' (in a manner reminiscent of Auden's counterpointing of 'Yesterday...today...tomorrow' in 'Spain') offering images of external chaos and disorder ('disfigured by a web of bulletholes') against the world of the domestic, 'a sort of life'. The poet appears in section four as 'a small child whom no one minds / intent on his own piece of anarchy'. The poem moves towards its conclusion through a superficially rhetorical question within which lurks the question asked by all these poems: 'Then what is left?' The words and images that make up this powerful sequence are, in a sense, the answer; 'The Courtyards' strives to construct the presence of the past in its repeated injunction to the reader to 'think of' ('imagine') the world imagined by the poem itself. Memory and history are here products of intellectual effort, aesthetic recollections of the past distilled by imagination and concentration from the 'inchoate' residues of 'what is left', restored momentarily in the activity of reading and responding to the poem. *The Photographer in Winter* is the verbal record of this effort of aesthetic recollection. It concludes with translations of poems by the Hungarian writers Miklós Radnóti, Ottó Orbán and Dezsö Kosztolányi (the earlier 'After Attila' reworks an Attila József poem). These are pointed choices: Radnóti's 'Forced March' prefigures the train journey to Ravensbrück in 'Metro' (Szirtes writes elsewhere of Radnóti that 'the material of his poetry lies somewhere between concentration camp and battlefield'),[82] while Orbán's 'Ars Poetica' (later reprinted under the title 'To Poetry')[83] responds to Ágnes Nemes Nagy, another poet later translated by Szirtes. Szirtes' translations mark his entry into the canons and exchanges of Hungarian poetry, a development that will be discussed later.

Metro

'Metro', the title-poem of Szirtes' next collection, returns to the theme of betrayal, constructing the human body as the metaphorical site of a betrayal that is physical in effect. Described inaccurately by one reviewer as an 'unrhymed sonnet sequence',[84] it clearly prefigures Szirtes' later experiments with different versions of sonnet sequence. Its ten sections, each comprising six curtailed, thirteen-line sonnets (formal incompleteness mimicking the absence of full knowledge – 'Even now I know so little about my mother', the poem laments) are irregular in metre and rhyme, holding only the familiar 'ghosts of form' with which Szirtes implies organisation. Section 5 is titled 'Betrayals', continuing this theme from the previous collection and opening with a question: 'Betrayed? She felt and thought she was'. Feeling comes first, the poem insists: its history is 'a subcutaneous universe' of 'this fair city', a space underpinned by the metaphorical Metro, its 'tunnels creep[ing] / Under the skin'. The 'bare bones' of narrative contribute to this 'thread' of the 'desire' that concerns the poem.

'Metro', central to the collection, transforms into the public realm of history the gothic, private nightmare of the earlier poem 'The House Dream' and its version of history's persistence in the unconscious of the dreamer, its language constructing the physicality of the dream as a material experience; the wall of 'The House

Dream' is 'dimpled', the wife is 'buxom', the legs of the desk are 'twisted', the dead man is 'smelly and ghastly', 'horribly' dead. His poems, amid the 'statues' and 'the wife of a drunken architect', offer only one version of the immortality imagined by the poem, which reworks Shelley's 'Ozymandias' in its expressed desire 'to leave / some tiny vestige of self, some collateral, / a History of Since Then'. A Romantic urge to transcend history, the poem suggests, resides in the writer's ('My dream or his?' it asks) unconscious. 'The House Dream' is an allegory of this urge, a dream of mortality masquerading as survival, offering itself as 'a poem to celebrate the peaceful and unnatural'.

Dream analysis is one way of "reading" the past and the future ('Siren Voices' evokes Freudian psychoanalysis in its singing of 'Viennese neurotics'). Other early poems deal with the interpretation of prophecy – the women in 'The Lukács Baths' (revived, perhaps, from the dead in 'The Swimmers') are sibyls, 'prepared to prophesy their own extinction' and 'To prophesy the past with unerring accuracy'; 'they can tell the future as it shrinks / to its faint determined pattern', we are told. Their powers return in allusions and repetitions throughout the collection, divining insights into the past and its possible futures. The sinister analogy of the 'walls' of the baths 'stuck with plaques' 'just as in crematoriums' alerts us to the directions that the future prophecies of this poem are likely to take, the drive towards death of the desire to know. The women's readings are taken up later in part 7 of 'En Route', 'Border Crossing', where physical transformations symbolise psychological changes in a condensed moment of transience; humanity itself is erased by the bureaucracy of deportation, leaving a physique 'As thin and transparent as glass'. The 'glass' becomes the mirror of a shattered, dislocating augury: 'You see the future in slivers and shards...I try to discover my disease in traces / Of tea leaves, life-lines, livers, tarot-cards'. Here 'leaves' puns alliteratively on 'life' and 'livers' and 'auguries' half-rhymes with 'surgeries', connecting the prophetic powers summoned by *Metro* with the collection's other main thread, the compromising of aesthetic distance by the more immediate world of the physical, the sufferings endured by the human body subjected to the violence of history.

In 'A Card Skull in Atlantis' the paper skull symbolises the skull constructed on paper by the poem, cementing the link implicit in 'The House Dream' between the reality of individual mortality and the horror of genocide. The skull metonymically evokes 'something politic / of skulls like paper, piled high in ditches' (later, in 'Metro', an uncle disappears, 'dropped' 'in the ditch / Among the rest'). The poem closes with a condensed echo of Eliot's Phlebas and his *The Dry Salvages*, 'sucked finally to a sea in salt-sour smells, / and settling dumbly among rocks and bells'. The *memento mori* of the skull, the poem realises, also dissolves. If 'The House Dream' extends the 'gossipy' histories of 'The Lukács Baths' into myth and Romantic legend, 'A Card Skull in Atlantis' returns us to the tension between history and myth, 'Atlantis' suggesting the mythic continent but really 'The *Atlantis Paper Co.*, to be precise'; in the manner of James Fenton's 'The Pitt-Rivers Museum', legend collapses into mundanity in this deflation, only to be resurrected by the allusion to the 'crystal skull' in 'the British Museum', a return to the material traces of the past and to the burgeoning archaeological imagery with which much of the central sequence will indirectly deal.

These poems address the interpretation of the past and the divining of the future, enquiring into poetry's potential as a vehicle for such acts. The poems in *Metro* are concerned with how language constructs the past in representing it – 'The sirens sang all this', 'Siren Voices' asserts, alluding to poetry's complicity in the histories that comprise Europe. It seeks a way of thinking and imagining the past as constituted in a space ('the cavity / Beneath the streets', in 'Metro') in between conventional categories, part-myth, part-history and part-memory, but wholly fitting into none of these, the space of family anecdote and inherited reminiscence. The title poem counterpoints 'facts' ('This is a fact', it asserts in section 2) with narrative imaginings, half-remembered events and encounters, speculative narratives, and recollected versions of the past.

The Budapest Metro system, its interchanges and underground tunnels offering rich metaphors of this form of narrative, extends the symbolic force of the train, allegorising the past as the depth, desire and displacement associated with a narrative constantly shimmering out of focus, dissolving or collapsing into uncertainty – 'The place below is treacherous', we're told, returning us to the theme of betrayal. Sean O'Brien remarks that *Metro* is 'pre-occupied with dissolution', a consequence of the failure of words and poetic forms to perform the functions demanded of them.[85] The haunting incompleteness of the project ('The missing items haunt me', we're warned in 'En Route 1: My Name') suggests that the totality of historical truth is both menacing and necessary; its fragmentary poetry seeks a language in which to contain the contradictory urges to confront and escape from the demand of the past. The poet's guides in negotiating this tension are family figures – the aunt at the opening of 'Metro' (a familiar version of the old women of

'The Lukács Baths'), and the figure of the mother mythologised as *'psychopompos'*, the Greek guide of souls who mediates (in Jungian theory) between conscious and unconscious worlds, which correspond in this collection to the present and the past.

'Metro' combines narratives of the poet's return to Budapest, his memories of childhood in the city, his mother's betrayal, capture and deportation to Ravensbrück forty years earlier, and the imagined experiences of other family members (particularly her brother) under Nazi rule. 'Escapades' and 'escape' are, in the fifth section, fatally confused; the poem's narrative of flight is also a flight from narrative, into something wholly unclear, a nightmare in a 'sleep' which, in the poem's penultimate sonnet, is 'a kind if emptiness'. Narrative appears primarily as a sequence of images in which 'voices' are seen': 'I see a voice'. 'Seeing' here is imbued with the sibylline power of second sight; the 'voice', one of the 'threads' of the poem itself, leads reader and poet into the 'crinkled, crenellated, creviced' city, affording insight and revelation. Writing of the poem in the 'Preface' to *The Budapest File*, Szirtes describes its 'half-haunted polyphony' (it incorporates, in italics, a monologue in the mother's 'voice'), a condition that arises in part from its attempt to reconcile history, memory, the written and the pictorial into a single, dissolute poetic form.[86] It descends allegorically into a past in which images are framed by words that signify and provide links between places, a space of Orphic resonance in which the poet can only look back 'to find a history which feels like truth', losing in the process that which he seeks. Just as the poem examines betrayal, the language it must use is treacherous, threateningly uncontrollable: 'the words / Are muddy, full of unintended puns / And nervy humour'.

Ironically language has to be 'watched' as if it were an image, which, in a sense, it is – a verbal image of a homeland turned hostile, a once-familiar city rendered forgotten and unfamiliar by exile and consequent historical and geographical distance, and by the residues and destructions of authoritarian rule. The poem addresses its past through another poetry, that belonging to the mother and therefore to the past, a poetry of photographic images initially 'unseen and without sound', which (*contra* Wilfred Owen) 'Lies not in pity but in charity' – precisely the 'charity' unforthcoming in the mother's betrayal: '*I whispered their names / But they did not answer to their lasting shame*'. In addition to poetry and the amoral silences to which it gives expression, 'Metro' offers photography as a discourse through which muteness, silence and indirection attempt to utter history. What is revealed is the subject-matter of the poetry, a past of 'Disorientation and loss'; its difficulty is the difficulty of a poetic language constantly struggling to say the unsayable of traumatic experience. Initially a quest for knowledge of origins ('Even now I know little about my mother'), 'Metro' extends into an enquiry into 'the fiction / of history which makes up Budapest / and what one thinks of as oneself', a daunting formal conflation of fiction, the past, the city, the nation and the self, in which each seems to present itself as origin of all the others. The quest for knowledge of the mother becomes a quest for knowledge of the self in and through the mother, who is discovered, in a now familiar metaphor, 'frozen' into photographs: 'He'll keep her face and others in the drawer, / With her own photographs, her frozen youth, / Her unsent letters, his unwritten reply'. Mother and 'others' thus persist in photographic images that fuel poetic images, the realism of the former challenging the tendency towards romance of the latter: 'My fiction turns to sepia', the poet notes, in an image which also ironically confirms poetry's aspiration, in 'Metro', to the condition of photography. '*Photography, I need you. Freeze me too*',[87] the mother's voice demands, echoing the chorus line of George MacBeth's 'Prayer to the White Lady': '*lighten my darkness, I / need you now*' (MacBeth's poem, interestingly, is a version of László Nagy's Hungarian poem '*Himnusz Minden Idoben*'). The poem's reply is its incomplete, half-frozen formalism, its recognition of the restricted capacity of words and poetic structures to recapture the past 'which remains forever another place'. In a moment of crisis precipitated by this recognition, the poem demands of us and of itself: 'How much is all this information worth?' Its answer resides in its lyrical and narrative density and in its conflation of digging into memory with the material act of 'excavating' historical events of middle years of the twentieth century, an undertaking that cements the poem's ultimate commitment to an unrepresentable core – human remains and human experiences as testimony to genocide and Holocaust.

'Metro' opens in private memory, a child's world, tangible and sensual, 'an insect friction' establishing tension and abrasion as primary elements of the past. The domestic interior of the opening stanza is counterpointed in the next by the city, itself comprised of multiple domestic spaces ('darkened rooms'). The city represents the extension of the private into the public, the personal into the general, suggesting a shared dimension of the experiences the poem will relate. 'Metro', with its deliberate Eliotesque echoes (a later poem in the collection is titled 'Preludes'), draws on the tradition of the modernist city-poem, and on the modernist construction of the city as poem. It presents a city of dreadful night, gothic in its potential otherness, existing at a point in history seemingly forsaken by God: 'this is not the time to speak of him', we're told in the first section. He is replaced, instead, by a private infant mythology of 'dwarfish furies of the forest' and 'lank rain-coated ghosts', products of 'the reading of a tale'. Divine dispassion taints its world: 'When we raise / Our holocausts to him he looks away'. Later, God is replaced by 'administration', secularising the ministering functions of the church, replacing it with a menacing bureaucracy foreshadowing Communist rule. Nevertheless this city is, early in the poem, a 'happy' place; the word is emphatically repeated in 'At my Aunt's', modulating to 'healthy', to 'Certain streets, hard cores of pleasure'. Its underside is embodied in the Metro, which functions immediately as a container of memories of the immediate past, the 'artillery' and the 'whole war', the 'heavy guns' of military action, invasion, occupation. The Underground is a repository of the violent otherness of the past, subterranean yet anchored (by stations) to the city surface, demanding (like dreams and nightmares) interpretation through these momentary surfacings.

In his analysis of the social-symbolic functions of the Paris Métro, Marc Augé argues that 'To speak of the Métro first of all means to speak of reading and of cartography'.[88] The Metro constitutes the city as a legible fiction, a mapped space with a subtext, a deep structure to be scrutinised – read – for short-circuits, junctions and connections not evident above ground. The city of 'Metro' is a sedimented space, built of layer upon layer of historical moments, demanding a forensic or archaeological reading to reveal depths of meaning at different historical moments. The poem conceives the city as a space similar to that imagined by Angela Carter: 'Consider the nature of a city. It is a vast repository of time, the discarded times of all the men and women who have lived, worked, dreamed and died in the streets...'.[89]

The city is a body, the occupying armies a physical presence – 'their all too tangible bodies' – a corpus (or corps/corpse) to be analysed, on which the ravages of time have left their traces; the city's 'subcutaneous universe' is also an underworld, demanding a guide – the '*psychopompos*', 'greyest of grey shadows', the imagined spirit of the dead mother – to lead us through its various infernal pasts. In Section 2, 'Undersongs', these various hells underpin the 'desire' to escape the mythologies and bureaucratic rewritings of the past, the memories and delusions of childhood and the family narratives. This 'desire' is felt in language itself, in 'the words', 'muddy, full of unintended puns', and in 'voices'. Desire exists in words that make up the poem itself; 'To give voice is to lip read, to construe / The contortions of a mouth,' the poem asserts, insisting on reading its imaginings of the mother's movements and activities, her meetings with the father, her biography encoded in fragments of memory, which are also its encodings of a desire to know, a yearning for comprehension mimicked in the questing uncertainty of irregular rhyme that characterises its form.

As it elaborates a fragmented biography through descriptions of photographs and through imaginary acts of impersonation ('*In Her Voice*'), the poem develops certain motifs as registers of a scale of pain it seeks to record and, perhaps, palliate. The city-as-body trope develops through the generalised assertion of 'the skeleton / Of something – body, city, staircase, wall' (in 'Portraits') to photography's construction of the mother as desired object and fragmented body reminiscent of the metonymic list of excavated fragments of the past: 'Her hair...her teeth...Her finger...her lap...her lips'. These 'frozen' images of body-fragments constitute memories, the image-repertoire of a memorial impetus working hard to piece together a shattered past. The Communist world of post-war Budapest ('in Uncle Joe's moustache') offers a backdrop to an imagined family romance which barely compensates for all that the poem has had to omit, 'the lost history / Of which she hardly spoke', which can only be faintly, inadequately apprehended by the poem.

The poem's Hamlet-like rhetorical dismissals – 'The rest is data', 'Facts, bare bones, the rest / Are silences' – reverberate most powerfully in the broken spaces that 'Metro' constructs and the shattered bodies ('bare bones', 'the skeleton') over which it moves. At its centre lies a despair that, in appealing for value, asserts the devaluation of all logic and form: 'How much is all this information worth?' It branches into genealogy and family histories in its seeking of an underlying pattern that differs from the menacing rumble of the *Metro* line; when the mother is given a voice in section 6, it is simple, dissociated, imagistic, befitting her '*thousand eyes*'. Her world is sensual, material, invested with significance beyond the capabilities of the rest of the poem to imagine adequately. She speaks of living on and enduring, of the body's persistence: '*My body is still standing. The wind blows through it / Like a language, of which not a word / Is what it seems, and yet it survives.*' She asserts identity in appealing for '*justice*' in the face of her imminent annihilation; later, she speaks '*of parts, / The one dissociated from the other*'. The fragmented self's desire, the poem suggests, matches its own desire for formal coherence, a desire continually threatened by the direction (the line on the Metro) its narrative drive is forced to take, which leads inexorably to the poem's final stanza with its 'horrible familiar stench / Of loss', where 'familiar' resonates with its full potential.

The poem searches for a space 'all dreams / And talk, and rumours of talk', but finds the mother's voice, 'unseen and without sound'. When it discreetly averts its eye from a parental liaison, it does so with a knowing omission: 'The rest is not my business', in which that which is 'not my business' is silence itself, silently completing the poem's embedded echo of Hamlet's final words. Repeated later in the poem, 'the rest' becomes 'reconstruction and conjecture', and 'data', the dimensions of narrative and fiction the poem is both bound to and seeks to avoid. Another implicit silence reigns, that implied by the concluding words of Geoffrey Hill's Holocaust elegy 'September Song': 'This is plenty. This is more than enough',[90] a line echoed, later in *Metro*, in the second part of 'The Love of Windows': 'Her words are not enough. Or far too much'. Silence, the refusal to add more than is needed in the face of the surfeit of the already-said, is also the form taken by betrayal, the moral (in)action the poem works hardest to comprehend, developing from the 'winter of betrayals' of 'The Photographer in Winter'. In her betrayal by her neighbours, the mother encounters their silence, the silence of political acquiescence that empowers totalitarianism: '*I whispered their names / But they did not answer to their lasting shame…/ They closed their mouths to my pitiful dole*'. Her voice is imagined out of the silences of history, distinct from that of the poem, constructing its own memories, its own encounters with history, in images uniting the train and language:

> The train is rushing past the fields and woods
> Of all that was. The words renew it,
> Rephrase its truths and falsehoods.

The poem's latter sections register a linguistic shift to a kind of directness of reference, speaking of 'witnesses' (in Section 7) and 'holocausts' (in Section 9) and making these words work amid the imagined events of which it despairs: 'To know is not to see or understand'. Its argument shifts discursive register to the philosophical language of proposition, distanced and enervated:

> I propose
> A yard, a hut, a fence, a row of beds
> And shins and shanks and ribs and collarbones
> And one familiar among shaven heads.

– where, again, 'familiar' is overburdened with meaning.

The ethical imperative of witnessing ultimately concerns 'Metro'. The poem, and the collection as a whole, constitutes a significant postmemorial text; the difficulty it addresses is that explored by Marianne Hirsch, the paradox of intense experience 'distinguished from memory by generational distance and from history by deep personal connection'.[91] The poem's polyphony, its refusal of a single narratorial voice, complements its tendency to irregular, inconsistent metrical and rhyming structures, its 'awkwardness' in relation to conventional patterns and forms. The 'parts' assumed by its voices – the 'walk-on parts / in history' of 'Burns Night on the Danube' – are also versions of the 'parts' or fragments of data, memories, bodies, histories and narratives in which it deals; their 'partial' status is also the 'partiality' that the 'I' of the poem declares, the 'familiar' as the personal ground of experiences it desires ('What should they do there but desire?') to contain and to universalise. This desire is also resisted – as Szirtes points out when discussing 'Metro' in an interview, 'The poem never goes inside Ravensbrück, it stops dead at the gates – I think that's as far as I can do. I don't think my imagination has the... – "permission" is the word used before, authority, in terms of that.'[92]

The poems of *The Photographer in Winter* and *Metro* constitute a series of provisional questions asked of poetry in relation to issues of 'permission' and 'authority'. They enquire into the poet's authority to remember and reconstruct in words the history he is permitted to access, indirectly and incompletely, via the memories and narratives which belong to others. 'Permission', the poet's permit to travel on the 'Metro' of desire into the winter of the past, is thus a form of legitimised trespass, a tolerated, guarded entrance into the 'underworld' of repressed pasts. The poems in these collections struggle, in articulating this sense of tolerated permission, to find forms and sequences of images through which to represent the past. These are transitional collections in the sense that they enact the poet's transition from his earlier observational 'cold pastorals' and smaller-scale formal experiments towards a deeper sense of poetry's obligations to engage with the complex and daunting intermeshing of self and other, present and past, proximate and distant, permitted and forbidden that is recognised in these collections. Questions of 'permission' and 'authority', of the poet's roles, responsibilities and abilities in relation to historical events, and in particular of his own relations to the newly recognised Hungarian poetic traditions that appear in *Metro*, will constitute major concerns of his next collection, *Bridge Passages*.

4

'A furious year': *Bridge Passages*

I shall forget it like a childhood illness
Or a sleepless night-crossing.

DEREK MAHON, 'The Prisoner'

A poem by the Hungarian poet Sándor Weöres (1913-88), 'Magyarok', translated by the Scottish poet Edwin Morgan as 'Hungarians', imagines the 'thousand years' that comprise the mythic and real history of the Magyars, the tribes of Hungary: 'all passed in my dream', the poem relates, a historical procession culminating in a vision of 'Budapest woven of bridges'. Death appears, finally, to lead the narrator and his 'little group', symbolic of the Hungarian nation, across the Styx (the Danube) with a face 'clouded by hammer and sickle of froth and foam', a nightmare vision of repressive history. The poem concludes with the beginning of the journey of death; '*A lerombolt híd tövén a kompot sötétben értük el*' – 'We reached the ferry at the end of the broken bridge in the dark'.

Weöres' poem is reprinted, in Morgan's English version, as 1988's entry in a recent anthology of 25 Hungarian poems spanning the years 1978-2002, entitled, after this concluding line, *At the End of the Broken Bridge*,[93] an entitlement that invests the line with a symbolic resonance as a thematic "summary" of the prevailing mood, if not the themes and styles, of modern Hungarian verse. Weöres died in 1988, just before the collapse of the Berlin Wall and the end of Communism in Eastern Europe. George Szirtes writes, in the 'Introduction' to *Leopard V: An Island of Sound*, that Weöres 'has good claim to be Hungary's greatest poet of the century'.[94] He is elegised by Szirtes in 'In Memoriam Sándor Weöres' as 'the conjuror' who 'could take / a parasol and out of it create / an ecosystem, or beneath / the parasol, meander in the wake / of *realpolitik* and contemplate / its dreadful colonnade of teeth.' The 'parasol' alludes to Weöres' long poem 'The Red Parasol', printed in Szirtes and George Gömöri's 1996 anthology of modern Hungarian poetry, *The Colonnade of Teeth* (itself a title borrowed from another poem by Weöres).

Szirtes' elegy to Weöres is printed towards the end of his 1991 collection *Bridge Passages*, a book comprising poems that also 'meander in the wake / of *realpolitik*' in their responses to the events

in Hungary and elsewhere in Eastern Europe in the autumn of 1989.
A series of 'decent, relatively peaceful'[95] revolutions, fuelled by
massive popular protest, saw one by one the downfall of the Eastern
European Communist states. Hungary, historically more liberal in
its Communism, led the way; Hans Magnus Enzensberger has
argued that 'without the Hungarian precedent it is hard to see how
the dissolution of the Eastern Bloc would have begun.'[96] On 23
August border controls with Austria were removed; on 10 September
foreign minister Gyula Horn declared the opening of Hungary's
borders to refugees from East Germany. Within five weeks the East
German leader, Erich Honecker, had been forced to stand down in
response to public protests and demands for democratic reforms.
On 23 October, Mátyás Szürös renamed the state the 'Hungarian
Republic', replacing the former 'Hungarian People's Republic'.
Events escalated across the Eastern bloc countries through Nov-
ember, with the opening of checkpoints along the Berlin Wall on
9 November sparking protests and eventual revolutions in Prague,
Timisoara and elsewhere.

The transformation of the previous Cold War environment was
rapid, total and bewildering, both to onlookers in the outside world
and to many of the people directly involved in the protests; even
Communist Party apparatchiks recognised immediately the impli-
cations of these events: 'This is the end of Yalta...the Stalinist
legacy and "the defeat of Hitlerite Germany",' noted Gorbachev's
foreign policy assistant Anatoly Chernyaev in his diary on 10 Nov-
ember, immediately after the fall of the Berlin Wall.[97] This official
sense of an ending was of course experienced elsewhere, amongst the
people whose protests were responsible for these transformations,
as a new beginning. The confluence of endings and beginnings, the
sheer ambiguous, uncertain dynamism of the period, contributed
powerfully to the effects that the experience of the period would
have upon the people involved, directly or indirectly, with the
events. What initially emerged, at social, political, economic and
cultural levels, were 'new, peculiar structures' that replaced the
'mutant, political constructions'[98] of Communism.

Hungary's specific role in the prising open of the Eastern Eur-
opean regimes was complex and definitive, and contributed to the
building of these 'new, peculiar structures'. Hungarian economic
and social reforms had been fermenting long before the uprisings
of 1989; the "liberal" version of Stalinism practised by premier
János Kádár from 1956 tolerated (despite its initially repressive
executions of Imre Nagy and other leaders of the 1956 revolution)
certain levels of dissent, and allowed the "goulash" economy (a

mixture of Stalinist and Western policies and strategies specific to Hungarian politics and history) that left Hungary in a distinctive position amongst other Communist bloc countries; visits by Western tourists, for example, were tolerated and contributed considerably to the economy, but at the expense of the Hungarians themselves, whose shops were frequently left empty by Westerners on shopping sprees in the cheap Eastern Europe. Stephen Brook, in a book published in 1989 but addressing pre-revolution Prague and Budapest, described the Hungary of Kádár as 'the most market-orientated and least repressive nation in the Eastern bloc'.[99]

Nevertheless Hungary remained a repressive Communist regime, until, in May 1988, Kádár was quietly removed from power by a makeshift, momentarily expedient coalition of radical reformers and conservative technocrats. The symbolic reburial of Imre Nagy in June 1989 provided an ambiguous focus for Hungary's movements for democracy; it was the central event in a series of strategic political renegotiations, re-organisations and restructurings that culminated in the declaration of the new state and constitution in October, and the eventual free election of March 1990. Hungary emerged from the events of 1989 with a political landscape significantly more Westernised than that of many former Eastern bloc countries, but marked by new divisions between contesting political forces, and the resurgence of old cultural and ethnic divides (like that between the "urbanist", integrationist movement and the "populist", separatist campaigns for a "pure" Hungarianness). While division itself was the defining experience of the emergence of Eastern and central Europe from four decades of imposed Communist unity, the recurrent rhetoric used by commentators on the events of 1989 exploits conventional images (endlessly recycled by American presidents through the 1990s) of the road, the way, the passage and the movement from the collapsing communist societies towards the potential market economies of the West.

For a poet in Szirtes' own culturally ambiguous position, between nations and languages, both a participant in and yet separate from events, the revolutions of 1989 demanded a complex literary response, a demand to which his poetry would offer a guarded, provisional set of answers. Szirtes was in Hungary for nine months in 1989 on his third British Council scholarship, the longest of his several visits to the country between 1984 and 1989, and therefore experienced at first hand the events leading up to the revolution. 'In 1989 I spent most of the year in Hungary when everything was crumbling around one,' he remarked to John Tusa in 2005.[100] Nevertheless he clearly expresses his own sense of disconnection from the events he witnessed; writing, in *The Dublin Review* in 2002, of his involvement in the protest march of March 1989, he notes that 'I felt ever more keenly that I had no right to be in the crowd; their fate, whatever it was to be, would not be mine'.[101] This perception of disconnection is an important constituent of the emotional tone that characterises the poems in *Bridge Passages*. Nevertheless the transformation in Hungarian realities was palpable and demanded a poetic response: 'Everything changed after 1989', he writes in the 'Introduction' to *Leopard V: An Island of Sound*; 'Reassessment is a normal part of literary life and moves with the generations, but post-1989 it has had a different edge. The re-orientation goes on while the body politic is in an anxious, almost fraught, state of transition.'[102]

'Reassessment' and 're-orientation', Szirtes implies, are the immediate duties – the dimensions of the initial response – of the poet when faced with rapid, inassimilable social and political transformations. *Bridge Passages* offers poems that address and seek symbolically to link Hungarian and English places and experiences, memories and perceptions. The collection maps out the possibility of a response to history that incorporates symbolic and literal connectivity as its key motivation. Connections are represented in the metaphorical functions of translations as well as in the prevailing imagery and the organising structure of the collection. 'Reassessment' and 're-orientation' afford motives for the analysis of interconnectivity enacted in form and content, and extending into the traditions on which Szirtes draws, and the relations to those traditions upon which his poetry has hitherto relied. Szirtes' voice in *Bridge Passages* develops the modernist tones of previous collections but is firmly adumbrated, now, by substantial contributions in the form of translations and versions of works by major Hungarian poets. This suggests a new confidence in and awareness of the possibilities (and perhaps urgencies) of Szirtes' dual linguistic situation. This new quality is tempered, in turn, by the collection's oscillation between first and second person, the lyric 'I' of poems like 'English Words' and the more familiar 'You', a surrogate 'I', addressed in poems like 'A Domestic Faust'. The movement between pronouns suggests a sense of a fractured, uncertain subjectivity corresponding to the fractured and uncertain times. His voice finds, furthermore, that its own residual timbres suddenly return as profoundly relevant to emerging scenarios, derived as they are from the Anglo-American tradition of poets like Auden, whose strategic responses to his own experiences of major political-historical events informed the relations of subsequent poetry to such events for half a century. *Bridge Passages* thus cements another form of connectivity, that between the poet and his chosen Anglophone tradition in terms of the adaptation or transformation of the effects of that tradition.

Szirtes' poetry in this collection develops out of an increasing sense of such familiar but contradictory requirements, suggesting the importance and the difficulty of *Bridge Passages* as a response to contemporary history. He outlines these factors, as he experienced them, in the 'Preface' to *The Budapest File*:

> The obligation to history at this point was particularly divisive. Everything was crying out for definition or redefinition, but the triangular relationship between Hungary, myself and England felt all the more uncomfortable for it being defined at all. None of the three parties involved knew how it felt about the other two.[103]

This three-way tension, a 'divisive' combination of the drive to identify oneself and the need to differentiate specific aspects of otherness, typifies Szirtes' poetic position in relation to the events of 1989. As a visitor from England he is outside these events, an observer separated by geography and history, able to comment, in the radio broadcast cited earlier, that 'The country is rolling down its present fearful and intoxicating historical path';[104] as a displaced Hungarian he is deeply involved, drawn, by the sense of an origin, by linguistic identity and political affiliation, into the urgent process of 'definition and redefinition'. From a position somewhere between these latter two, furthermore, he was both observer and participant, sending reports on the developments in Budapest and elsewhere back to England to be published in *Poetry Review*.

One of these essays, published in the autumn of 1989, expresses clearly the poetic aspect of this difficult position: 'If only I can twist my words round this room, or get them to scrape the façade off that building, I will have accomplished something.'[105] This desire for language to be able to intervene in the materiality of the world (and therefore to transcend the division between word and thing) or to penetrate beneath surface appearances, represented in the metaphorical roles played by architectural features and constructions, is, as we shall see, central to *Bridge Passages*. It is manifest in 'Drawing the Curtain', where the poet expresses the desire to experience the material world at first hand,

> To slide your hand behind the stucco, seize
> the mortar and move gently round inside
> makes sensuous and tangible.

The desire expressed here is for physical contact, a desire for writing to exceed the limits of words and enter into the world of things, a world in which, in 'Bridge Passages', 'things must quickly find a sign / to live by, to remain mere things'. This desire for the tangible reality of the world of things represents a contradictory recognition of and frustration with the limitations of language, while also articulating, through the sheer pleasure of verbal expression, the materiality of words themselves, their ability to provide 'a sign / to live by', to embody experience, 'to slide' and 'to move gently' within the parameters of the line and the sentence, making the world the poem constructs 'sensuous and tangible.' Nevertheless that world is uncertain, its material absence signified by the lack of direct object in the sentence – at one level, the poems in *Bridge Passages* enquire broadly into exactly what is made 'sensuous and tangible' by words.

Dedicated 'For my friends in Hungary', the lyrics in *Bridge Passages* address the historical transformations of 1989 tangentially, through poems that work within the spaces provided by apposite clichés like 'A Sea Change' or 'Drawing the Curtain', and through natural metaphors of historical agency like the 'storm' in the latter poem. Language, the collection implies, may be too abrupt in its assessment of the new reality dependent upon moments of social and political upheaval and consequent periods of rapid transition; to the descriptive and declarative assertions available to poetry, caveats need to be added that allow alternative responses to be encrypted within the words used. Discussing poetry's responses to 1989 in an essay published two years later, Szirtes notes of the younger generation of Hungarian poets that 'They withdraw from direct political statement and are concerned with questions of identity and integrity' (although he also concedes that under Communism 'Effective, voluntary self-censorship operated').[106] Such a diagnosis can be applied to his own poetic response. When 'Drawing the Curtain' refers to 'the storm / that lays the human pattern waste', the metaphorical force of the image is tangible, but 'the human pattern' remains indeterminate – a pattern of oppression or of freedom? A pattern detected and represented by the poem, or imposed? A pattern of creativity or of destruction? The general import of the image lacks the specificity necessary to pin down the poem's opinion of it, leading, instead, to contingent, unspecific and equally ambiguous details, 'the loud convergence of external moments / threatening familiar sound' (is 'familiar sound' threatened or promised, or do the 'external moments' 'threaten' to perpetuate, or destroy, 'familiar sound'?). An awkward syntactic looseness (counterpointing formal rigidity) enables the avoidance of the directness of political engagement, allowing (or forcing) the poem instead to rely on the ambiguous implications of its metaphors.

The prevailing metaphor in 'Drawing the Curtain' derives, like that of much of *Bridge Passages*, from architecture, with 'the convolutions of this frieze' offering masonry, 'stucco' and 'mortar', as products of 'the human pattern' that symbolises its immersion in history, like the 'rooms that live within / and yet without the history' in 'The Comfort of Rooms'. The 'sensuous and tangible' reality of buildings is reassuringly solid and present; each end-stopped stanza of 'Drawing the Curtain' (signifying, perhaps, enclosed rooms, allowing 'stanza' to return momentarily to its literal meaning) offers an internal closure that relates its own evasion of the import of architecture's potential friability, itself a metaphor for the 'flickering / inconsequentiality / of every human movement'. Emphasised as an isolated line, 'inconsequentiality' here begs a series of questions about agency, human self-determination and action, and the poem's underlying uncertainty about what it calls 'an expanding, shapeless ring / of meaning and capacity'. The poem seems to rely upon its own formal inertia (those end-stopped stanzas making it repeatedly judder to a halt); but agency resides, instead, in the departure of 'history', who 'packs her bags and pays the bill / long owing', offering up the raw details of the city as 'her discarded materials'. The conception of history indebted to a new economy and a new concept of liberty also expresses another kind of movement, 'a moral fall' or 'a moving curtain' in which 'everything uncertain / hurts and gathers in the folds'.

Bridge Passages opens where Sándor Weöres' poem 'Hungarians' ends, at the end of the bridge in the dark, with a short poem called 'Night Ferry', which addresses the navigation of history as an experience of disturbed, disturbing motion, 'A deep slow swell' as 'The vessel rolls'. Seasickness, and more broadly 'the idea of sea', permeates the poem's lexis and recurs throughout the collection as a contrastive locus differentiating landlocked Hungary from Szirtes' adopted England ('Nachtmusik' later tells us of its being written, in Hungary, 'miles away / from any sea'). It establishes reluctant movement and physical discomfort as the initial conditions, traumas of the body politic, to which *Bridge Passages* responds. Importantly, 'Night Ferry' begins with the word 'And': 'And our idea of hell is the night ferry', conjoining itself to the narrative and the final line of Weöres' poem, as well as to the tradition to which Weöres belongs. Szirtes' *in medias res* conjunction immediately asserts *Bridge Passages*' concern with linkage, just as 'Night Ferry' itself initiates the themes of the bridging of gaps and the interlinking of geographies and histories. The night ferry connects the world preceding the present to that of the present and the future, but also establishes that future as potentially infernal, conceivable in menacingly mythic terms. It connotes the ferry of Greek myth, which transports the dead across the Lethe to Hades. Szirtes' ferry, 'our idea of hell', also transports its passengers from an indeterminate departure point – the past – towards an uncertain future.

At a deeper level, 'Night Ferry' (its title also evoking Derek Mahon's first collection *Night Crossing* [1968] and the 'sleepless night-crossing' in his 'The Prisoner') enacts the transition or passage from a residual, symbolic history of 'pain' and 'nightmare' from which the poem, and, by extension, the collection as a whole, struggles to awaken into the world of *Bridge Passages* (although that awakening may in fact be a kind of resurrection, an entry into a posthumous world like the underworld of *Metro*). The movement of the night ferry traverses the 'deep slow swell' of the unconscious of history, which, in its revolutionary and unknowable forms, will constitute the chronotope, the undeclared territory and history, in which the poems of *Bridge Passages* locate themselves. The past persists into the present in the amnesiac world of 'Night Ferry' as 'emptiness', 'meaning nothing', and the poem's express concern is to record, however briefly and indirectly, the 'pain that art cannot refine', to alarm and inform in the face of poetry's own problematic agency. 'Hungarians', Szirtes and Gömöri contest in their 'Introduction' to *The Colonnade of Teeth*, 'have tended to cling to the belief that poetry can change social life'.[107] *Bridge Passages* explores the possibility of sustaining this belief in post-Communist Hungary, focussing its attention on the moment of revolution – 1989 – and its immediate aftermath. Its provisional, tentative approach – characterised by poetry of dense formal consistency, comprised largely of sequences of four-, six- and eight-line end-stopped stanzas of consistent metre and rhyme that resemble, in their fragmented totality, a shattered sonnet sequence or a dismantled, once monolithic regime – responds to the difficulty of addressing in poetry the events of what is described, in a 'Rondeau' late in the collection, as 'a furious year'.

The negative, Lethean resonances of 'Night Ferry' introduce thematic tensions between memory and forgetfulness, offering in 'the bottom line of nightmare' – later elaborated as the 'continual nightmare of the wall' – an implicitly modernist, Joycean vision of a history lying beyond aesthetic redemption, in a space that, in a further Joycean echo, 'art cannot refine'. Joyce's artist, 'refined out of existence', is echoed in the artwork itself in its failure to refine, to 'make good again' in some way the 'nightmare' experience of history. The poem offers a painful, sluggish transition tainted by a hangover – 'a thumping head no aspirin can soothe' suggesting, rather than the anaesthetic unfeeling of sleep or the 'soothing' aspirin, the aesthetic feeling of painful wakefulness as a compulsory option in the face of history's demands. The hangover signifies the trace of the past in the present, a persistence that enacts another kind of connectedness, the ineradicable past symbolically exerting its baleful influence over the present, persisting in the present as a painful disorder of the body politic.

'Night Ferry' is followed by 'Recording', which extends the collection's modernist undertones, opening with images reminiscent of thirties' poetry – 'A distant night-train and a dog' are objective correlatives of Auden-like compression, evoking both the documentary ballad 'Night Mail' (1935) and the surrealistic farce *The Dog Beneath the Skin* (1934), suggesting that the poem draws on an image-repertoire seen as "reliable" in the context of addressing tumultuous political events. The act of reading in this poem (the act, also, of the reader of the poem), a moment of apparently stable subjective perception and authority again implicitly pastoral in its import ('Crickets' and 'Insects' populate its two stanzas), degenerates into the indeterminate voice ('somebody') that 'goes on quoting / fragments, unattributable, without memory'. This fall from the potential authority of reading into the anonymous 'recordings' of unremembered history is experienced as a kind of death, again imbued with powerfully modernist undertones ('and there's the horror' alludes to Conrad's Mr Kurtz; the 'fragments' echo the 'fragments shored against my ruin' at the end of Eliot's *The Waste Land*). 'Recording' (perhaps the 'recording' of cultural debts) suggests that the shift from the stability of readerly agency matches the shift towards a kind of modernity characterised by recording without agency or memory, as if 'recording' itself became a meaningless, faintly menacing activity, a vaguely Beckettian 'repeating', redolent, of course, of the paranoia associated with pre-1989 eastern Europe. As in 'Night Ferry', death is not too far away; 'The final sensations' evokes a kind of death, or at least a transition from consciousness to the anaesthetic unconscious, an entry into the fragmentary, 'unattributable' world of dreams and nightmares which, it seems, will be the world of *Bridge Passages*.

'Night Ferry' presents three quatrains like a gate barring such an entrance into *Bridge Passages*; it both invites and resists movement and progression into the world of the collection. It establishes a mood of fraught anxiety of subject and language that it calls, for the moment, 'normal', and which the rest of the collection both resists and explores, through 'the continual nightmare / of the wall' (the constraining walls of domestic horror, as well as the Berlin Wall) in 'A Game of Statues', and the 'idea so macabre it cannot picture / its own desperation' in 'Smog', right up to the concluding translations of Ágnes Nemes Nagy's 'Diary', where the second entry reiterates the 'Nightmare' of the opening poem. Here, at the end of *Bridge Passages*, the 'nightmare' becomes pure Gothic melodrama, an epigrammatic howl of stock images of horror and mortality – 'the corpse', 'the softening skull', 'the naked row of teeth' (another 'colonnade') – depicting the historical realities the collection has negotiated as 'a world of rotting rags and clout' on which 'the marsh-light of cold reason' shines. Nemes Nagy, a founding editor of *Ujhold* (New Moon), a major Western-facing literary magazine, was 'silenced' by the Communists – 'She found work as a school-teacher', Szirtes notes in the 'Introduction' to his translations of her poetry, *The Night of Akhenaton* (which contains the same selections from 'Diary' under the title 'Journal' – both words translate Nemes Nagy's 'Napló').[108] Prohibited from producing her own work, she wrote children's books and translated foreign poetry. *Bridge Passages* seems sometimes burdened by its author's awareness that the freedoms and choices he has by historical circumstance been able to take for granted have been denied those of (and to) whom he writes; choosing (and having the freedom to choose) to conclude the collection with his translations of Nemes Nagy's work offers something of what Seamus Heaney would call 'redress'.

'Choice' is a concept that troubles *Bridge Passages*; an essential element of the ideological shift from Communism to free market economics, 'choice', and the 'freedoms' associated with it, undergo interrogation as ethical and aesthetic problems. 'Choice' is closely linked in these poems to agency and action: 'To act, to make things happen, to make choices / are all conditions of the beautiful / and the exact', asserts 'Nachtmusik' – 'exact' bears the adjectival weight of aesthetic precision but also the verbal implication of the demand and enforcement of payment (reminiscent of Heaney's 'exact / and tribal, intimate revenge'),[109] returning attention to history's 'bill long owing'. The framing of 'choice' in relation to aesthetics is a move that 'The Flies' extends further to geographical and historical situations: 'Being here is an aesthetic choice / for those who have it'. Some, the poem suggests, with a nod to the choices available to its author, are more equal than others in the new democratic world. The poem continues: 'We give the wall a voice. The cut worm forgives the plough.' Here 'choice' rhymes with 'voice', establishing in the notion of the *vox populi* connections between aesthetic choices, liberal values of democratic representation, and echoes of Blakean democratic radicalism. Blake's *Proverbs of Hell* is appropriate to the 'infernal' world of immediately post-1989 Budapest; further echoes of his poetry are found in 'The Flies', which imagines the coming of capitalism shrouded in the 'stink' of individualism, each 'fly' 'groping' towards his 'personal heap'. At the same time, other flies for whom 'the time is wrong' die in the new spring; the 'spring', in turn, heralds 'the cold wind / brewing beyond the Buda hills, the frost / making a belated entrance'. Whether the post-1989 thaw is real or not is already, in 1991, an issue – in 'A Sea Change', 'things are done / precisely as before but feel / a little different'. The Cold War climate remains embedded, domesticated in the poem's language but inflected by the tiny echo of other, older atrocities, as 'Behind the frosted glass / someone takes a shower'.

The cold dawn (the 'frosted glass') of capitalist freedoms is, in *Bridge Passages*, an ambivalent transformation, 'a conjectural landscape' described by the German word 'Heimat' in 'Nachtmusik', possibly in allusion to Ottó Orbán's poem for Sándor Weöres, 'Sinking Orpheus', in which (in Szirtes' own translation) the 'dying poet' 'writes in the dust with his blood the word: *heimat*'.[110] '*Heimat*', post *Waste Land*, resonates with Wagnerian and Eliotesque longing – '*Frisch weht der Wind / Der Heimat zu / Mein irisch Kind / Wo weilest du?*' 'Nachtmusik' refers to 'The lull / of belonging', the pause at the line's end imitating this 'lulling', before we return to the infinitive 'To act' and the transitive 'to make choices'. The 'lull' hesitates before asserting its own choice: music tells us that 'though we die / we nevertheless belong', the poem claims, with another caveat: 'It doesn't tell us where, that is the catch'. We're left with 'something without form', not art or music or poetry but 'The empty noise / of radio waves' (returning momentarily to *Short Wave*), a disorientating dislocation that recurs throughout the collection. 'You could be anywhere', the next poem, 'Bridge Passage', begins, repeating a line from the earlier 'A Domestic Faust': 'You could be anywhere. Indeed you are...'. In 'Bodies' we're told that 'it is hard to know just where to place a thing'; 'The Comfort of Rooms' worries that 'the layers of vision shift in alarming parallax'. The transitional experience of 'Night Ferry' imbues the subsequent poems with this sense of dislocated, fluctuating unreality, of perceptual confusion, a mood that matches itself to the giddy uncertainties of the events of 1989. The 'furious year' constitutes a historical moment that, to Szirtes' poems, is also present in all its confusing, sometimes bewildering new dimensions and transitions;

within the anger and energy implicit in 'furious' lies also (in 'In a Strong Light') 'the everyday news / of bridges, trees and grass'.

Such momentary pastoral interludes punctuate the collection, here connecting 'bridges' with simple symbols of nature. The conjunction throughout *Bridge Passages* of architectural and pastoral motifs with the underlying symbolism of the journey to death and the afterlife can be compared with Martin Heidegger's vision of an ordered pastoral social world in his 1951 lecture 'Building, Dwelling, Thinking', which argues for the connections between the accommodating functions of buildings and the act of thinking as a kind of accommodation of the possibilities of thought. Bridges, Heidegger notes, work to signify the beginnings of the processes of building and thinking in the possibility of connection, in linking things (building bricks, ideas) together; bridges, he writes, 'initiate in many ways':

> The city bridge leads from the precincts of the castle to the cathedral square; the river bridge near the country town brings wagons and horse teams to the surrounding villages. The old stone bridge's humble brook crossing gives to the harvest wagon its passage from the fields into the village [...]. Always and ever differently the bridge initiates the lingering and hastening ways of men to and fro, so that they may get to other banks and, in the end, as mortals to the other side.[111]

Heidegger's pastoral vision of the bridge as the 'initiation' and crossing-point of a community envisioned as wholly facilitated by bridges and bridging resonates with the poems in *Bridge Passages*. His misreading of the 'bridge' as the 'passage' for 'mortals to the other side' is silently rectified by Szirtes' 'Night Ferry'; but Szirtes elsewhere registers the importance of the Budapest bridges as facilitators of cross-city passages and signifiers of new freedoms during the protest marches of June 1989: 'Then across the bridge to the last two stations. ...We set off across the bridge towards the palace.'[112]

Szirtes' familiar and problematic pastoral forms, and their reliance (in poems like 'Wild Garden') on new configurations of the 'cold pastoral' of his earlier works, offer the 'bridge' and the 'passage' as allegories of multiple interconnections in the ways the words ramify through the collection. 'Bridge' and 'passage' share many meanings and containing multiple nuanced differences of meaning. Both terms can operate as nouns and verbs within this network of significances, which centres on the potentiality of movement through time and space and within formal and aesthetic structures. In an essay published in the *Times Literary Supplement* in November 1989 (amid the events in Eastern Europe), Geoffrey Hill wrote of

the contemporary world as 'the world of amnesia and commodity'.[113]
Szirtes offers his own version of this world in 'Learning from
Brezhnev' where he notes the different relations of East and West
to history: 'The history of Eastern Europe is unhappy and that un-
happiness permeates its consciousness. We live in a world that is
losing its history. We know it as consumable unexperienced infor-
mation. In Eastern Europe writers could articulate and preserve
historical experience in the face of tyranny. We appear to be haunted
by historical thinness, they by historical density'.[114]

  This conception of the 'density' of Eastern European history
saturates *Bridge Passages*, not least in its relation to the words it
uses. The histories embedded in words, revealed by their etym-
ologies, offer useful tools for comprehending the status of other
histories in *Bridge Passages*, and for resisting the 'amnesia' of the
new world. Etymologies of the words of the title expose these his-
tories, and shed further light on their significances across the col-
lection. The *Shorter OED* tells us that the noun 'bridge', from the
Old Frisian *brigge* and Old Norse *bryggja*, signifies 'A structure
forming or carrying a road over a river or ravine, etc., or affording
passage between two points at a height above the ground'; other
nautical, musical, technical and physiognomical meanings are also
listed. The verb 'To bridge' is also 'To make a bridge over; to span
with a means of passage.' 'Passage', from French *passer*, to pass,
offers a range of meanings concerned with movement: the passing
of people 'onward, across or past'; the migratory flight of birds;
passing from life to death; a journey or voyage. It also refers to
that which is passed along – 'a way, road, path, route, channel'; 'a
crossing, ford, ferry or bridge'. Then there are meanings, which
assume significance connotations in Szirtes' uses of the word, to
do with transactions and 'negotiations between two persons', and
a 'passage' as 'a portion of a composition' (as in E.M. Forster's *A
Passage to India*); and, finally, a series of more tangential meanings
to do with horse riding.

  'Bridge', we can conclude, is therefore something that affords or
constitutes or facilitates 'passage', while 'passage' can be a kind of
'bridge'; the two terms interlink or mirror each other in their mean-
ings, so that, for example, the 'passage' of 'a portion of composition'
can become, within this etymology, a figure of the way writing
can bridge the gap between writer and reader, or the way specific
poems act as 'bridges' between the different sections into which
the book is organised. Bridging and passages together constitute a
double movement, a linkage that effects a transference or trans-
mission between self and other, English and Hungarian, present

and past. Writing, as a form of passage, contributes to the architecture implied by the bridge; each is a constructed link between things, an attempt to join things together in order to make 'sense' out of them.

The dominant meaning of the title, however, derives from classical music, where a 'bridge passage' refers to the transition from first to second subject in operatic or sonata form, in which it is 'a passage of subordinate importance serving to connect two themes. It consists of figurations, sequences, or other subsidiary material'.[115] The structure of the collection approximates, without ever fully conforming to, the demands of sonata form, suggesting that the collection's formal organisation can be understood in musical terms, much as T.S. Eliot's *Four Quartets* has sustained readings like Helen Gardner's *The Music of the 'Four Quartets'*, or, as Simon Critchley has recently argued, Wallace Stevens' poetry invites musical analogies ('Stevens' poetry...is a poetry of notes, often musical notes').[116] The Polish poet Tadeusz Rózewicz has argued that the 1989 revolutions failed to engender formally innovative responses in the arts: 'No new forms', he writes, 'emerged in literature, painting, music or the theatre'.[117] Szirtes himself has written that 'The revolution – in so far as it was a revolution and not simply a collapse – produced some poetry but of a fairly inferior kind'.[118] This absence of formal invention and innovation in representing the events of 1989 suggests the difficulty of forming an aesthetic response to the new and quickly changeable situation, and, simultaneously, implies an awareness on the part of artists of what George Steiner called 'the shadows at the heart of the carnival'.[119] This awareness of formal difficulty lurks in the heart of *Bridge Passages*, and accounts for the degree of prevarication prevalent in the collection.

The six 'Bridge Passages' sections of the collection, corresponding to the six bridges that, in 1989, traversed the Danube in Budapest – a seventh, the Lágymányosi Bridge, was added in 1995 – work as a central and linking group of poems that, together, affords passage through the collection and between the other sections. They also, collectively, stand for Hungary itself at the particular historical moment addressed in the collection. Szirtes commented, in a radio broadcast in November 1989, on Hungary's emergent position in relation to East and West: 'As Austria and Hungary edge closer and Hungary strains to become the international bridge between East and West the concept of President Gorbachev's "common European house" gains ever greater importance.'[120] Hungary's historical and contemporary status as an international bridge between East and West offers a further dimension of significance to *Bridge Passages*.

Not so much subordinate to as organising of the other material by separating it and connecting it, the 'Bridge Passages' sections offer lexical and symbolic continuities and repetitions as structuring motifs, allowing the other poems in the collection to differentiate and diversify its themes. The 'Bridge' and the 'Passage' work throughout as figurative linking devices connecting present and past, autobiography and history, English and Hungarian, self and other. Angela Carter opened her final novel, *Wise Children* (published in the same year as *Bridge Passages*) with the question 'Why is London like Budapest?...Because it is two cities divided by a river.'[121] The divisions in both cities are, of course, spanned by bridges, and *Bridge Passages* assumes division in its reliance upon the metaphor of connectivity.

'Bridges' and 'passages' appear, recursively, throughout *Bridge Passages*, not least as titles of the collection, of the six 'Bridge Passages' sections and of the central poem of the third of these sections. The words also pepper other poems: 'A Woman with a Rug' offers 'unlit passages / of dialogue'; '*Somewhere there's a bridge / between the actor and his ghosts*', opines 'Funeral Oration' (the 'bridge' here spanning the space between stanzas); in 'Chinese White', '*An image hangs and drops / in a grey passageway or alley*'; 'Bridge Passage' meditates on 'passing time, and time too passing on / to things a passage can adjust'. The 'bridge' and the 'passage' are in one sense symptoms of the author's 'pretty desperate attempt...to discover bridges between my life in England and my history in Hungary'.[122] Nevertheless they transcend this biographical confine to express also the moment and movement – the momentum – which the collection perceives as its responsibility, to which it fastidiously responds, with the 'Responsibility / to every piece of unforgiving matter' of 'A Domestic Faust'. Their reiteration, punctuating and emphasising the collection's rhythm, adds to the poetry's formalism, its metrical and thematic consistency.

'English Words', significantly placed in the near centre of *Bridge Passages* as the opening poem of the section 'Appropriations' (which turns the collection's attention onto Szirtes' English memories and experiences), also demands an etymological engagement in order to address the poem's response to language. In returning us to the linguistic connectivity asserted in the collection's opening poem, refracted now through memories of the act of taking possession of a language, 'English Words' also re-introduces the first-person lyric voice to the collection as a momentarily stable, authoritative position from which to speak. Drawing on images and lexis (the 'drain' and the 'poppies') derived from Edward Thomas' poem 'Words', it relates the childhood experience of encountering, learning and 'appropriating' the English language as something 'exotic', 'Peculiar', and ultimately 'absurd', tracing the stages of a relationship to words that begins in their 'hostility' and ends in their untrustworthiness.

The poem opens with an assertion that firmly establishes this stability: 'My first three English words were AND, BUT, SO', words that signify in English only in grammatical terms (the opening word of the collection, we recall, is 'And'). Their 'exotic' sound also affords accommodation in the symbolic spaces afforded by language – 'Imagination made / houses of them' out of their resemblance to wooden 'Froebel blocks', an image that draws on Anthony Hecht's 'unbuttressed balancing of wooden blocks / Into a Tower of Babel' in *The Venetian Vespers*[123] (Eva Hoffman writes of 'whole literatures, histories and cultural formations' looked at 'as if they were toy blocks, ours to construct and deconstruct').[124] But, like the 'architecture, not of form / but aberration' that describes the tangible experience of the past in 'Drawing the Curtain', Szirtes' English words are also 'Genii from a gazetteer / of deformations or a *sprechgesang*'; to account for their specific English 'foreignness' (to the ear of the newly arrived Hungarian child), the poem resorts to descriptions reliant on foreign words ('gazetteer' from French and Italian, Latin 'Genii', German *sprechgesang*, or 'sing-song'). Foreignness thus resides within the language of the familiar, an emblem of the knowable world that reassures: 'somehow it was possible to know / the otherness of people and not be afraid'. Words are closely linked in this poem to 'people' – its version of 'learning how to speak' is, at one level, simply the difficult entrance into a new cultural symbolic, but in another sense it glosses the democratic anxieties expressed later in the collection in 'Wild Garden', offering a different slant on the learning of speech in which the 'crass / hostility' of what one says with the language one learns – the use to which words are put – assumes a degree of urgency.

English words are, in the immigrant's experience of linguistic unfamiliarity, 'foreign', and embody for the young Hungarian child the 'abyss' of unmeaning: 'Their emptiness appals one', 'their crass hostility' leads, paradoxically, to dumbness. Julia Kristeva has noted that, for the foreigner, 'the foreign language remains an artificial one', and becomes, no matter how well learnt or performed, 'an artificial language, a prosthesis'.[125] In Kristeva's powerful analysis of the experience of foreignness, 'prosthetic' language replaces a lost or repressed organic, native language. 'English Words' explores this process as predominantly one of enculturation, a displacement of the subject into a deceptive linguistic present characterised by mistrust: 'I cannot trust words now'. One response to this, an extreme one, perhaps, is dumbness, the refusal or inability to utter words: 'One is dumb / with surprise at their inertia, their crass / hostility. They are beautiful opiates, / as brilliant as poppies, as absurd.' 'Beautiful opiates' invites a contrast with Keats' 'Ode to a Nightingale', with its description of the experience of the melancholy invoked by hearing the nightingale's song as like a 'dull opiate' 'emptied...to the drains'.

Not birdsong or music but words, in 'English Words', are emptied of meaning, evacuated of semantic force only to return like 'poppies', suggesting a further symbolic twist that renders words as conventional symbols of memorialisation and links this poem to the thread of poems Szirtes has written on the question of how words and things relate to each other. The emphasis on the final rhyme-word 'absurd', linking back to 'heard' earlier in the same stanza, also connects it implicitly to 'word' itself, 'absurd words' summarising, perhaps, one surface meaning of the poem. But the etymology of the final rhyming syllable 'surd' extends the poem's complexity and its effectiveness, 'surd' meaning both an irrational number (hence 'absurd') and, in phonetics, a voiceless sound, thereby linking semantically with 'dumb' ('One is dumb / with surprise at their inertia') to express silently the linguistic exclusion and silencing, the word's power of excommunication, against which the poem appeals. 'English Words' exploits this latent absurdity of 'surd', the linguistic error recorded in the *OED* as a 'mistranslation of Latin into Greek *alagos*, "irrational", "speechless"', a lexical slippage allowing a word to signify wordlessness as absurdity. In appealing against the 'sheer inanity / of idiom' it detects in contemporary usage, the poem situates its critique on the basis of nostalgia: for the child, the words were 'lovely'; for the adult, they are 'dead'. 'I cannot trust words now': the statement of fact returns us to the 'now' of the present moment, and the immediacy of the poet's relation to words not 'dead' but living, 'dangerous'. Words, and the poet's ability to use them, delineate the dimensions of the present; their etymologies embed the histories behind the present moment, the products of conflicting, contradictory forces.

Miroslav Holub's essay 'The Dimension of the Present Moment' is informative in this context. The 'present moment' in *Bridge Passages* is the 'now' of 'English Words', the resigned location (and locution) of 'now' in 'The Service of Remembrance' ('And this is where we are, at least for now'), the time in which things 'feel a little different now' in 'A Sea Change', or the Ted Hughes-like ('again now, and now, and now')[126] in the same poem: 'Even now, something begins…These things are done / precisely as before but feel / a little different now…Now's the time perhaps / for understanding what remains the same'. These adverbial 'nows' assert the immediacy of the present moment as a linguistic dimension (and 'now' is also a conjunction, a joining of present to present). Its presence is also emphasised by Szirtes' pitching of most of the poems in *Bridge Passages* in the simple present, and his intermittent use of the present continuous, as in 'the band is gaily signalling' in 'A Woman with a Rug'.

Holub, considering the limits of human perception in relation to the experience of the immediate 'now', writes that 'Every musical composition, especially of classic or romantic tradition, has its basic tempo, which the musician either keeps or breaks. This tempo should be in some relation to the dimension of the present moment.'[127] The sonata-like form and 'tempo' of *Bridge Passages*, the rhythmic order and pace underpinning its concerns with surface variations, is perceptible in its metrical consistency (predominantly four- or five-stress lines). Keeping or breaking with such a demand is another ideological choice, one adhered to in the collection's concern with reparation (paying the debts of history) and with repairing what it perceives as a 'damaged' or compromised language. This is implicit in 'the language games' of 'A Domestic Faust' or 'the foreignness of languages' in 'English Words'; in 'Rain', linguistic frailty becomes palpable: '*You can't pronounce the words, nor can you shout / for lack of vowels. The language starts to ache / and slowly crumbles*'.

'The Dimension of the Present Moment', Holub's scientific allegory of endurance and suffering, is translated in Szirtes' poetry into a possession of the Hungarians who populate it, but not of the poet himself: 'A Woman with a Rug' addresses, as does all of *Bridge Passages*, 'The tragic dimension which is rightly theirs'. In doing so, it also establishes the poetic space – form, metre, density and responsibility of language, the proper and the due, the poets' authority and permission of access into this space – in relation to what Holub (citing Turner and Pöpel's *Poetry*) calls 'rhythmic community': 'In addition, 'metre clearly synchronises the speaker with the audience and provokes a "rhythmic community" essential to the "social solidarity"' – the great presence and simultaneity of people – which is about the best that poetry can do.'[128] Synchronicity of poem and audience – 'about the best poetry can do' – is a form of 'bridging', the establishment of passages for intercommunication and exchange between reader and text.

'Wild Garden', one of the key poems in *Bridge Passages*, grounds this intercommunication and exchange in translation and the exchange of languages. The poem opens with the Hungarian word '*Vadkert*' (a neologistic compounding of '*vad*', 'wild' or 'untamed', from Lapp '*vuow'de*' meaning forest, and '*kert*' meaning 'garden', giving the familiar Hungarian surname 'Kertész', meaning 'gardener'), which it immediately glosses as 'The wild garden', an English phrase for a Hungarian neologism that roughly translates as 'natural park'. The 'wild garden' offers a pastoral space circumscribed, in the collection's now-familiar conjunction of pastoral and architectural motifs, by 'bridges, masonry and trees / which spread themselves like railway stations': the 'airless music' repeating the 'dissolving' airs of 'Nachtmusik'. But this pastoral is tainted: it appears as 'this grave / ceremonial greenness', a Marvellian tincture hamstrung by that hanging 'grave', both a demeanour and a final resting place, reiterating the poet's caveat disclaimer of the final stanza of 'Street Entertainment': 'I'm only a reporter whose truth lies / in diction clear as water', water which 'darkens like a bruise'.

Where Blake's Piper 'stain'd the water clear', Szirtes as 'reporter' here offers 'truth' and 'lies' in immediate collocation, fatally compromising each. The 'reporter' returns in the penultimate stanza of 'Wild Garden' in an allusion to Isherwood's *Goodbye to Berlin*: where Isherwood writes fatalistically, of a Berlin about to elect the Nazis, 'Over there, in the city, the votes were being counted',[129] Szirtes emphasises the popular voice of democratic freedom: 'In the city they're counting votes / and learning how to speak'. In 1989, speech and freedom of speech accompany, and are the end product of, the movement towards democracy: 'Wild Garden''s 'grave / ceremonial greenness' is also, in relation to 'learning how to speak', the 'greenness of innocence and inexperience', a colour for a nation finding its voice. Holub warns us that 'The dimension of the psychological present probably does not only concern speech; speech is a phenomenon suitable for demonstration and measuring.'[130] Speech, in 'Wild Garden', leads almost inexorably to the 'society of worms and ants and clods' which 'lived in terror of the creatures / of the garden'. The garden's wildness is now not untamed but bestial; as the thrice-mentioned peacock should alert us to the deception of appearances, so the ambiguity of 'lie' is again embedded in the otherwise Audenesque 'Bucolics' of the world outside: 'And beyond them lie the woods, / the lakes, the sea and the enormous waves / on which we inscribe our human features'. The poem concludes with the immense force of the 'enormous waves' as figures of irresistible historical transformation; not speech, but the 'inscription' of 'human features' – the anthropomorphisation of nature – provides the closing image, leading to the next poem, the elegy to Sándor

Weöres, who, continuing writing's sudden pre-eminence in the col-
lection, 'signed my book / in a childish trembling hand'.

The 'incongruity' that 'Wild Garden' detects in the '*Vadkert*', its
proclivity for the politically blinkered 'game of let's pretend', is,
finally, a concession that the collection's concern with the present
moment is interminable, a concern that can only gesture, MacNeice-
like, to the 'variousness' of things. In 'A Woman with a Rug', 'world'
is palpably unconcerned: 'The world of things remains as various /
and indifferent as the leaves / in the garden which itself is lost...'.
The 'lost' garden evokes Biblical innocence; speech succumbs to
music as 'The human voice surrenders to the air', language trans-
lated (by words) into music. Translation from one medium or lan-
guage to another, as indicated by the interchange between 'Wild
garden' and *Vadkert*, affords a particular kind of 'Bridge Passage',
the possibility of connection between peoples and nations and his-
tories through linguistic equivalence. What Walter Benjamin calls
the 'vital connection', 'the central reciprocal relationship between
languages' or between original and translation is, for Szirtes, ex-
tended to the cultural level, affording bridges that seek to evade
the 'plunging of meaning from abyss to abyss' by which Benjamin
describes Hölderlin's translations of Sophocles.[131] For Szirtes, in a
self-conscious metaphor, translations are 'a kind of love affair with
the complementary Other whose shadow you have decided tempor-
arily to become'.[132]

Translation is, of course, central to the ideological project ex-
plored in *Bridge Passages*, and assumes significance in relation to
Szirtes' developing relationship with Hungarian poetry, his involve-
ment in its translation into English, and his awareness of the pos-
sibilities offered by versions of Hungarian poetry within the frame-
works constructed by his own poetry. In 'bridging' gaps between
languages and cultures, translation emerges as a vital activity of
exchange and communication, a key re-situating of the translated
poem as the medium of at least a potential exchange. Nevertheless
translation, like 'choice', also presents a problem, the significance of
which is evident in the dramatic shift in tone and register between
Szirtes' own poems and those reprinted here.

The choice of works by Ottó Orbán and Ágnes Nemes Nagy
(both poets with whom Szirtes had social contact: in May 2002 he
published an obituary for Orbán in *The Guardian*) suggests a
deliberate association with poetic voices clearly distinct from and
yet connected to Szirtes' own, voices which nevertheless represent
(in some exemplary, demonstrative fashion) dimensions of the pre-
sent moment of modern Hungarian poetry necessary to adumbrate

or develop the themes of the collection. Nemes Nagy's position as a 'silenced' poet has already been noted; Szirtes' translations of her work were collected in *The Night of Akhenaton*, thirteen years after the publication of *Bridge Passages*. Orbán, on the other hand, is represented in English in a volume of translations by various hands, *The Blood of the Walsungs*, first published in the same year as *Bridge Passages* and edited (and partly translated) by Szirtes, in the introduction to which he notes that Orbán (1936-2002) 'has become the leading commentator on the politics and social life of his times'.[133] Szirtes' description of Orbán's poetry, in the same introduction, is instructive:

> Marked by a brisk, vernacular, apparently unliterary, unconfined energy, they carry an authority blended of the humorous and tragic, of the commonplace and extraordinary. Often they take the form of anecdote or comment. A voice buttonholes the reader, carries him along in its narrative sweep, then detonates a mine (or several mines) under his feet before returning to the texture of dialogue. The voice appears almost garrulous at first, afflatus and deflation quickly succeeding each other, seemingly engaged in some violent internal argument. The whole procedure seems to have a dizzy, scat quality about it which spins free of formal constraint.[134]

Orbán, from this description, is, on the surface, a markedly different poet from George Szirtes. His general use of ironised dialogic forms differs from Szirtes' tendency towards the monologic lyric voice; his 'garrulousness' resists comparison, in particular, with the restrained, almost understated, tones of *Bridge Passages*. The sequence of seven translated sonnets (drawn from a longer sequence published in *The Blood of the Walsungs*) constitutes a potentially disruptive presence in *Bridge Passages*, a deliberate interrupting of the tones and registers developed in the first two 'Bridge Passages' sequences. In wider terms, Orbán's poetry offers orientation points for several motifs in Szirtes' collection: the second part of 'A Small Country' describes 'A Central European Hell' and asserts, in terms echoed in 'Night Ferry', that 'it's easier for the bookkeepers if each generation's placed, when it comes to the bottom line, under Loss'; 'The Flying Faust' is echoed in Szirtes' 'A Domestic Faust'.[135]

The insertion of another voice into the sequence of lyrics offers the potential of dialogue; but Orbán's sonnets, drawing on the 'conversational/confessional' moods of Robert Lowell's loose sonnets, offer not dialogue but a series of informal, conversational monologues. All were originally published in Orbán's collection from 1990 (*A kosmikus gavallér* [The Cosmic Cavalier]) and a later collection (post-dating *Bridge Passages*) from 1992 (*Egyik oldaláról a másikra fordul: él* [He Turns from One Side to the Other; He's Alive]). Both are collections which, like *Bridge Passages*, respond to the events of 1989. In the context of *Bridge Passages*, their 'garrulousness' ('Forgive this garrulousness', Szirtes' 'The Flies' begins), their linear sprawl and metrical variations, compensate for the tight, reserved stanzas of poems like 'The Flies' and 'A Woman with a Rug'. Imagery like 'darkness and nothing, and nothing and darkness' confirms the deep pessimism that seems to preoccupy the early sections of *Bridge Passages*, and, in the penultimate and most directly politicised of these poems, 'Witchfinder General', the opening 'idea of hell' of 'Night Ferry' acquires a specific historical and geographical location: 'the address and postcode of hell: Paris, 1789'.

The French Revolution thus symbolically substitutes, in Orbán's oblique political commentary, for the Hungarian ones (of 1956 and 1989) addressed or shadowed in Szirtes' collection, but it does so ironically, in an 'imagined TV-series' in which 'history is exhausted / and bored of the bloodbath'. The poem, an extraordinary allegory of historical process, imagines Rousseau, figurehead of the French revolution, opening the 'Pandora's box' of revolutionary dictatorship that bedevils subsequent centuries. This cynical vision of historical dispassion is framed by the poem's conceit that the demonic modernity it imagines is a fantasy of 'neo-conservative ideology' or 'mass ideology', directly loaded political terms that add to the poem's rhetorical armour a language redolent of mass-cultural shorthand for political allegiances. This shorthand is evident too in the references to 'the bloodbath at Vendée and Katyn Forest', references respectively to the slaughter in western France of the counter-revolutionary forces (up to 250,000 deaths, by some estimates) of the Vendée army between 1794-96, and to the Russian execution of over 4000 Polish service personnel in the Katyn Forest in 1940 (a massacre blamed by the Russians on the Nazis, who discovered the mass graves in 1943, but acknowledged in 1989 by Gorbachev as a Soviet crime). French revolutionary and Communist atrocities are thus directly paralleled, and allowed to echo in relation to the Soviet occupation of Hungary; contemporary history's 'bored' attitude to genocide, its postmodern, distanced desire for 'a bit of home-cooking and TV in front of the fire', exemplifies the vicious satire of Orbán's poem; the power of historical naming counterpoints the banality of the contemporary. Such a position is clearly one that the author of *Bridge Passages* simultaneously aspires towards and repudiates.

The importance to Szirtes' project of Orbán's critique of Hungarian history and politics emerges in his analysis of what, in 'The Father of the People', Szirtes translates as 'the tombstone / of common memory'. Orbán's wariness concerning the 1989 revolutions is indicated in the closing lines of the last sonnet, 'A Roman Considers the Christians':

> out of the screaming and bloodshed
> something emerges...the same thing? the worse? Or the better?
> the gods only know, if they know, what lies in the future...

The poem clearly asserts uncertainty; Szirtes' translation draws attention again to the potential ambiguity of 'lies'.

If Orbán's poems lend historical ballast and his voice the authority of 'presence' – linguistic, cultural and national – to Szirtes' meditations on the events of 1989, Nemes Nagy's 'Diary', written in response to the banning of her poetry in 1948 by the Hungarian Communist authorities (under the advice of the Marxist literary critic George Lukács) continues their uncertainty at the end of *Bridge Passages*, concluding the collection with a series of strange, dislocated voices. Nemes Nagy's assertion, in an essay (translated by J.E. Sollosy, first published in 1980 and appended to *The Night of Akhenaton*) that discusses the linguistic and moral bases of her poetry, that 'All poetry is untranslatable, Hungarian poetry is even more untranslatable',[136] invests translations of her work with added levels of difficulty. When she writes, in the same essay, that 'it is the duty of the poet to obtain citizenship for an increasing horde of nameless emotions',[137] one senses the potential that her theories of poetry, and her poetry itself, might offer for the projects of Szirtes' collection, which has struggled throughout to articulate its own responses to 'an increasing horde of nameless emotions'.

These brief, highly objectivist lyrics, fragments of the 'crystalline mountain'[138] which Szirtes evokes to describe her work, suggest an implicit commentary on the themes of the preceding poems. In his introductory paragraph on Nemes Nagy in *Leopard V: An Island of Sound*, which also reprints these poems, Szirtes comments that they meditate 'both on her own nature and on the nature of those who banned her work'.[139] They contrast markedly with Orbán's sonnets, adding in this difference a further tonal shift to *Bridge Passages*. From the fractured mental processes of 'Mind', where 'knowledge', 'thinking', 'contempt' and 'intellect' jostle for a kind of intransitive position in the absence of any objective world or thing (only an 'act', the 'act' perhaps of thought itself, assumes a ghostly object position), to the fantasies, in 'Contemplative', of abandoning 'the face fate assigned you' in 'In front of the mirror' and shedding 'the old pose', these poems delineate a subjectivity at the limits of coherence, seeking to abandon itself to intricate word-play and deep condensed imagery. Their contribution the mood of *Bridge Passages* consists of a reinforcement of the connections between complex poetic expression and historical movements; the final poem, 'Sincerity', articulates a kind of despair even as it finds a poetic image through which to do so:

> Inspecting myself makes me bilious.
> It's easier for the spontaneous.
> I would if I could, be the driver of the dray
> who washes great blonde horses all the day
> and has nothing to say.

Poetry, this epigrammatic conclusion suggests, is a kind of introspective activity at odds with the sheer materiality of physical rather than intellectual or aesthetic labour suggested by the 'driver of the dray' and the 'great blonde horses'; having 'nothing to say' might, it suggests (perhaps, in Szirtes' translation, echoing Seamus Heaney's despairing 'Whatever you say, say nothing' in his *North*),[140] be a safer, less 'bilious', response to history.

Bridge Passages thus concludes, ventriloquistically, in the problematic English-rendered voice of a Hungarian poet whose career was interrupted by (and seeks to avenge through 'redress', in 'Revenge') the Communist regime of which Szirtes' collection marks the passing. In ending in the words of a poet who died in 1991, the year of its own publication, *Bridge Passages* offers a final gesture of mourning and commemoration that links it back to Szirtes' earlier commemorations of his mother; the collection is, in this sense, a text of mourning. But this is balanced by the optimism of 'Clumsy Music', the second of the 'Two Rondeaus' that conclude Szirtes' own voice in *Bridge Passages*, which asserts that 'Important things remain undone'. *Bridge Passages* seeks simultaneously a language and a form in which to imagine, from its historical grounding in a period of deep and threatening uncertainty, that the future, in which such things may be done, is still possible.

4

'A whole life external': *Blind Field*

...I clutch at things, plain things
I've lifted to symbols;
...Why, then, back there on
That warm pew do they prick me?
GEORGE MACBETH, 'St Andrew's'

Bridge Passages offers a personal response to public historical events, and punctuates Szirtes' career just as the events to which it responds punctuated Western history. *Blind Field*, published three years later in 1994, constitutes by contrast a concentrated return to Szirtes' concerns with poetry and the image, and the possibilities they offer for an analysis of the traces left by human lives and historical events. This chapter will examine the ways in which *Blind Field* explores the workings of the visual and verbal image in relation to memory, history and representation. Through the metaphorical potential of the concept of the 'blind field', and through the structuring device of counterpointing, the collection offers complex, imagistic constructions of the real as mechanisms through which reality – the real of perception, experience and history – can be questioned and deconstructed. In doing so it also questions the interdependence of image and narrative, pushing a stage further the analysis of each in long poems like 'Metro' and 'The Photographer in Winter'. Its enquiry seeks connections between the different ways images work within these contexts, and focuses on a sceptical reading of how, within the space of the image, 'even appearance becomes something other / than imagined'. This assertion is made in the second poem of a short sequence 'For Diane Arbus' entitled 'On a Young Lady's Photograph Album'; the line-break at the word 'other' emphasises the collection's concern with the 'other' qualities of the world of appearance offered by the image.

The tension between 'appearance' and 'imagination' is central to *Blind Field* and, retrospectively, can be seen as a recurrent and developing concern of Szirtes' work. Images, it seems, are not to be trusted in *Blind Field*; they present a world of seeming rather than of being, in which ethical questions are momentarily suspended in the act of looking. In the specific case of Diane Arbus' photographs, they invite through their to-be-looked-at-ness the potential confusion of the image with the real thing, as well as the confusion of point of view (photographer's, viewer's, subject's) that Szirtes' poems explore.[141] Martha Rosler has noted that 'Even in the fading of liberal sentiments one recognises that it is dangerous or impolite to stare in person, as Diane Arbus knew when she arranged her satisfyingly immobilised imagery as a surrogate *for the real thing*, the real freak show'.[142] Arbus' deliberate presentation of reality as constructed, her offering of the photograph as 'surrogate', affords Szirtes spaces in which to consider the 'imagining' of 'appearance' as a form of deception, and to explore the possibilities opened up by such a deception. Another poem in this sequence, 'Bichonnade', responds (via reference to a photograph by Jacques-Henri Lartigue) to an epigraph from Arbus that summarises the concerns of this collection: '...that we may wonder all over again what is veritable and inevitable and possible and what it is to become whoever we may be'.

New York photographer Arbus (who committed suicide in 1971, aged 48), the younger sister of the American formalist poet Howard Nemerov, was famous – notorious, even – for her images of the dispossessed and the freakish, the underclasses and the excluded. She represents those who populate the underground spaces of America, just as Szirtes' previous two collections explored the symbolic underworlds of Budapest and Hungary. Szirtes has commented of Arbus that 'She is the off-stage subject of a number of poems in [*Blind Field*]' because he 'identified some aspects of' his mother with 'the photographer of the extreme'.[143] This possibility – that the photographer Magdalena Szirtes might, in different historical circumstances, have been a figure like Arbus or produced work comparable to hers – haunts *Blind Field*. Arbus' photographs 'represent the troubled psyche of America and the torments of individual souls', argues critic Anne Marsh,[144] just as Magdalena Szirtes' images and experiences constitute one major element of the 'troubled soul' of her son's poetry.

Szirtes' poems respond explicitly to Arbus' writings as much as to her images, but the aura surrounding her photographs is also invoked in the poems' concern with 'the scapegrace, / the lost and the squalid' ('Paragons'). Arbus' questions of the 'veritable' and the 'possible' concern Szirtes: he constructs, in the poems' spaces, other 'spaces / with the smell of the past trapped in their unstable walls'. This structural instability (always implicit but formally resisted in the rigid stanzaic poems of *Bridge Passages*) is integral to the worlds of *Blind Field*. It elaborates the tendency towards

'dissolution' noted in earlier collections, a quality that resides con-
tradictorily within the solidity of the material world, the 'thingness'
that is a recurrent concern of the collection, evident in descriptions
like the 'hard and joyful' light of 'Bichonnade'. It suggests, in
contrast, a fragility in the material world which the image and the
poem expose; solidity (the quality of 'frozenness' of earlier poems)
is present, but exists in counterpoint to new kinds of fluidity and
movement in these new poems, which in turn map Szirtes' char-
acteristic tensions between movement and frozen stasis, in the con-
flict between the static image and the fluidity of the word. The use
in 'For Diane Arbus' of the photographer's words as epigraphs is
important – *Blind Field* negotiates the terrain of the image through
words via the space of the image in words, and through words
discussing, describing or analysing images. Above all the collection
is concerned with what reading can mean in relation to words and
images.

Reading is the motivating activity of most of the poems in *Blind
Field*, whether they read images, or other words and texts (in cita-
tions or translations), or momentary perceptions, or moments of
historical or remembered experience. Szirtes arranges poems about
reading to counterpoint or comment upon poems that 'read' images
or read into them. Reading, as a constructive, analytical engage-
ment with the text, the image and the real world, also inaugurates
dialogue with the world of texts, images and historically material
experiences. Michael Murphy notes the series of literary references
in 'The Baths on Monroe Street' and comments that 'At this point
in the sequence it is increasingly difficult to separate the various
strands of literary allusion from which Szirtes constructs his poem'.[145]
This density of literary and cultural allusion (incorporating lines
from T.S. Eliot, Matthew Arnold, and allusions to Dante and to
Greek mythology, as well as to iconic figures from the world of
images like Marilyn Monroe) emphasises the "written-ness" of
Szirtes' exploration of the image, suggesting that the poems in *Blind
Field* also read the traditions out of which they develop.

The results are densely imagistic and allusive poems presented,
in the sequence 'For Diane Arbus', as a series of meditations on
reliability, truthfulness and the potential authority invested in the
pseudo-objectivity of the photograph and the poem. The first poem
in the sequence, 'Paragons', advises us to 'Distrust everything', in
particular the freakish world constructed in Arbus' notorious photo-
graphs, 'the man with a tail, / the man who smokes cigars with his
eyes'; at the same time, as Murphy has carefully explicated, Szirtes'
responses to Arbus explore an infernal dimension of the real that

finds expression in what Susan Sontag described as Arbus' 'Dantesque vision of the city'.[146] Death lurks within these poems: 'On a Young Lady's Photograph Album' explores the question of 'what remains' of human lives after death (a question addressed from a different angle in 'Metro'), and addresses the unreliability of the images held in the memory, in which, as we age and die, our self-images, the visual fictions by which we construct our identities, become 'blurrier, vaster, ever more unfocused, full of grains'.

The poems respond to historical questions and pressures in complex, sometimes difficult ways, opening further biographical and autobiographical spaces of enquiry. *Blind Field* contains, in the long poem 'Transylvana', a third instalment of Szirtes' extended enquiry into his mother's life and its connections to Hungarian history, in which eastern European histories and traditions merge with mythic Western narratives to provide a new allegorical descent into the past. It also incorporates new short sequences of poems responding to photographs (by Arbus and by the Hungarian photographer André Kertész [1894–1985]); and it includes translations from Ágnes Nemes Nagy's 'Balaton Cycle' (two of which are later reprinted in Szirtes' edition of translations of Nagy, *The Night of Akhenaton*), and a tribute to the Hungarian poet István Vas. In the same year as *Blind Field* Szirtes published a collection of translations of works by a younger Hungarian Poet, Zsuzsa Rakovszky's *New Life: Selected Poems*; like translations between image and text, translation between languages was becoming an increasingly important element in the trajectory of Szirtes' development.

Blind Field is structured into three sections. The first, 'Blind Field', is a poetic series taking several cues from photography, in order effectively to offer lyric meditations on the relations between writing, poetry, photography, history and memory. 'Transylvana' constitutes the second section, returning to Szirtes' extended elegiac remembering of his mother. The third part, 'Blindfold', offers a further series of poetic translations, threnodies and elegies, and constitutes a short sequence that might be read as an honouring of poetic debts (several of the poems are dedicated to other poets) that nevertheless continues the thematic preoccupation with memory and history. After the sometimes claustrophobic functional formalism of *Bridge Passages*, *Blind Field* exudes a confident sense of creative energy and freedom, as if its author had emerged from a dark period to discover a wealth of new opportunities to explore. Formal patterning is markedly diverse in appearance and motivation (after the blocked stanzas of *Bridge Passages*), and Szirtes offers a fluid deployment of stanzas, line lengths, metres and rhyme-schemes throughout to emphasise the formal range of possible responses to the questions posed in the collection. And questions are frequently posed, suggesting that Szirtes is developing (in the wake of the political uncertainties of *Bridge Passages*) a poetry of possibility and proposition, of interrogation and enquiry, rather than any dogmatic seeking of solutions.

While history remains a central concern of *Blind Field*, its status is now mediated through theory, specifically theorisations of the photographic image. The new work is bolstered by a critical and theoretical awareness flagged in the collection's title, which derives from Roland Barthes' meditation on photography, *La Chambre Claire* (1980), translated into English in 1982 as *Camera Lucida*. Barthes' book, apart from being one of the most profound and influential theorisations of photography and its symbolic functions, is also an extended elegy for its author's mother, whose death in 1977 was effectively the inspiration for the book. The connections with Szirtes' extended poetic mourning for his own mother are obvious; 'Transylvana' imagines Szirtes' mother's childhood, extending the archaeologies of 'The Photographer in Winter' and 'Metro' further into the biographical and historical past, away from Hungary and into new Eastern European contexts. 'On a Young Lady's Photograph Album' suggests that the word 'mother' is central to the collection: 'and what remains / is perhaps a voice saying (for instance) "mother"'. The carefully tentative phrasing, prevaricating and deflecting certainties, draws the question of 'what remains' (a question central to the ontology of the photograph as it is theorised by Barthes) towards its focus in the word 'mother'. Like the hypotheses and assertions of Barthes' *Camera Lucida*, the poems in *Blind Field* examine 'what remains' in and around and as a consequence of images of the dead, and specifically of the figure of the mother.

Blind Field provides, and works through, a new metaphor for this 'archaeological' process of excavating 'what remains' of the past. In Barthes' theorisation of photography a 'blind field' describes the excavated space that lurks 'within' and 'behind' certain photographs, a space opened up within what Barthes calls the *studium* of the image (that which resides in it for study, that which attracts the viewer towards it out of historical, cultural, personal or nostalgic interests) by the action of what he describes as the image's *punctum*. This is the element or detail of the particular image that 'pricks' or 'pierces' the individual viewer, making them suddenly aware of the real world that lies outside, and yet establishes its presence within and through, the image. Photographs are not reality – they represent a fraction or moment of real experience, fixed and recorded in an unreal, contrived or constructed way. Photographs are bound to reality by reference (they can, Barthes insists, only refer in some way to the real world), but are also separate from reality, offering an image of that reality which no longer exists, because the photograph fixes a moment in time which has immediately passed, constructing an imagistic 'dimension of the present moment' fixed and recorded. Barthes examines how certain images, in their fixing of time and of the details of reality that might otherwise escape everyday notice, seem to affect the viewer, inviting them through a particular detail captured in the image into a space seemingly contained within the image itself but really an imagined vestige of the reality outside and before the image. Such a detail – the *punctum* – becomes the focus of critical scrutiny, which, in turn, is led to imagine and to seek to reconstruct the 'blind field' behind the image.

That imaginative reconstruction is the object of many of the poems in *Blind Field*. Expanding and redirecting both the visually descriptive impetus of earlier works, and the movement towards narrative demanded by Szirtes' encounters in the 1980s with Hungarian histories, the collection takes its cue from Barthes, who, referring to the film theory of André Bazin, argues that 'The screen (as Bazin has remarked) is not a frame but a hideout; the man or woman who emerges from it continues living: a "blind field" constantly doubles our partial vision.' The 'blind field' here adds depth and volume to the incomplete perception of the viewer – it doubles, in the viewer's imagination, the potentiality embedded within the image. 'Yet once there is a *punctum*,' Barthes goes on, 'a blind field is created...'. The 'blind field' is thus a space that 'doubles' the viewer's relation to the image, opening up another dimension in the ways that the image affects the viewer; it is an imaginary space into which the viewer's imagination is led by the gently insistent ambiguity and uncertainty of the image. For Barthes, the 'blind field' characterises certain images and is apparently absent from others: 'The presence (the dynamics) of this blind field is, I believe, what distinguishes the erotic photograph from the pornographic photograph...the *punctum*, then, is a kind of subtle beyond...'. Barthes discusses Robert Mapplethorpe's *Young Man With Arm Extended* in order to examine how this 'beyond', inculcated within the experience of the image by the *punctum*, can be appreciated. He refers to the *punctum* as 'this "thinking eye" which makes me add something to the photograph.'[147]

The *punctum*, in 'piercing' the viewer, opens up the possibility of the blind field as a necessary adjunct of the process of reading or an outcome of the process of interpretative association – in the context of poetry, the *punctum* might be understood as a phrase, an image, a simile, a line that stimulates the 'blind field' of significance and depth of meaning that the reader adduces from the poem, the space of critical or interpretive creativity that the poem implicitly contains within itself and that becomes available, in the performance of a given reading, for an individual reader to imagine and critically explore. The critical process of imagining and exploring can be understood in terms of another concept from Roland Barthes' writings, that of the *scriptible* or "writerly" text, the text that draws attention to its own written-ness, its 'perpetual present' status as writing, and in particular (in this context) its writing of the photographic images it represents. The reader, in turn, becomes involved in the *scriptible* text, engaged through the necessity of interpreting it in the active process of producing meaning from the text.[148]

The aesthetic moments excavated by Szirtes' poems reside in the effect of the *punctum*, the penetration of an aspect of a photograph into the consciousness of the viewer, a viscerally experienced moment of apprehension. In this 'accidental' moment, described by Barthes as 'this wound, this prick, this mark made by a pointed instrument', 'that accident which pricks me', something is inscribed into the image to be seen.[149] Alluding to this moment of the encounter with the *punctum*, Szirtes opens *Blind Field* with a poem titled 'An Accident', a sonnet that emphasises the materiality of the experience of reading, of 'sitting down' to 'turn the page' in order to enter the space of the text, the 'blind field' of *Blind Field*. The accident literalises the 'accidental pricking' of Barthes' *punctum*, the point which opens up the space of association which eventually constitutes the collection of poems. In a manner reminiscent of Italo Calvino's postmodernist novel *If on a Winter's Night a Traveller* (1979) (the chapter headings of which combine to form the novel's final paragraph, as is the case with the interlocking opening and closing lines of the Hungarian sonnet sequence later used by Szirtes), the poem imagines its own reading, staging the scene of the act of reading in its addressing of the reader as 'you': 'You're simply sitting down. It's getting late.' The poem opens out momentarily into Barthes' 'blind field', its own version of the 'whole life external to [the] portrait': 'a child / killed in a car, a freak wind raising hell / in an obscure American town…'.

These are the spaces outside of the frames of the image and of the act of reading that Szirtes' poems attempt to capture and insert into themselves. Each poem in *Blind Field* offers a speculative foray outside the frame of the image into that external life which lies beyond the immediate evidence, the *studium*, which the poem presents. The "written-ness" of these forays is emphasised from the outset in 'An Accident', but so are the physicality of the reader and the aesthetic solidity of the experience of reading: 'it's like the room is just too full of you, / your senses, your own presence in the chair'. The 'thingness' of the world, indeed, is what constitutes the context of the 'accident', in which 'The sky is a thick slab of premature dark, / metallic, of imponderable weight'. The solid, 'imponderable' presence of the real returns throughout *Blind Field* as a quality of the world beyond word and image, the 'heaviness' of things a marker of their solidity and permanence, but above all of their presence; photographs and poems may fabricate versions of the real, the collection implies, but the real remains – indeed, it may be, in the later poem 'Hortus Conclusus', 'what remains' after 'languages dissolve'.

'An Accident' meditates on accidents as objects of reading ('Sometimes you read of accidents') but offers 'an accident', a specific moment of contingent encounter that directly addresses the reader. Its second person address emphasises the physical action of reading as an entrance into the unknowing but tangible opening of the book, and into the unawareness of what lies beyond the first page, within the book, the contingency of experience contained within the book that constitutes its 'blind field'; accidents of birth, accidents of nature, accidents of death, accidental happenings, coincidences, random occurrences. The attention to detail required by the experience of reading is embodied in the expectation engendered, in this opening poem, by the written book's ability to sensitise the reader to certain kinds of accidental or contingent experience, whether natural ('wild / storms of atoms raging') or meteorological ('a freak wind') or human ('a child / killed in a car'), but always, in this short poem, experiences of violence. The opening poem initiates furthermore a sequence of colours ('The sky is a thick slab of premature dark') and sounds ('And noises start: a scratch, a whoosh, a bark') that establish sensory perception as the ground of the material experience of reading – not merely sight but also feeling and sound combine in a synaesthetic experience inculcated by the power of words to re-present the world.

Blind Field, then, begins in a world of seemingly accidental disorder and violence, both man-made and natural. 'An Accident' sketches out the collection's themes and moods, describing the reader's actions in entering the 'blind field', the space within the volume: 'You turn the page'. But reading has also to relate to the

writing, to the *punctum* of each poem and each verbally represent-
ed image. The 'visible integument of air' of 'An Accident' materi-
alises the intangible as a visible and material skin or husk, just as
the 'you' becomes the (physical) contents of the room, a subjectiv-
ity swelling into the spaces that contain it, collapsing the distinc-
tions between self and externality (later, the Doctor "becomes" the
contents of his room in the third poem in the collection, 'A
Doctor's Room'). The room becomes a 'stage' on which the reader
is placed as object of the book's gaze: 'I watch you sitting down as
on a stage', and momentarily the poles are reversed as book watches,
or reads, reader, positioning the reader's self as a performance, sit-
uating the reader as performer. The act of reading, the poem sug-
gests, is acted out on the stage of the reader's subjectivity, and act
collides with accident, suggesting the deeper philosophical impli-
cation that subjectivity itself might be an accidental effect, a prod-
uct of contingent events. This possibility is present throughout
Blind Field and becomes an overt concern in the book's concluding
section.

If subjectivity can be understood, in 'An Accident', as a kind of
performance, it is one that is watched. The self is a spectacle seen
by others, and, in this sense, might not be dissimilar to the other
images that preoccupy the poems in *Blind Field*, many of which (like
Diane Arbus' photographs) are concerned with different kinds of
self and different experiences of selfhood. The Greek word *ekphrasis*,
meaning (in James Heffernan's phrase) 'the verbal representation
of graphic representation', has already been used in Chapter 2 to
describe Szirtes' exploration of word–image relations.[150] In *Blind
Field*, ekphrastic poetry emerges as a dominant mode of poetic
expression and a central concern. Nevertheless, for all its imagistic
qualities, Szirtes' 'blind field' is, like his earlier poetry, profoundly
literary, informed at key moments by the phraseology and the for-
mal dynamics of poetic modernism. In 'The Baths on Monroe
Street' (a sequel to 'The Lukács Baths' in *Metro*) 'The walls are
patched and blistered like Eliot's Jew'; in another echo of Eliot,
the people in the image are 'anaesthetised and fastened down, like
butterflies' (echoing Prufrock's 'When I am formulated, and fixed
upon a pin'). 'Passenger', an extension and reworking of Edward
Thomas' 'Adlestrop' and of the 'Trains' sequence in *The Photo-
grapher in Winter*, concludes with an allusion to Miroslav Holub's
poem 'Wings', adapting Holub's image into a metaphor for the
transport offered by reading. Three 'Chandleresques' are titled
after Raymond Chandler's novels; there are three further poems
offering 'Variations on Angela Carter'.

Blind Field contributes further to the theorisation of word and image through Szirtes' characteristic device of counterpoint. He effects, in this collection, a poetry that deliberately operates in the interstices between those clearly defined contrapuntal positions – Hungarian and English languages, Hungary and England as geographical and historical spaces, the past and the present, the poetic image and the photographic image, formal dexterity and precision and calculated vaguenesses of content – that have organised his earlier work. Counterpoint allows a comprehension of oppositions working in tandem across the text, generating meanings out of tensions between them. Counterpointing sentence and stanza structure, Szirtes effects a poetry in which rhythm and line work to produce syntactic and thematic continuities and fractures; form and grammar relate, through counterpoint, in ways that generate further consistencies and inconsistencies of meaning.

But Szirtes develops counterpoint to go much further than this. It organises the themes and ideological frames in *Blind Field*, providing a metaphor for the ways in which form and content relate to each other. This is clear in the formal choice of *terza rima* settled on for the central poem of the collection, 'Transylvana'. The Dantesque connotations of terza rima are wholly appropriate for the theme and mood of the poem; where Szirtes has effected similar themes and moods (in the preceding instalments of the trilogy about his mother) different formal choices have been experimented with. The interlocking, contrapuntal structure of *terza rima* affords precisely the formal progression, hesitation and gradual development required in a poem returning carefully to a fractured, irredeemable past and juxtaposing that past with an equally damaged present. The form's canonical pedigree affords the infernal connotations appropriate to its symbolic content; and its emphasis on rhyme as a structuring pattern, posted against the line and the stanza as formal constraints regulating sentences, affords the right productive tension between different levels of form.

'Transylvana', described by its author as 'in many respects a highly photo-journalistic poem', relies on formal and thematic counterpoint to establish and develop its internal logic.[151] It can even be counterpointed with a different version of the same poem published in *The Budapest File*, in which the first italicised paragraph (the eighth paragraph of the poem in *Blind Field*) is moved to the beginning of the poem to act as an introductory sequence, and the poem's second section, 'Virgil's Georgics', is reprinted as a separate (but succeeding) poem. These variations give some insight into Szirtes' difficult relationship to this poem, which he describes as 'the record of a visit to Romania, to see my mother's birthplace and her one surviving relative (called Virgil in the poem), [and] the registering of a cultural shock at what I saw there'.[152] The 'cultural shock' of returning to Romania is registered in the poem's fractured images and in its own adaptable form. The poem is preceded by an epigraph comprising the opening words of Auden's Bucolics poem 'Woods' (1952): 'Sylvan meant savage'. Auden's poem continues, '[...] in those primal woods / Piero di Cosimo so loved to draw';[153] the bucolic fantasy in Auden's poems is always domesticated and circumscribed, in this case by the rendering of the 'savage' woods in the conventional codes of Renaissance art, the poetic image becoming a painted one. In Szirtes' poem Transylvania's mythic and gothic primitivism takes on a contemporary hue, tainted by intervening decades of communist and fascist rule. The poem seeks a moral register appropriate for a verbal representation of its shattered 'world-of-what-remains', repeating in this phrase the question central to another poem, 'On a Young Lady's Photograph Album'.

As in 'Metro' and 'The Photographer in Winter', the mythic narrative underpinning 'Transylvana' is the descent into Hell, this time signalled by the poem's form and by the naming of the author's Romanian relative as Virgil, the guide to Szirtes' Dante. Its form enacts the movement that the poem quickly establishes – the movement of the eye across the view, of the tourist through the town – in counterpoint with the (political, historical, cultural) stasis met in Romania. People seek what the poem calls 'an honest apposition' in negotiating their lives against the balance of political power, which rests between 'old' and 'new dispensations'. Personal experience is counterpointed with the public performance of the 'leader', and different temporal orders counterpoint each other; the journey along Romanian roads where 'only patience is its own reward' is balanced by the 'barely noticeable' moment (a tiny *punctum*) in which 'the leader...smiles'. Temporality is confused in the opening sections, time stretched and compressed according to activity and perception. The 'moment' contains within it the potential to be recalled 'twenty years later'; the 'instant' leads to 'thirty years of trouble'.

Memories and the process of memorialisation, within this distorted temporal framework, become problematic; Virgil's memorialisation of his wife, 'not long dead', involves a domestic ritualisation with sinister, historical overtones: 'suitcases of old shoes, dead soles, / dead arches, metaphors of emptiness'. The poem's symbolic territory is now very similar to that of 'Metro'. These remainders seem to 'accuse' the world of 'innocence, / complicity, not knowing' – an accusation that hovers between the veritable and the unacceptable. The 'intense thickening' of the 'denser universe' stored in Virgil's wardrobe reintroduces the motif of 'thingness', the presence of 'the world-of-what-remains'. These traces parallel the domestic details of Virgil's life, which, in turn, counterpoint the public spectacle of the leader's life (and his death: 'The leader is dead?', we're later asked; 'The ways remain'); both are fleshed out by curt, abbreviated sentences describing in metonymic detail the moral order of a country reduced to 'rubble' that, like the traces of the past and of the dead, also 'remains', a climate of 'defiance first, then sloth'. The world of 'Transylvana' is recorded in fragmented detail, a further refinement of the poetic style Szirtes has developed in order to detail reality while suppressing overt or simple emotion and empathy.

In switching as the poem does from roman to italics in order to record motive and discovery (italics were also used to represent the mother's voice in 'Metro') the poem typographically marks its underlying contrapuntal structure, between experienced and imagined scenarios. Whereas in the world experienced by the narrator 'It's spring', the imagined world of the past is trapped in a winter where 'Snow falls on the branches' and 'a mob of skaters wheel and weave'. Suddenly, in this frozen past, the season changes to 'Summer' and 'The trees are thick with green'. This confusion of seasons (referring forward, perhaps, to the second section of 'Transylvana') represents the mother's desire as she watches her brother skating; it encapsulates Szirtes' connection of seasonal moods with emotions, metaphorising the 'in-between' conditions surveyed by his poetry: the climate and landscape figure internal conditions in such similes as 'vague herds / of clouds meander like soldiers on patrol / at a border station between two absurd countries'. The 'two absurd countries', the present and the past, are the territories of desire in Blind Field. In the overwhelmingly specular world of the poem (in the present, 'light is stored patiently under the eyelids'; in the past, 'The city is full of...quick, evasive eyes'; Virgil 'smiles / with sad, sharp eyes') desire resides in images and imagination; it is a luxury repressed by a grim experience of reality.

The reality of Romania stretches even the versatility of terza rima, as the poem, seeking further details and connections, finds the form collapsing underneath it; stanzas peter out incomplete, sections diminish dramatically in size, and the two worlds draw closer to each other as the poem progresses through 'murky waters everywhere', a world of 'ghosts' that 'stand in queues / at holes' where people 'survive / as long as possible', towards the only conclusion that awaits it, that of death, the ending of 'pain' that 'remains / to be tidied up' in 'the final indispensable dignity'. 'Transylvana' reveals itself in these final lines as a compressed elegy for a country as well as for an individual; it laments the decline of dignity that allows an entire nation to live fixed, for reasons of political and economic expediency, in a present where people 'remember everything' and, in actively so doing, are forced to 'make their peace / with consciences, authorities'.

The second section of 'Transylvana, 'Virgil's Georgics', combines the allusion to Latin pastoral with further ekphrastic description. It consists of twelve quatrains '*After the illustrated calendar of Béla Gy. Szabó*', a year's worth of poems (reminiscent in language and style of Ted Hughes) that combine detailed, syntactically curt description with moments of memory ('On my first day at school my mother cried'), images of nature with images of death, and hark back in style and function to some aspects of Szirtes' poetry of the 1970s as well as to the sequence of short lyrics translated from Ágnes Nemes Nagy that concluded *Bridge Passages*. These are threatening, dark poems of transition, expressive of anger and frustration, part fairy-tale and part gothic horror ('A frosty creature, half bat, half bear, / clings to a tree'). The world of this sequence, like that of 'Transylvana' as a whole, is, the poem concludes, one of violence and disorder in which, in 'December', 'All things [are] given over to destruction.' The poem ends with a bizarre juxtaposition, 'A Gun. A Joke' – the destructive thing is, finally, balanced by the creative imagination, or at least by a linguistic coping mechanism.

'Thingness', the materiality of the world, is implicitly connected throughout *Blind Field* to mortality, to the 'thinglike' residue of the body that 'remains' (a word recurrently used in 'Transylvana') after death. In a further acknowledgement of the influence of Barthes' *Camera Lucida*, Szirtes frequently connects the photograph with death, allowing another level of the analysis of the kinds of fixing and stasis involved in photographic and poetic images. In 'Elegy for a Blind Woman', which alludes to Paul Strand's photograph *Blind Woman* taken in New York in 1917, the physical domestic world of 'high pink walls and recessed panels' (reminiscent of the world of 'The Courtyards') embodies the visible world's embarrassment at the old woman's blindness, mocked by her being surrounded by images: 'Her mother's eyes / stared piteously down at all she could not see'. The colours and imagery of light and darkness that saturate the poem – pink, dark, sun, yellow, darkness, clear, greyness, 'grey / Turned to black or whatever colour she

called it', red, lilac, sepia, 'the green park' – map out a visual field
of experience which the poem uses to contrast the blind woman's
experience with that of the (seeing) reader (and all these colours
are, ironically, only symbolically connoted by words in the poem).

The woman's blindness, characteristically, seems a consequence
of a combination of social exclusion and emotional coldness: 'her
pebble glasses / misted at weddings, froze in brutal February ice, /
and there never were children'; it becomes, like the cold in Orwell's
Nineteen Eighty-Four (already alluded to in *The Photographer in
Winter*), allegorical for the national condition, a symbol of the
country's decay into 'uniform dereliction'. The poem, structured
by a delicate system of half-rhymes, eye-rhymes and slant-rhymes,
seeks out in a clatter of onomatopoeic words and synaesthetic meta-
phors of hearing and touch ('her stethoscope fingers', the 'pittering
feet and small beaks' and 'tangible faces' of children) a language of
feminine tact and tactility – 'the tapping about in the kitchen' – in
which to represent the external reality of the woman's blindness.
Poetry's rendering of the visible is stretched to an accommodation
of the lexicon of the invisible, 'unobserved', 'all she could not see',
'unseeable', which constitutes reality as 'a hostile crowd / of animate
objects'.

The image here is of an experience of the world deprived of
images. Enjambment and syntactic flow ensure that the 'blind field'
excavated in this poem is the field of the domestic, expanding fluidly
into that of biographical experience. Its contrapuntal relation to
history ('the ancien régime') is almost incidental in the poem's
internalisation of experience, its refraction of the woman's biography
into a series of memories 'visible in her head'. Narrative becomes
images, a sequence leading to a conclusion: the poem, after all, is
an elegy, lamenting a death, and invisibility and blindness are
explicitly connected to the condition of death. If the blind woman
may be read as another version of the elderly sybils who populated
'The Lukács Baths', her prophetic powers are turned inwards; it
is, instead, the reader's task to divine meanings from the world she
inhabits and is unable to see. Writing, this poem asserts, enables
the 'seeing' of the unseen, in the sense that the poetic image encap-
sulates in verbal forms the physical responses to an unseen event.

In 'Inuit' the *punctum* is provided by the dead baby's eyes. Their
'pricking' of the narrator enables the poem's imagining of the child
as symbol, 'essence of baby' and 'a perfect pathos'. The image
leads the poem introspectively towards itself as simile – 'still as a
photograph / of stillness, without potential energy'. The poem,
approaching tautology in its circling around the 'blind field' opened

up by the photograph, then shifts to anecdote as a different form of accounting. Death, here counterpointing babyhood, is immobility (with the added implication of the familiar 'frozen' present through the associations of Arctic coldness accruing to 'Inuit'). The child's gaze disconcerts in its failure to reassure the viewing narrator of his presence – instead he observes 'how he looks and does not look at me'. The dead baby's symbolic living-on in the image is firstly mythologised: 'Could he be the Christchild under an Eskimo moon...?' before returning mortality to the material – he becomes 'a comforting thing' 'registering surprise / at the thingness of anything and everything'. The poem shifts intellectual register from myth to philosophy, where 'The thingness of anything and everything' registers the shocking material reality of this image of death.

The poet's disconcertedness is the overwhelming sense conveyed by the poem: he is, in this 'accidental' world, 'unable / to adjust to his appearance'. The 'empty eyes' of the baby are linked, by the associative play between Eskimo and north, with the 'startled eyes' of the deer hit by the poet's car (another accident, a further momentary 'pricking' of the *punctum*); the poem compares a perception of death in representation, and the accident (an experience) which causes the deer's death. In both cases, death happens to the paradigmatically innocent; it is explicitly connected to the icy north. Things in the material sense intrude upon any complacent attempt to intuit ('Inuit'?) their meaning; instead the poem offers half-explained, half-true happenstances and seeks parallels or connections or associative links through which some sense or coherence may be found. The poem ends with an appeal, almost a prayer for the dead child (like 'Elegy for a Blind Woman', it laments death), counterpointed now with the wish for the child to experience not reality, but the 'live deer crashing out of sight'. Concluding with the word 'sight', the poem, in its desire to 'speak light / for the baby', places the visual sense 'out of' reach, in end-focus, in contrast to the 'thingness' or tangibility associated with the baby, 'more touching than any live baby'.

The experience in the third paragraph of 'Inuit', in which the narrator recalls driving into a deer, is recalled, revisioned, by the poet as something unseen: 'I didn't see him fall / But felt his dark soft leg'. In an analogous way the X-ray machine (a kind of camera) in the following poem, 'A Doctor's Room', 'could pinpoint organs, bones and heart / With light as hard as a jewel'. The description of the doctor's room metonymically slides into a description of the doctor himself, his life, domestic spaces and desires, his body damaged by 'that hard, invisible light' which illuminates the 'blind

field' of the poem, the space into which invisible light is poured
in order to reveal the concealed, the 'beyond' of the visible world,
the (physical and psychological) inside of the human body itself.
The X-ray machine links together communication and death, being
'part coffin, part phonebooth', so that its 'light as hard as a jewel'
(like the 'hard / and joyful' light of 'Bichonnade') develops the
poet's desire in 'Inuit' 'to speak light / for the baby', just as the
machine penetrates with light the body of the patient, 'protected,
naked, still decent' as a baby (the doctor, 'growing old', regresses
into an infantile dotage: 'His servant brought his boots in. Who
was she?').

Seeing and illumination are explicitly connected in these poems.
Sight leads conventionally to insight, blindness to different kinds
of insights, and technologies (the X-ray machine and the camera)
provide new kinds of sights and insights. 'Window' develops these
themes by exploring the latent metaphorical meanings of its title,
being a 'window of opportunity' as well as a 'window into the
soul', the letting in of light and the letting out of air, the window
shutters suggesting that of the camera eye. The poem's 'single
moment', unspecified but elaborated, unlocated except in the gen-
eral sense of 'the city', seems to be a moment of violence, media-
fixed by the camera as by the *punctum* of the gun, a moment in
the Hungarian revolution of '56 perhaps, captured in memory as
in photographs. The 'spent cases' immediately connote cartridge
cases but could also be film cases, while the 'others' who 'are still
fighting' do so in the present memory of the poem's narrating con-
sciousness.

From the link between guns and cameras the poem forges a
conclusion that links cameras and writing, both being recordings
of events ('a shutter keeps opening and closing / to trap them in
mere words'), but the ending note of despair hints at the inade-
quacy of such recordings in the face of the reality of lived and
remembered experience. A photographic metaphor ('our lips blur')
overrides the exhausted drive to narrative ('and there is nothing
left to tell'), leaving nothing of history but poetic and photographic
images, disconnected except by the poem's formal insistence on
their rhymed interconnectedness. In an echo of 'The Swimmers',
'The dead swim through their pictures' (rather than in the frozen
floors of the church). The poem both desires and laments its com-
pulsion to 'Trap them in mere words', gesturing again towards the
futility of trying to write the immensity of the historical moment.
It also prepares the ground for later poems in *Blind Field* and their
preoccupation with images of verbal entrapment: 'I write to hold

you there in the subtle / nets that words can weave' ('The Word House'), 'a box of caught / echoes or photographs of names that ring bells' ('The Japanese Hive').

The short sequence of four poems dedicated 'For André Kertész' makes deeply problematic the relations between words and images. Like Szirtes, Kertész was a Hungarian operating in displaced circumstances; born in 1894 in Budapest, he worked in Paris in the 1920s, and emigrated to the USA in 1936. His photographs offer a remarkable chronicle of the twentieth century, insisting on realistic depiction of often bizarre or unreal moments. A major Hungarian photographer in a long tradition of major figures, Kertész's earliest work, alluded to in these poems, offers a documentary record of Hungarian life before and during the First World War. Implicit within Szirtes' attention to them is the recognition that these images provide contexts for a further consideration of memory; family memories and memories of nation are being explored here, as well as relations between written and pictorial images. Szirtes' poems allude to four well-known photographs in order to elaborate their 'blind fields'; if, for Barthes, the *punctum* is the 'thinking eye' at work in the image, Paul Dermée has described Kertész in similar terms: 'In our home for the blind, Kertész is a Brother Seeing-Eye'.[154]

Szirtes writes four thematically, structurally and linguistically linked short poems, each elaborating a 'reading' of a particular photograph, not necessarily indicated by the poem's title. The photograph presents itself within the poem as a springboard for the poem's meditation, which in turn is initiated or inspired by the image. The poems contain images which correspond to or describe the photo's image, but these images are often associative in their connections with the photograph. In 'Two Aunts Appearing' Szirtes offers description that modulates into the surreal imagery of a Dalí painting: 'their legs are thin glass monuments that sway / with the gentle nudging of the wind'. Based on Kertész's *Iskola Tér, February 19th, 1920, Budapest* ('Iskola Tér' means 'School Place'), the poem effectively narrates the photograph, in which a woman sits on a bench in the square, surrounded by trees, wearing a headscarf so that her face cannot be seen. In the top corner of the image a suited man is about to walk towards her across the square. Two other figures are just visible in the distance. Kertész's image is redolent of stasis, of waiting, of time elapsing in quietness and inactivity; the woman's clothes imply mourning, but signify to a twenty-first century viewer the symbolic rendering of the female refugee, the image so familiar from news footage of Bosnia, Kosovo,

Afghanistan. The *punctum* is the presence of the two figures in the distance, who might have wandered out of a painting by de Chirico or Magritte, and lend the photograph the faintly surrealist air to which Szirtes' poem responds. Above all it is an image of stillness despite the evident motion of the suited man. A meeting is implicit, but the photograph also implies that this is a passing.

The poem opens with description that modulates into historically specific association: 'It is the winter of the year after the commune' (the 1919 Commune, Hungary's first experience of communism, which Kertész photographed after serving as a War photographer and which collapsed on August 2nd, leading to the 'White Terror' Szirtes mentions in 'The Swimmers'). The woman becomes the poem's imaginative focus, as the 'emptiness' of the square inscribes itself onto and into her body, 'skin-scaffoldings' echoing 'the visible integument of skin' in 'An Accident'. The Aunts of the poem's title are imagined as figures descending from this woman, presumably aunts of the narrating voice, so his family history merges with that of Hungarian history (the Commune) and of the history implicit in the photograph – the histories of its subjects, the narratives implicit within the image and evoked by it. The poem translates the photograph to fit its themes – the woman's scarf is white, not 'black' (in 'Translating Zsuzsa Rakovszky', Szirtes notes that he translated Rakovszky's use of 'fehér', the Hungarian word for 'White', as 'Black'). Iskola Tér is transformed by the poem's imaginative force into an embodiment of 'the squares and streets of the mind', the imagined spaces of memory and experience.

The poem's surrealistic conclusion sustains multiple ambiguities, destabilising the apparent authority of the photographic image and inserting instead the uncertainties of linguistic reference: does 'they' refer to 'two heavy black aunts', or to 'a generation', or to 'the squares and streets'? The 'thin glass monuments' offer contradictory images of solidity and fragility (compounded by 'brittle bones' as signifiers of age, poverty and malnourishment). The photograph, the poem suggests, relies for its meanings upon words which rely, in turn, on ambiguity and uncertainty of reference for their meanings. Photographic image and verbal poem are radically incommensurate even as each draws upon the metaphorical potential evident in the other to legitimate its own claims to referential authority.

This is further developed in the next poem, 'Accordionist', which is based on Kertész's photo of an accordionist (wearing glasses, so probably not 'blind', despite the poem's description of him as a 'blind intellectual') taken at Esztergom on 21 October 1916. The accordion provides the vehicle of the poem's metaphor, as an image which mutates from 'typewriter' to 'hat'; the image of the accordion as hat develops from the headscarf of the preceding poem. The musician as 'blind intellectual' suggests the ethical and moral functions of art; the accordion as 'typewriter' connects musician and poet as creative figures confronting the destructive forces of history. The poem's conceit is to read the photograph against the history that surrounds it, resituating the image in relation to an embedded discourse, that of poetry of the First World War: 'We are the poppies sprinkled along the field. / We are simple crosses dotted with blood.' In switching to a secondhand rhetoric derived from the War poets (and specifically John McCrae's 'In Flanders Fields', its line 'We are the dead' repeated in Orwell's *Nineteen Eighty-Four*), Szirtes establishes conventional imagery as untrustworthy, its conventionality a source of suspicious 'sentiments'.

The poem provides the allegorical framework for a broad historical judgement summarising the violence and destruction of the 20th century (and specifically of the First World War, the immediate historical background of Kertész's photograph) as 'one of collapses', momentous historical tragedies inscribed onto the bodies of the dead. 'The concertina of the chest' aestheticises the human body through association with the accordion, an image which combines echoes of War poetry with further implications of poverty and malnourishment. 'The flattened ellipses / of our skulls' evokes the distorted skull – a painterly special effect that provides the painting's *punctum* – that functions as a dramatic *memento mori* in Hans Holbein's *The Ambassadors* (1533). As the 'century' is 'one of collapses', so 'Tubercular' collapses into 'tubular' as the poem deflates from associative tour-de-force into generalised historical condemnation, into the bathos of self-repudiation expressed in warnings about poetry rather than history: 'Beware the sentiments concealed / in this short rhyme', and then into the simple admonitions 'Be wise. Be good'. The 'blind' accordionist (repeating the motif of 'Elegy for a Blind Woman') reminds us of the paradoxical invisible presence of the 'blind field' of the poem, and implies that the *punctum* of the photograph (as in 'Inuit') is the accordionist's eyes, which can't be seen behind his spectacles. The poem implies that music is a kind of 'blind' writing; the 'keys / grow wings' just as the aunts 'flap free' in the preceding poem (and just as the reading girl in the later 'Passenger' is given 'Wings', Holub-like, by the open halves of her book).

'Hortus Conclusus', meaning a concealed garden, is based on Kertész's *Tisza-Szalka, July 6th 1920, Hungary*. Again the poem opens with description, which matches the photograph, but then shifts focus into the realm of Christian mythology, suggesting that this is an Edenic garden, a contained space of innocence. This reading is to an extent sustained by the innocence of the image, of another headscarved woman feeding geese while sat on a step before an indeterminate building, again with a tree whose shadows dapple the wall and ground behind her. Another blurred, indeterminate figure (the *punctum*) seems to lurk half way round the corner of the house. Kertész's photograph symbolises 'peasant culture', depicting a rural idyll marked by the signifiers of poverty, and perhaps establishes the disjunction he maps in these early images, which consists in the implicit contrast between the (ancient) world represented and the (modern) technologies of representation. 'Geese …rabbits and birds' contrast with the supernatural Christian myth summarised in the 'angel' and the 'child' 'born, out of air'. The poem addresses the advent of writing as record and proclamation of the event: 'a scroll flew like a pennant'. The dissolution evident in 'Now languages dissolve' implies both modernity as personally experienced by the poet, the shift from Hungarian to English, and the power of words to dissolve things, necessitating the 'start again' (in words) but also in photographs ('shadows'), and the two sensual modes of the collection, 'touch and sight'. The final declaration: 'I'll reinvent a world of geese whose reign / will seek new synonyms for white', implies the role of the poet in relation to language and its potential urge towards representational purity, words as *tabulae rasae*, erased of their associations of meaning. 'Hortus Conclusus' raises questions about the association of words and things and meanings. Its promise to 'reinvent' implies a loss, a historical need to rediscover innocence / purity, but also implicitly concedes the false-ness of these values as things already 'invented' in the first place.

The final poem for Kertész, 'The Voyeurs', is the one most explicitly connected to its referent photograph, *Circus, May 19th 1920, Budapest*. The voyeurs, 'in transit', as the poem puts it, are looking through cracks in a fence, presumably at the circus; the poem imagines what they see as 'something perfectly new / and terrifying that light will not let through'. The man wears a worker's boots, a jacket and a slightly incongruous straw boater; the woman, a black dress and a silken headscarf with a black stripe (the head-scarf links this to two of the other images alluded to). The pic-ture's meaning lies in their activity of watching, leading to the recognition that, as they peer through the hole in the fence, so the photographer peers at them through his viewfinder, and we peer at them peering; everyone involved in the presentation, produc-tion and consumption of the image is included in the reference of the title – as in the world of Diane Arbus, we are all voyeurs. The poem asks a question (answered by Kertész's title), but then asks the question of the voyeurs, extrapolating from the image to an implied disgust with voyeurism. The associative image of the 'lighted window' (connecting this poem to 'Window') in which the 'wealth of alien stuff', the detail and detritus making up the world of private domestic lives, is displayed for visual consumption. 'Lustful, lost and afraid' summarises the condition of the voyeur. The figures in the image correspond to the imputed movement of the viewer, allegorically the movement through life: 'They too are in transit'. Again movement is written into a static image – the poem uses its own form and language to counter the tendency of every photograph to become 'a photograph of stillness'.

In each of the four Kertész poems, a photograph enables a philo-sophical contemplation of the nature of looking, and of the symbolic structures (history, memory, myth) which become attached to looking as a voyeuristic but necessarily interpretive process. The poems run in counterpoint to the images, invoking movement where there is stasis, colour in place of contrast, transience in place of permanence, verbal imagery in place of photographic real-ism, and associatively constructed narratives comprised of verbally formed images in place of framed visual representation. The poems meditate upon the relationships between image, word, reader and viewer, and less explicitly on the differences and similarities between poet and photographer, poem and photograph.

The poems seek to account for the world of Kertész's images, or rather for the disappearance of this world into the images. Szirtes offers poetry as a formal language which allows the reconstitution of a different version of the worlds in the photographic images ('I'll reinvent a world'), but a version which remains potential, momentarily fixed at the level of possibility and speculation. We return in each of these poems to the blind field, the *punctum* indi-cating something beyond the image in spatial and metaphysical terms; the 'something perfectly new / and terrifying' is perhaps the moment of sublime apprehension towards which each poem gestures, which each poem seeks in its photographic equivalent, but which also lies beyond language itself. The blindness here is the occlusion of vision by light (a consequence of the world 'that light will not let through'), the recognition that enlightenment interrupts vision as much as it allows it. Description modulates into meditative association, disconcerting any simple correlation between poem and photograph but inviting instead an associative counterpoint between the respective formal purities of the image and of poetry and their relations to content. Association in turn invests the figures in the photographs with histories and memories which may or may not belong to them but which certainly belong to the poems themselves. The poems construct, in words and sequences of poetic images and devices, a series of posthumous lives for the photographs, a series of metaphysical extensions of frames into the bounded forms of poetic framing.

Two poems separate the Kertész sequence from its companion, 'For Diane Arbus'. 'Voluptuousness' returns to images already familiar in *Blind Field* and in earlier collections; a 'child dancing', a 'sister' described as an 'enclosed garden', a 'dancing underground' with 'bones unsettling swathes of thought', and the poet's children, their 'eyes illegible, a foreign writing'. 'Voluptuousness' is close, physical, tangible, the remembered presence of the mother-photographer 'behind the lens, her face hidden, rich in voluptuousness'; in its opening assertion – 'I think of a child dancing' – the poem imagines the intimacy of photography as itself a form of imagining, a method of rendering in images the material bases of remembered experience.

As noted above, 'Passenger' rewrites Edward Thomas' 'Adlestrop', transforming its quatrains into *terza rima* and reworking the older poem into a post-industrial pastoral, offering a moment of sublime transcendence firmly located in the perception of the act of reading. The poem opens with an extended *punctum*, 'A long stop at a hot provincial station', giving the narrator pause for thick description of the surrounding wasteland. Images of the decaying external world inscribe themselves onto the body of the perceiving consciousness as pains and irritants, physical manifestations of discomfort and disease: 'rivulets of perspiration...pustules...their heads ache'; in this last image the external world is finally anthropomorphised into an internal image. The poem expresses restraint to the extent of physical discomfort, both the discomfort of the journey (alleviated by the identification, in the second section, with 'The girl', and, through her, the Czech poet Miroslav Holub). The narrator becomes a watcher (another 'voyeur') balancing, through acts of constructive imagination and poetic insight, the ominous decay of the landscape, its dereliction and disuse. 'The girl', by contrast with this world, 'is far too smart' in appearance and, perhaps, intellect – the poem insists on the disjunction between landscape and the feminine in an almost over-conscious evasion of the stock cliché, and offers instead an image of the girl as fastidiously over-ornamented, counterpointed by her book, 'the History of France', which offers a mirror for the external dereliction, being 'an ancient faded copy'. The decayed industrial empire of the opening section is thus mirrored by the book's decay, and by implication the decay of the grandeur of the book's subject-matter. It is poetry itself that allows a transcendent quality to this set of mirrorings and disjunctions: Miroslav Holub's description of the reading girl as a winged angel, the open halves of the book as her wings, allows the poem momentarily to draw a conclusion which pushes beyond its frames of reference, enabling the reading girl to become the poem's new *punctum*, and her reading itself the blind field, of the poem.

'Blindfold' constitutes the third section of *Blind Field*. Its title implies enforced blindness, the inability or refusal to see rather than the symbolic and real sights and insights of the rest of the volume. It continues the collection's concern with representation and the solidity of the real, and focuses on the traces left by those who have died. 'Blind Fold' thus engages with a world that is tangible and perceptible to senses other than sight – like the smell of the gas that has 'eaten' the grandfather in the extended sonnet 'Grandfather's Dog': 'Even now as I walk through the town it is there, sharp / and pervasive' (the adjective 'sharp' reminding us of Virgil's 'sad, sharp eyes' in 'Transylvana'). The section opens with an elegy for Ágnes Nemes Nagy, described here as the 'monumental' Hungarian poet of the materiality of history, whose 'images were engraved / or scratched (more physical than this) into the ice'. The physical exertion of writing, and its persistence as trace of the effort of its author to create and represent, concerns these poems; in 'The Japanese Hive', the 'crowds' 'leave traces / then they disappear'; 'Threnody', dedicated to poet Matt Simpson, details traces of natural mortality in 'shells of dead insects, / heaps of moth-wings, beetle shards, disinfected, no thought of flight now or crawling, they lurk / in the annals, sad husks…'. The circular construction of *Blind Field* returns us, in this final section, to the opening poem of the collection: the 'visible integument of air' of 'An Accident' becomes, in these closing poems, a 'sad husk', a remainder of a life completed. The 'Blind Fold' is also a 'folding', a conclusion, which leaves traces recorded in these closing poems. In the concluding memorial poem, 'István Vas', Szirtes offers the clearest statement yet of his poetic credo: 'it's only the wind that blows / between words not through them / that constitutes poetry'. The in-between-ness of Szirtes' cultural position emerges here as defining of poetry itself – the 'freak wind raising hell' of 'An Accident' takes on a new meaning as a version of what Szirtes will later call (in *Reel*'s 'Shoulder') 'the space of the word'.

In 'Variations on Angela Carter' and 'Soil' this credo, applied to the experience of self, opens spaces that will be explored in Szirtes' subsequent collections. The poems sketch out a new series of movements, symbols and tropes that allow selfhood to be perceived contrapuntally, as a product both of language and of history and geography. The second poem of 'Variations' eulogises the word made flesh in the child's experience of the mother's body: 'It is not so much in the saying / as in what the word does', the poem asserts – the effect of language, its tangible force in the world, is Szirtes' concern here, 'which you feel', 'which is yours'. In this effect resides the possibility of selfhood, with all the narratives, images, memories and histories upon which the very concept of selfhood relies: the poem (in a Whitmanesque turn that Szirtes will develop over subsequent collections) becomes a celebration of the self within the word, 'singing of the entire self that is, / with its history, tenderness, / self's infinite capacity.'

If the word allows this sublime conception of the self liberated by language, 'Soil' repositions the self as an unstable product of history and territory, bound ('caught by your heels') to the 'lyrical earth' but also stranded upon the same soil. The poem (discussed in the Introduction) offers a dialogue which asks unanswered questions about perception and classification ('What colour would you call that now?'), which allude to the unknowable-ness of the self's origins. Its main recourse through this Heaneyesque, unfamiliar 'landscape that's a mood / or a thought / in mid-birth' is (in keeping with the rest of the collection) to literary and photographic traditions; the 'dull music' and the 'violin / scraped and scratched' recall Eliot's 'dull tom-tom', 'defunctive music' and 'insistent out of tune / of a violin', and also, perhaps, allude to the violin-player of Kertész's famous 1921 photograph. 'Soil' explores origins as endings (hence its subsequent function as the concluding poem to two of Szirtes' retrospective selections); its 'grudging lyrical earth' is both 'home' and 'nowhere', prefiguring the symbolic 'English landscapes' of Szirtes' later collections.

Blind Field concludes with a consideration of new categories of the 'accident' with which it opened – accidents of birth, of language, of geography and history, which allow meditations on the constitution of subjectivity, and effect a subtle shift of emphasis away from the postmemorial commemoration of Szirtes' mother towards a new focus, the consideration of the effects of history (including the mother's life and its contexts) upon the individual subject. In effect, Szirtes' poetry returns to a sophisticated mode of imagistic autobiography, and focuses on the effects of its familiar concerns upon the possibilities of poetry to afford an enquiry into the construction of identity. *Blind Field* has of course been concerned with establishing the grounds of this enquiry; its contrapuntal structure mimics the dialectic of self and other, the dialogue between subject and object and the oppositions between past and present, Hungary and England and parent and child that will be the focus of Szirtes' next collection, *Portrait of My Father in an English Landscape.*

6

'Ghost in a photograph': *Portrait of My Father in an English Landscape*

My father's past is now arranged into anecdotes –
which is an art of sorts – not raw material at all.
CRAIG RAINE, interviewed by JOHN HAFFENDEN

In the 'Preface' to *The Budapest File* Szirtes comments on his relations to the different histories of his parents: 'The history of my mother took me to Hungary: the history of my father has brought me back.' He acknowledges the centrality of another history, his own, which begins in and returns to Hungary but belongs, problematically, to England – 'I have spent 43 of my 51 years in England,' he points out.[155] This 'taking' of the self away from, and 'bringing' it back to, a world – England – that is both familiar and unfamiliar, the place where one lives but to which one doesn't fully belong, is of course a recurrent concern of Szirtes' poetry, but becomes the central impetus of work published since the mid-1990s. A continuous exploration of the tension between familiarity and unfamiliarity structures the explorations of perception, of surrealist or 'slant' vision and juxtaposition, of condensed imagery and sometimes awkward or difficult poetics and symbolism that we have seen in his poetry. The self's displacement and return from one version of home to another in response to historical events invests these experiences with significances which are deeply political in their implications. Occurring at historical moments distant from each other, the movements between countries of parents and child/ adult poet are contingent in part upon powerful historical forces (revolution, war, genocide and invasion) that transform the world and the subject's experience of it, rendering the familiar unfamiliar in ways characteristic of poetry itself; furthermore they embody the defamiliarised experience of the exile, doubly displaced from his past and present homes, inhabiting the condition Szirtes refers to in interviews as 'in-between-ness'.

In his eighth collection, *Portrait of My Father in an English Landscape*, published by Oxford in 1998, Szirtes explores his condition of 'in-between-ness' as an aesthetic figuring of the hopes and delusions of the difficult experiences of displacement, loss, desire and hope, and pushes poetic form into the foreground as a metaphor for paternal authority, the authority of tradition and of familial inheritance. Szirtes describes this inheritance, in the collection's title poem, as 'the figure I feel I have to build / into and out of language'. This movement 'into and out of language' (like the movement away from and back to experience) can be seen as a recurrent dynamic in his poetry; the obligation it seems to incur in the poet will be examined below. Here it's important to note the self-reflexive compulsion, an expression of obligation in 'feeling' and 'building'. In-between-ness, as an indeterminate location, doesn't offer an escape from this obligation; instead it confirms its demand, because it is a condition linked to the experience of selfhood which develops out of an awareness of one's obligations to different kinds of pasts – 'which', the final poem asserts, 'must be interpreted'. A poem in *Blind Field*, 'Eat Good Bread Dear Father', uses its acronymic title to refer to 'the space between lines / measuring distances'; this space is invoked again in a long poem late in *Portrait of My Father*, 'Travel Book', which narrates an abbreviated history of the movements and displacements suffered by Szirtes and his family, describing them as 'gross events' from which 'the brittle hide'. The hiding place is offered by the 'space between the lines', where the 'lines' are those of the poem and of history, the 'pure narrative lines' that, in the preceding poem 'The Looking-Glass Dictionary', 'run through' the semi-mythical figure of the poet's father. In 'Mouth Music' this 'space' narrows down to that 'between words', suggesting that the unsaid and the unsayable, the gaps and silences in language, as figures of the forgotten or unrecorded events of history, are opened up as objects of scrutiny in this collection. The reader encounters its meanings in these 'spaces between', which become metaphors of the 'in-between-ness' symptomatic of Szirtes' identity.

We've seen throughout this book how Szirtes uses what he calls the 'whispers' and 'ghosts' of form to structure poems that, in turn, explore the 'in-between' and subterranean places and spaces of Budapest – the underground, the courtyards – as well as the symbolic and ideological spaces of the home, the family, the past, memory and history. These different spaces and places contrast repeatedly with the informal or formless realities of histories of displacement and dispossession experienced by Szirtes and by different generations of his family. This in-between location is itself a form of dispossession or of not-belonging, but it also offers a kind of freedom that allows the generation of Szirtes' characteristic fluidity of image and syntax out of the solid architecture of poetic forms, and the lightness of poetry out of the 'gross events' of history. History, Szirtes asserts in an earlier poem, 'The Lukács Baths', is 'a constant shadow' located 'half way between myth and memory', or, in 'Metro', in the 'cool / Shadows of biography'. In these 'shadowy' spaces his poems come into being; they are often haunted, in turn, by the ghosts produced by the 'gross events' with which they deal, the victims and casualties of historical events and forces, that figure themselves in formal traces, elements of a larger, deeper pattern implicit within each poem and stretching across collections. Form, in Szirtes' developing conception of it, is a quality both internal to the poem and imposed upon it; its in-between-ness corresponds at times to the 'inner cartography' by which Szirtes describes his own earlier work, providing a mapping of internal experiences by external poetic structures.[156]

Portrait of My Father in an English Landscape revisits the specific territories on which these spaces 'between myth and memory' are mapped, in order to reconstitute them as terrains and resources for further poetic exploration. The myths and memories of the self and of family, occupying a shadowy border territory between the personal and the historical, constitute large areas of these territories, as do literary and artistic traditions (English and Hungarian, as well as wider European traditions to which the poems sometimes allude), functioning as repositories of linguistic and cultural resources through which memories can be encoded. These territories – 'landscapes', in the rhetoric of this collection – delineate in general terms the central themes of Szirtes' poetry, offering heavily contested and overlapping spaces, described by one reviewer of the collection as 'strikingly un-English'.[157] The in-between space that his poems both construct and inhabit makes possible the enquiries into identity, the status and use-value of forms of historical knowledge, and sometimes the very possibility of knowledge itself, that characterise the poems of *Portrait of My Father*.

Szirtes has noted in autobiographical writings that his father was the only member of the family to speak any English at the time of their enforced migration from Hungary in 1956, first to Austria, then to London. 'His journey,' Szirtes writes of his father, 'like mine, has been through culture and language. Above all his has been through history. That history is part of the English landscape now.'[158] The 'English landscape' is thus a space connected, in Szirtes' poetry to a key paternal attribute, the ability to speak English, and to the family's movement into the histories and geographies that delineate the English landscape and language. The poems in *Portrait of My Father* explore how the experiences of one generation of migrants are both assimilated into and differentiated from the residual, mythical properties of Englishness associated with landscape and language – and how each is altered by the experience of the other. As its title suggests, the collection signals a change of thematic emphasis. The significant theme is still parental in focus; but now, Szirtes' father, and the 'English landscape' that his poetry will associate with him, are concerns refracted through the collection's focus on observing and recording the traces of reality, and pondering their rendering in words.

The surface themes of the collection address Hungarian and English memories and experiences, but the underlying drive, as with previous collections, is towards an extended analysis of the self and its origins in history and in the processes of perception, a self culturally and aesthetically mediated. Painting and film, rather than photography, emerge initially as the dominant visual modes of representation; music provides a further medium extending Szirtes' exploration of poetry's relation to other arts as well as to its own traditions. The 'English Landscape' is, furthermore, almost wholly experienced through the art, film, poetry and dance of non-English traditions that pervade the collection, from 'Directing an Edward Hopper' to 'Three Songs for Ana Maria Pacheco' to 'Four Villonesques on Desire' to 'Busby Berkeley in the Soviet Union'. Implicit in this symbolic displacement is an underlying concern (that emerges more clearly in later collections) with exactly what constitutes 'Englishness'. Different arts interchange in a maelstrom of celebrations of the creative force and its trans-national, rather than national, manifestations. 'England' comes to signify, in this network of interrelations, an 'effect', a space in which artistic freedom is made manifest, and 'Englishness' becomes, in this signification, a hybrid, profoundly European, concept.

The world, in these poems, develops further from its role as object of perception and observation, becoming increasingly complex in its poetic construction; moments of perception, like the 'deep raw umber' 'under the eyes' in 'Romanian Brown', become (in a phrase returning us to Louis MacNeice's 'Snow') 'strange as the world' and ' as disturbing in its brilliant intimacy'. The world is, ultimately, the 'brilliant intimacy' of words, the word made strange as the world by poetry; 'To sit in the dark settees of the eye is to know / the heart as literature,' asserts 'Romanian Brown', linking the mundane domesticity of 'settees' with the bodily truth of art, but reminding us also that the poem is aware that the 'heart', despite its centrality to poetic myths of identity and emotion, is only, here, a 'metaphor', a 'literary / device'.

Portrait of My Father is divided into two sections. The first offers a variety of forms exploring different aspects of artistic and historical themes in order to construct a kind of 'prehistory' or shadow history, situated sometimes in Hungarian as well as English landscapes, a series of observations and parables preparing the ground for the poems of the second section by marking out different art forms, different genres and traditions, and different poetic possibilities. Some of these poems are miniature formal *tours de force*, like the single extended sentences of 'Golden Bream', 'Tinseltown' and 'Daffodils'. Others, like 'Mouth Music', are densely allusive in a manner reminiscent of some of the poems in *Short Wave*. The second section, the last ten poems of the book, comprises two untitled 'sequences' exploring 'the short half-life of sonnets' ('Flesh Pink: The Face in the Coat'). The first sequence uses artists' colours to explore the spaces afforded by the sonnet for observation, analysis, reminiscence and experience; the second comprises three 'Hungarian' sonnet sequences, also known as double coronae or *sonnets redoublé*, remarkably dexterous and intricate sequences of fifteen interlinked sonnets in which the last line of the first sonnet becomes the first line of the next, and so on until the fifteenth, which comprises the concluding lines of the preceding fourteen sonnets. Szirtes varies the form in these poems so that each line is a version, rather than a repetition, of the preceding one; this kind of inter-poem linkage and variation was first explored in *Bridge Passages*, where the final line of 'A Sea Change' – 'The water thunders in the shower' – modulates into the opening line of the next poem, 'In a Strong Light': 'Behind the shower curtain thunder sharpens'.

Portrait of My Father is clearly organised so that it develops towards this closing formal performance, suggesting a new level of confidence in Szirtes. The tone of the collection is assured and measured, a long way from the fractured uncertainties of *Bridge Passages*; his preoccupation with the poetic representation of visual art reaches new levels of complexity; and the range of literary, cultural and historical allusion lends the collection a new kind of cultural authority, mapping experience in different territories and spaces in order to demonstrate both the interconnectedness of different histories and the poet's increasing willingness to focus on his own position in relation to different, competing narratives of origin and destiny.

These narratives, the historical properties of the various familial figures in Szirtes' poetic 'landscape', are the collection's ultimate concern. In constructing its verbal 'portrait', the poetry – confined to the medium of language – necessarily has recourse to narratives as containers of information. Szirtes, in a brief introduction to the title poem, has written that 'Human lives often seem to be composed of more or less colourful anecdotes, which get polished up as they are repeated, becoming entertainments, perhaps even fictions. Slowly their meaning drains away. I think traces of our meanings lurk in the crevices of these entertainments.'[159] The collection is concerned with the transformation of 'life' into 'anecdote', then into 'entertainment' and 'fiction'. In seeking 'traces of meanings' in the landscapes and spaces it explores, and expanding them into a poetic language of memory and analysis, the collection develops into a sustained intellectual enquiry the familiar focus on words and things, the excavations and interrogations of the everyday and the contingent as potential sources of the strange logics of human existence. The 'crevices' within these 'entertainments' are also, of course, the spaces 'between words' in 'Mouth Music', where perceptions reside, 'the senses one hears in the night-time / or smells in the daytime'.

Such moments of perception, residing in-between the solidities of experience and history, are the fundamental province of these poems. In 'Rabbits', the collection's opening poem, the image of rabbits emerging into the fields at dusk, seen from a passing train, provides a vehicle for a consideration of poetry's ability to capture such transient moments of perception and invest them with meaning. The apparently conventional pastoral world constructed here is always already compromised by the presence of the train, indicating that the poem's version of nature is actually denatured, artificially rendered, subjectively reorganised. The poem alludes perhaps to Wallace Stevens' 'A Rabbit as King of the Ghosts', in which the rabbit embodies initially 'The difficulty to think at the end of the day'; many of the poems in *Portrait of My Father* seem indebted to Stevens' poetry and the 'difficulties' it explores. The 'difficulty' of Szirtes' rabbits – a version of the moments of perceptual, verbal or formal 'difficulty' that punctuate his poetry – resides in their being material and real, a 'softening' and a 'thickening' of the world, 'something earth- and dropping-scented'; they embody the natural world 'for which woolly words have to be invented'. Their 'presence' concerns the first stanza, in which nouns construct the pastoral world of an apparently English landscape, a world of 'hedgerows', 'clouds', 'fields', 'sky', 'flowers' and 'wind'; and present-tense verb forms emphasise movement and development ('congregate', 'overtake', 'bolt', 'opens and shuts', 'purpling', 'plumps'), investing that landscape with activity, making it a dynamic, immediately

tangible space and cementing its own presence as an active force
in the poem.

Only in the third and fourth stanzas do deeper significances
emerge, rendering the 'English' landscape rather more problematic;
adjectives shift the poem's tone, as the rabbits 'run off scared' and
the 'train swoops down its sinister track'. 'Swoops' suggests a pre-
datory movement; the 'sky', 'purpling with the scent / of evening'
in the first stanza, is now 'dropping like a blind' as night threatens.
And with night, 'the negative of daylight', comes 'something of
terror'. The train's residual symbolism (reminiscent of the trains
in *Blind Field* and *Metro*, and therefore of the train's function in
the history of the Holocaust) develops in implication as the poem
shifts attention away from the world outside onto that within. The
'old man', the only human presence in the poem (the 'father' of
the collection's title, perhaps?), signifies human frailty, in contrast
with the 'curl of soft metal' of the rabbits and their world. The
'trembling' of the train signifies its impact on the natural world
around it (in 'Romanian Brown' this extends to its effect on people,
as 'the train shakes like a tremor in the breast'). As it flits by during
the train journey the world becomes, like the rabbits, 'soft', 'a fog
of names', 'insignificant'. It loses definition, blurring into 'a stain'.
The final image, shifting from the implicitly narrative form of the
train journey, offers a blurred snapshot of startled nature: 'a bird
or a figure caught in mid flight', an image that prefigures the 'Mad
flight, sane flight' of the seventh sonnet of the title poem, the mig-
ration of the poet's father, a fugitive subjectivity that the poems seek
to capture and portray within a landscape that becomes increasingly
European rather than simply 'English', rendering the discreteness
of national identities and traditions increasingly blurred.

An indication of these new 'European' dimensions sought by
Szirtes is given in the collection's title (and that of its final poem),
which may owe something to a poem entitled 'Contained in the
Order of an English Landscape' by the Polish poet Adam Czern-
iawski, published in the special 1991 'Europe comes to Cheltenham'
issue of *Poetry Review*. In the same edition Szirtes published a
long piece on East European poetry, 'Learning from Brezhnev',
along with translations of poems by Gyözö Ferenc and Zsuzsa
Rakovszky. Czerniawski's poem uses pastoral to meditate upon
history: its 'neatly ordered dreams' are tempered by 'a sharper
measure / of justice' through which the 'Space and time' symbolised
in the English landscape come to signify a 'tribute' to a suffering
that extends beyond the borders of such a world into an expressly
European space and time of violent historical experience, 'to those /
who have not known peace: / bloodily mutilated, crushed / against

walls'.[160] The poem's closing image of 'ashes / silently invad[ing] / herbaceous borders, verandahs and lawns' captures a momentary horror, the insidious permeating of English pastoral tranquillity by the destructive realities of European and other twentieth-century genocides, a historical process foreshadowed most powerfully in the English pastorals of Edward Thomas, and implicit in Szirtes' poems.

Ideas of order (the 'neatly ordered dreams' punningly echoed in the 'borders' of Czerniawski's poem) pervade the formal regularities of *Portrait of My Father in an English Landscape* – indeed a major tension of the collection is that between order and disorder, form and the formless. An early prevailing metaphor is provided by the dance: from the East Coker-like 'concord of dancing' in 'Daffodils' (Wordsworth's daffodils were 'fluttering and dancing in the breeze') to the rain 'starting to dance / on the pavement' in 'Tinseltown', the dance suggests the close and rhythmic allegiance, almost a physical interdependence, between the orders of nature and of the English landscape and the forms of poetry. It also embodies the creative potential of art, suggested by the use of choreographer and director Busby Berkeley in two poems in the collection. Order itself is a recurring motif: Szirtes' versions of Czerniawski's 'neatly ordered dreams' are inflected with Wallace Stevens' meditations on ideas of order, a connection implied in 'The Idea of Order at the Jószef Attila Estate', where 'the architect's fiction of order' suppresses a level of social and political disorder residing beneath the surface of the Communist housing Estate, one of the first built in the Ferencváros district of Budapest in the early 1960s.

Aesthetics conflict with historical and social realities here. The 'Idea of Order', after all, is not 'Order' itself; the 'Arranging, deepening, enchanting night' of Wallace Stevens' 'The Idea of Order at Key West' is an order produced within the space of the song the woman sings and the poem the poet writes, a product of what Stevens calls 'The maker's rage to order words'.[161] The poet, Stevens suggests, is 'Master' of the world within the poem; in the 'glassy lights' that have 'Mastered the night and portioned out the sea' resides the enlightening power of words to create, their power to 'portion out' the implicit chaos ('the sea') of the natural world. The interdependence of the poem and the real world, Stevens' theme, is also a significant concern of Szirtes' collection; 'The Idea of Order at the József Attila Estate' imagines a social world alarmingly structured by the ideologies and rhetoric of Communism, but persisting in a post-Communist age. The poem meditates on the lives of the Estate's inhabitants, which 'fit together as if in a

programme, a drawing / In a department': the bureaucratic vision of
the Estate's 'Order' is this absolute, a vision akin to that of John
Betjeman's Planster.

Within this idea of order lurks death, which, in this ordered
'dream of files and cabinets', 'entails merely a comfortless distanc-
ing'. The poem eschews the 'comfortlessness' of such a 'dream'.
Its closing images of familial and social worlds beyond the Estate
– 'The voices of children scrambling upstairs, / And the distant
suburban railway coming and going' – return us to a different kind
of order that exists not in planning and control but in perception
and the aesthetic registering of reality. The poem hovers, however,
on the brink of social disorder, the entropy and decay implicit in
'rubbish' in the second line and in 'Waste materials' in the final
stanza; its version of 'order' seems to be a barely maintained veneer,
suggesting a world in which 'all has an explanation' but the 'explan-
ation' might not be convincing.

The order imposed upon reality by grammar's ordering of words
concerns 'The First, Second, Third and Fourth Circles'. Suggest-
ing Szirtes' recurrent troping of Budapest as a Dantesque inferno,
the poem offers four single-sentence sections in which the city's
ring roads provide metaphors for its structure, sprawling from the
long, detailed list of the first section, which exploits a long sequence
of co-ordinated and subordinated clauses to symbolise the immense
complexity at the heart of the city, to the concluding image of
alienation in the 'fourth circle', of 'a lost voice' that 'interrogates
itself at the mirror'. As in 'The Idea of Order at the József Attila
Estate' (and in an echo of 'Wild Garden'), the 'suburban' world lies
outside metropolitan concerns, in 'the distant industrial suburbs'
and beyond, in 'an uncharted country' that suggests an alternative
landscape towards which the poem, and the collection, is moving.
Order resides, in this poem, in the ability of poetry to order and
represent experience; the sentences circulate words in a flow of
verbal traffic that is potentially endless, a complex variety of the
lists noted in earlier collections. Budapest represents a kind of
totality of Europeanness and all that it assimilates: it contains
'migrant workers from Romania', 'East German' domestic artefacts,
'Ottoman carpets' and 'domed turkish baths', a 'Prussian style
academy' and 'the Westminster Gothic of Parliament', 'baroque
excrescences' and 'secessionist doors' – all signifiers of the ethnic,
geographical, cultural and historical diversity characteristic of the
modern European city. Architecture, in particular, offers traces of
the different constituencies of the city, imposing again its own for-
mal order on the chaos of history.

Order is also a metaphor for control, implicit in its potential to mean 'command'. In 'The Manchurian Candidate' the plot of the 1962 John Frankenheimer film (and the 1959 Richard Condon novel) is condensed to signify the fear of losing control of the self, the reduction of the human subject to 'a puppet waiting for a sign', a volitionless product of (Communist, in this context) brain-washing. 'This', the poem asserts, in a tongue-in-cheek cliché, 'is the stuff / of nightmares', whereas 'order' is the stuff of 'ideas' and dreams. The poem's second stanza relates the conceit of *The Blob* (Irvine S. Yeaworth, 1958), a science-fiction B-movie starring Steve McQueen; like *The Manchurian Candidate*, the film also allegorises the ideological tensions of the Cold War, as a giant alien blob (again symbolic of Communism) attacks and dissolves the teenage population of small-town America. The poem tantalises with its enjambment: 'Perhaps it's best / not to think of this.' As with 'The Idea of Order at the József Attila Estate', memories of the Cold War and Communist rule, the past returning in the present, embody the fear of disorder. The poem's third stanza imagines 'a place, a clean white house, some chairs / set out on porches', an image of American domestic bliss and peacefulness (politically coded by the 'white house'). The tranquil 'view / of lawns and streets the whole neighbourhood shares' is, like the films of the previous stanzas, not the imaginary world of capitalist fears of Communism, but the consumer dream of private ownership – 'This place belongs to you' – a dream where the world is 'like a mind, fresh washed, hung out to dry'. Consumerism, the poem suggests, brainwashes just as Communism did; if the consumerist world isn't one of pure horror in which the subject is excavated by ideology (the 'blob' that 'comes and eats / folks' innards out'), it nevertheless mimics its effects by erasing the past: 'rain comes down to wash the memory out'.

Memory, history and the burden of the past are transformed in such poems into narrative and poetic forms, standing as exemplars of Szirtes' ability to reconstruct moments of perception. He is aware of the tendency in poems for words to replace things, for poems to become verbal spaces meditating on their own formal directions. Later in *Portrait of My Father*, sonnet 2 of the short sequence, 'Chalk White: The Moon in the Pool' demonstrates how, for Szirtes, poetic words tend to reflect only themselves, constructing the space occupied by the poem itself:

In any case
there are no columns, no moon, only sounds
made by words whispering, a mouth, a face,
lack and desire, language doing its rounds.

This moment of self-reflexive diagnosis points towards the increasing recognition in Szirtes' poetry that the space constructed in words differs in fundamental ways from that understood as reality. This difference affords the poet massive freedoms and massive responsibilities, which become the implicit concern of the poems that make up the second section of this collection. The 'rounds' of language in 'Chalk White: The Moon in the Pool' prefigure the circular structure of the Hungarian sonnet sequence, its 'sounds' the incessant murmur of the historical and literary pasts that permeate all Szirtes' literary spaces; each of the short sonnet sequences that precedes these concluding poems offers its own version of the role of the sonnet form in recording and meditating upon experience.

Form and technique merge in these sonnets, producing poetry of careful emotional intensity that constructs its worlds with an increasingly subtle awareness of the effects of verbal positioning and counterpointing. The opening lines of 'Sap Green: Old School' indicate how Szirtes manipulates the balancing of word, line, sentence and form to generate these intensities:

> The copper dome of the old school had turned
> into the colour of soup they used to serve
> on certain Fridays. The dining-hall lights burned,
> low in the autumn gloom. You boys deserve
>
> all you get, muttered the head into his gown.

'Turned' is carefully placed as the rhyme word on which the line turns, its meaning shifting from the expected verb of movement to one of transformation, a shift of colour rather than place, that effects the subtle shifting, in turn, of the focus of the collection onto the artist's colours that preoccupy these sequences. 'Soup' links forward semantically to the 'dining-hall lights', further aspects of the 'old-school' environment and architecture of memory that the poem constructs and inhabits. 'Burned', rhyming with 'turned' and also potentially a verb of transformation, becomes instead one of action and is also balanced by its own turn to 'low' and 'gloom'. 'Lights' and 'gloom', along with the 'colour of soup', emphasise luminescence and its absence as vital constituents of mood, enhancing and deepening the poem's burgeoning nostalgia, which is further emphasised by the 'desperate smell of tobacco' and the head's 'bad smoker's cough', cohering later in 'the fog' which is also 'memory' seen through 'dark translucent glass'. The poem's figure of history as 'the pool / of memory' returns us to the images of Hungarian and English history represented in the swimming pools and other watery places – places of dissolution, of escape from the frozen and the fixed – familiar from earlier collections.

The tangible mood of these poems, with their explicit concern with the problem of how to represent others, is deeply nostalgic. 'Sap Green: Old School' remembers 'the class / of '65', while 'Prussian Blue: Dead Planets' considers the 'music in space' as 'violins and sentimental songs'. 'Whole years drown / in your coffee' in 'Cerulean Blue: Footnote on Wim Wenders', which also imagines 'the dream-film of all those other lives which are / not yours'. 'Romanian Brown' returns to territories explored in 'Transylvana', exploring how 'A deep smudge of brown, something like a forest, / suggests an entrance into a possible past' where 'the dead come and go'. The movement of these poems is relentless, 'backwards into youth, backwards into childhood, back / into something formless yet vital, a directionless force' that is refigured as 'the remembered form / of the reaching hand as it grasps the bar and grips'. These sonnet sequences impose form upon this 'formless' past, offering remembrance as the imperative driving the poems in *Portrait of My Father*. 'Cerulean Blue's' 'dream-film of the life of others' is developed in 'Flesh Pink; The Face in the Coat', where the cinematic trope foreshadows Szirtes' next major collection, *Reel*: the poem asks of the faces of the world, 'Where can we store / all their knowledge? On some machine with a reel / of film inside it?' Another answer might be in poetry itself, and the poem goes on to allude forward to 'journeys and films or any kind of sequence', a brief summary of the collection's concluding poems.

The order and control available to well-managed poetic form are exercised most clearly in the three sequences of Shakespearean sonnets that conclude the collection. These poems are impressive technical achievements that also perform important thematic and ideological functions in the context of the collection, symbolically 'completing' the projects of remembrance that began as early as some of the poems in *November and May*. Their structure motivates form to achieve closure and completeness, suggesting that *Portrait of My Father in an English Landscape* is underpinned by a narrative logic, working towards certain symbolic closures and completions. The complex patterning of these three sequences is heavily reliant on local repetition and general circularity; it also introduces ideological questions of continuity and disruption, connection and disjunction, and progression and regression. The deliberately baroque form of the Hungarian sonnet sequence offers an exaggerated version of the ways Szirtes uses an overdetermined counterpoint between broken and enjambed syntax and rigid, structural line and stanza patterns, to regulate the emotional distance and intensity of the themes his poetry addresses. Szirtes states, in the 'Acknowledgements' to *Portrait of My Father*, that he has 'taken some minor liberties' with the form, chiefly the relaxing of the requirement that the first line of each sonnet repeat exactly the preceding closing line. Such liberties suggest that formal strictness counterpoints a less formal tendency towards flexibility, allowing development in the form's complexity, and emphasising self-consciousness within the demands of the form. Above all this tension between flexible and inflexible formal constraints corresponds to the specific difficulties addressed in these poems, which together offer a symbolic autobiography constructed out of the traces and remains (in narratives, anecdotes, memories and photographs) of the poet's childhood.

The central concern of this emphasis on form and its variations can be traced through the recurrent attention Szirtes' poetry pays to the potential failure of the poem and the word adequately to represent. This failure returns in the insistent concern of each of the closing sequences with its own mechanisms, evident in the relentless, self-reflexive exploration of language, words, speech, voices, writing, graffiti and other forms of linguistic expression. This emphasis on language and on the poem's writing of spoken words and utterances also draws attention to the act of reading, and to the fact that each sonnet sequence takes its own place, in turn, in the tradition or sequence of its literary precursors. Again, Szirtes' 'liberties with the form' have important effects in this context. Variation reinforces and subverts tradition, marking Szirtes' sonnet sequences as developments from as well as continuations of preceding versions of the sonnet sequence, and drawing on the reader's competence to establish and sustain the significance of form. Szirtes' sonnet sequences become origins of new formal possibilities as well as culminations of traditions, and the formal oscillation between beginnings and endings frames poetry which aspires towards a total but shattered representation of the past, an 'emergent complexity' of literary figurings of history. Szirtes has developed this style to address his own sense of what Michael Murphy has called 'the burden and responsibility of writing about historical events from the sanctuary of the present',[162] the responsibility of the exiled writer rediscovering and making amends in poetry for his dispossession and disconnection from history.

The personal and familial experience of history as disruption emerges as the ideological motivation of these concluding poems. The Hungarian sonnet sequence, considered in relation to Szirtes' Hungarian lineage, offers an alternative, literary lineage that, he notes in discussing these poems, goes back to the 16th century, a form that is both stable and unstable, consistent and inconsistent, repetitive of itself and different from itself. In this form Szirtes inscribes the specific verbal terrain that constitutes what is designated, in sonnet 12 of 'The Looking-Glass Dictionary', his own 'lexical demesne'. Memories are fractured by history and then reconstituted in the form of sonnets, affording a specific kind of insight into a dislocated historical experience of the twentieth century. The underlying quest of these three concluding sonnet sequences is for origins; conclusions and origins circulate each other in a complex, recursive oscillation that is sustained across 630 lines of dense, autobiographically and culturally allusive verse.

The beginning of this structural oscillation between beginnings and endings lies in the poem that precedes the first of the sonnet sequences. 'Flesh Pink: The Face in the Coat' meditates on eternity – 'such an eternity / without dimension' – as a counterpoint to the dimensions of the present moment that hitherto have preoccupied different aspects of Szirtes' *œuvre*. Cameras and film record the passage of time, the poem notes, but time itself remains mysterious, its passage (and its effects on human lives) 'something no-one understands'. The final sonnet concludes with lines that nod to Andy Warhol:

Everyone is a star, for more than fifteen minutes,
more than enough to fill the short half-life of sonnets.

This 'half-life' suggests incompleteness and transience, a decay that is enacted in the sonnet's structured movement towards closure, and the 'fifteen minutes' of stardom prefigure the fifteen sonnets of the Hungarian sonnet sequence, summarised in 'the short half-life of sonnets'.

'The Looking-Glass Dictionary', the first of the concluding sequences, begins this 'short half-life' with the narrator's fraught entry into a symbolic universe of language, 'an otherness' that modulates into 'a world of forms'. This opening 'otherness' disturbs the familiarity of formal convention, marking the 'world' or 'universe' as 'other' and establishing the poem's wider concern with linguistic and formal differences. The tension between verbal constraint and release and between the freedoms and constraints of form focuses the poem's attention on itself. The opening line, 'Words withheld. Words loosed in angry swarms', establishes this tension. 'Swarms' immediately implies further movements between form and formlessness, inviting but semantically resisting line 3's rhyme 'forms'. The repetition of certain rhymes is an important limiting factor of the form Szirtes has chosen to work in: in sonnet 3, 'forms' rhymes with 'storms', and 'storms' and 'swarms' provide the concluding rhyme words of sonnet 14; the tension between 'withheld' and 'loosed' recurs in line 9 of the opening sonnet. These repetitions provide a conspicuously artificial constraining limit on the patterning of the verse, suggesting that repetition and thematic return – the dynamics of memory and nightmare – are major elements of the poem's universe.

The poem maps out a world defined by traumatic childhood experiences of the self's emergence from otherness, fragmented memories, confusions, myths and fears. The world of memory is rendered wholly unfamiliar in the first sonnet, and then, in the second, restructured into a manageable, condensed autobiographical scenario intertextually dependent upon a poem to which Szirtes has frequently alluded, Auden's 'In Memory of W. B. Yeats' – 'The airport. Night. December.' In the third sonnet, this scenario (a memory of the family's migration in 1956) is reconstituted again in terms of narrative, leading to the closing linear image of 'deserted rails'. This image, alluding back to the 'sinister' train of 'Rabbits' and further, to earlier train motifs in Szirtes' poetry, introduces travel, destination and arrival as the themes of 'Travel Book', but marks them also as anxieties. 'Deserted rails' leads to the pseudo-repetition of the line to open the fourth sonnet: 'Faint vibrations of trains along the rails', inculcating a traumatic locational confusion that founds (and founders) the speaking, questioning child on an experience of loss that, we now understand, is central to Szirtes' *œuvre*: 'where are we now? Abroad again or home?' The answer, characteristically, is 'between': 'between two kinds of sound', that of the mother's 'voice' and her 'internal traffic', the subterranean noise of her past and her unconscious. The mother's body is the origin and destiny of the child in this sonnet, 'desire and loss' marking the conflicting drives that orchestrate childhood memory and its reduction of the articulate self to onomatopoeic mutterings (the 'thrum,' the 'croak' and the 'blub' of bodily sounds replacing the meaningful sense of adult expression).

This internalisation of childhood experience within the confines of the maternal body continues into the next sonnet, which asks: 'Where do the inner journeys go? They end / in trails of words…'. 'Trails of words' constitute the sonnet sequence itself, which always moves towards the possibility of words, a 'coming-to-speech' that is also a 'coming-to-writing' in the written expression of 'sound / that was articulate'. 'Articulation' signifies both the child's emergence into a coherent, connected position from which it can articulate its own experience, and the connecting-together of experience as linguistic expression that constitutes the sonnet sequence itself. It also hints forward to sonnet 12's attention to 'the macaronic my parents speak'. A macaronic is a verse mixing different languages, but here the word is used with the imbedded critique of the immigrant's failure to master the native tongue, or the peasant's inadequate grasp of Latinate speech. A complex nexus of class consciousness, linguistic exclusion and immigrant status is implied in Szirtes' use of the term. 'Macaronic' here stands in for the parents' speech itself, absent from the poem but perhaps indicative of Szirtes' use elsewhere of Hungarian words and place names, and his range of European cultural reference. The latter half of the sequence addresses a divided experience of language ('The language outside meets the ur-language within'), in which the speaking subject finds itself alienated, linguistically displaced: 'The words my mother spoke were rarely home / to her' (where 'her' echoes 'ur-').

The sequence returns insistently to this theme of alienation in language in order to seek a home there. Sonnet 8, formally central, concludes by recognising the tension between poetic and temporal (formal) linearity and the different linearity of lived experience, of living in time: 'The clock goes ticking on but your life runs / straight down the hill of poetry and puns'. It offers a collage of images culminating in 'Your parents' voices...arguing', an expression of familial division that the sequence enacts by turning, in the next sonnet, to 'My father's voice', replacing the mother's; he later appears (in the context of the poem's emphasis on formal development) as reassuringly solid, composed of 'Pure narrative lines'. The father's voice announces the paternal authority the poem has been seeking, and introduces the poem's central symbolic movement – the development of a patrilinear ideology invested with the authority of symbolic exchange from father to son, via the voice / law of the father, the word / law of formal and genealogical transmission.

In Sonnet 10, this process of exchange is made explicit as the father's symbolic authority is rendered in monetary terms, in the 'notes / shuffled through the cold hands of the dead' and in 'The coins' that 'bear his own head / as guarantee'. In contrast with the uncertainty and traumatic horror of the mother's experience towards which the sequence gestures, its focus shifts to patrilinearity, the transmission of paternal inheritance as symbolic authority in words and 'notes' and 'coins' from father to son, in order to ground its symbolic narrative of origins and conclusions. In sonnet 11 his overtly symbolic exchange resituates language and subjectivity into more comfortable and familiar domestic relations: 'home / among the words that mean us and reflect / our faces and possessions', a resituating and re-stabilisation of the self in a language (English?) now welcoming and simply 'reflective' in its symbolic functions. The shift in these latter sonnets to the law and authority symbolically situated in the father's voice suggests that at a level slightly below consciousness *Portrait of My Father in an English Landscape* is much concerned with the paying off of patrilinear debts with the tokens of words.

Sonnet 12 presents the narrating self as an object to be spoken by language, within the 'macaronic', the 'multicoloured chatter' where 'sounds mean me', 'the me I vaguely sense, that free- / standing monument', endowed with self-possession – 'owner of that lexical demesne'. 'Ownership' implies possession and self-possession in language, another difference between the 'macaronic' parental speech and that of the son, inheritor and transformer of the 'lexical demesne' of English verse. The self is, like the poem itself, a 'monument' to the force of language, to the self's ability to construct form (itself, and its own recognition of itself in words used by others) out of 'chatter', coherence out of chaos, and to endow its speakers with powers of ownership, in which linguistic control ensures self-possession. But language here is also divorced from the self and the usage that selfhood implies: the 'lexical demesne' is qualified by its elaboration as a space 'of spotless glass where words may sit and preen'. Its 'spotlessness' asserts the paternalistic world of 'pure narrative lines', separate from the real, constructing instead the world of difference that exists through the 'looking-glass'.

The 'Looking-Glass' of the title (another version, perhaps, of the windows that periodically feature in Szirtes' work) appears in the linking lines of the twelfth and thirteenth sonnets as the mirror of language, in which the self sees itself constructed; one objective of the poem is to chart the emergence into the symbolic world of its narrating consciousness, but this is haunted by the threat to subjective stability offered by the 'constant shadow' of history, alluded to by the 'pain' that is 'drowned / and resurrected' in sonnet 6 and by the mother's alienation from the familiar 'home' of the English language and landscape ('Somehow the room / was never hers'). In sonnet 13 historical reality, a 'grimace / in forty-five', an experience addressed so powerfully elsewhere in Szirtes' poetry, 'creeps under the screen' of the symbolic world the poem has carefully constructed, the narrative of the poet's self as end-point of history; this 'history' refuses, in its return, 'to mean', to allow subjective stability as a luxury within 'the sanctuary of the present'. This refusal is re-enacted in the final sonnet, which reiterates in approximate form the preceding linking lines, condensing the movement of the sequence from 'Words withheld' to words 'refus[ing] to mean', and confirming, in doing so, the allegorical function of 'The Looking-Glass Dictionary' as a version of the struggle to represent such historical experience in poetic language.

The poem seeks ultimately to mirror the deconstruction of the poetic self that constructs. It explores the effects of the resistances, movements and displacements that are products of historical traumas and are generated by generic and formal laws in the process of their enforcement. It is a deeply complex personal narrative of the emergence of the poet-as-subject, enabled by his own distortion of the tradition (his 'liberties' taken with the form) to evade the parental 'macaronic' and speak anew in writing, and it maps the poet's entry into the symbolic world of language at the cost of maternal, historical allegiance, enacting the sequence of symbolic patrilinear inheritance, from father to son, that is simultaneously the inheritance and the renunciation of the formal demands of tradition.

'Travel Book' develops the tracing of the poet's development from childhood, figured now as a Woolfian 'voyage out', through a series of images presented as data in the recording of a life, initially located in the earliest years after Szirtes' arrival in England ('at nine', we're told in sonnet 4). Its opening line – 'The ego grinds and grates like a machine' – immediately renders the self as a mechanical process, engaged in the noisy, potentially destructive process of self-creation, which is the deep theme of the poem, its argument with itself being also its argument about its selfhood. In the minutiae of childhood memories significant figures – the blind woman of sonnet 2 (who also appears in 'The Courtyards' and in 'Elegy for a Blind Woman'), 'Mr Shane, the violinist' of sonnet 3, the 'two tiny flirtatious girls' of sonnet 4, and eventually 'My darling', 'the body whose pools you have swum in', echoing the imagery of 'Chalk White: The Moon in the Pool' – assume the proportions of prophetic figures encountered on an epic journey, avatars of deep but indeterminate significance. 'The self cooked through' is the emergent theme, transmuting into the central question 'But what is self?' in sonnet 6.

As the most overtly autobiographical of the three sonnet sequences, 'Travel Book' is also the most subjectively encrypted, drawing on resonances that remain for the most part implicit within the image-repertoire of the poem. In the third sonnet, comments on art reflect the sequence itself and provide a key to its comprehension:

Art has no gender,
is an uneasy comfort zone where the mad
briefly settle and the sane diminish in wonder
at their predicament, which is a sad
and brilliant obsession with pattern   .
both raw and cooked, so soft and yet hard-bitten.

The sequence itself evinces a 'sad [i.e. nostalgic] / and brilliant obsession with pattern'; the comprehension of art as 'a comfort zone' registers its affording of safety as well as its offering of a place of strategic withdrawal from the vicissitudes of the real. The patterning is rhetorical as well as formal: each sonnet asks a question or develops an argument, before providing more fragmentary images and parts of narratives that accumulate, as the poem progresses, into the 'Travel Book' of an unfinished life.

Sonnet 4 recollects a 'refugee party' charged with nascent infant sexuality, connecting photography with 'saucy pictures for calendars' and (referring back to 'The Looking-Glass Dictionary') noting the mirror's symbolic role in confirming identity: 'The mirror is no censor but tells you who is who'. This final line interrupts the iambic patterning of the poem by the addition of an extra, stumbling foot (a disruption repeated in sonnets 1, 7, 9, and 11, offering the ghost of a deforming patterning to the poem). The 'frail' ego' of sonnet 5 develops from the 'I / me' structure of sonnet 4 into a repeated 'You', that informal first-person code characteristic of Szirtes' displaced autobiographical persona. 'Frozenness' returns in 'the Christmas chill', a guarantee of an authentic code of experience that the poem recognises (again self-reflexively) as 'special, undisguised'; but it is also the coldness of 'rejection' which, the poem recognises with adult wisdom, is 'the law / of late childhood'.

Anxieties about identity and subjectivity modulate into ontological uncertainties about what exactly can be known about the past. Sonnet 7 begins with the kind of caveat-question that assumes increasing urgency in Szirtes' work, a rhetorical self-questioning that the poem seeks to answer: 'But how do you know what is valid or true / when there is no sense of being, no fixed space / to move in, no vantage point or overview?' The modality here is important – the question asks 'How do you know', not 'How can you know', suggesting not the impossibility of knowledge but its difficulty. The lack of a 'fixed space', a disorientating sense of dislocation that has pre-occupied Szirtes' poetry since *Bridge Passages*, is experienced as the lack of 'overview', the difficulty the poem encounters in trying to coordinate its fragments and narratives into a coherent, plotted, whole – the difficulty of moving, in the space of the word, from

memories to life. The fictions it necessarily constructs are also fic-
tions of selfhood, which, the poem recognises, ultimately resides
only in the performances demanded of it: 'you yourself must appear
with appropriate mask', 'the conscious mask' of the next sonnet.
Mirrors, film (the Bergmanesque 'filmic Death') and photography
('the photograph of a youthful father', the inspiration of the next
poem and of the collection) constitute the media through which
subjectivity is imagined, 'the slow moment' which imbeds the sub-
ject in the histories it encounters.

   In sonnet 9, real (but darkly gothic) history – 'Peter Sutcliffe /
stalks through Harehills and Chapeltown' – allows us to locate the
poem's chronological progression in the late 1970s (and reminds us
of Szirtes' connection to Leeds). But history, too, contributes to the
sense that the world is 'a dangerous romance' 'relying on memories
to get through its nightmares'. This 'Northern' interlude, featuring
a tiny vignette of Martin Bell as 'The Poet in his chair / reciting
Pope and Desnos', becomes increasingly compressed, oscillating
between massive general commentary ('Why stop at the universe?')
and detailed domestic allusion ('My father picks / a stamp up with
his tweezers and consults / his Stanley Gibbons'). Such differenti-
ation is the dynamic of 'Travel Book': the minutiae of a personal
history is counterpointed with the sense of a national progression,
constructing the intermediate point – 'the space between the lines' of
sonnet 11 – which emerges as the space of the poem itself, avail-
able to the self as it reads, in another echo of Wallace Stevens' 'A
Rabbit as King of the Ghosts', 'in negative at the end of the day'.

   'Reading in negative' summarises the interpretative strategies
harnessed in 'Travel Book'. Its counterpoint structure allows the
seemingly trivial events of childhood, adolescence and young adult-
hood to emerge as formative experiences, functioning like a relief
map of the self, set against the terrains of wider history. The find-
ing of love, which preoccupies the thirteenth and fourteenth son-
nets, offers a further episode in the 'grating and grinding' of the
'ego'; in an echo of earlier poems like 'A Domestic Faust' and 'A
Doctor's Room', the poem equates autobiography with domestic
space – 'your life expands to fill the room' – rendering the self
domesticated and familiar in doing so. 'Travel Book' forces its
way to the conclusion of this self-domestication, asserting at the
end of sonnet 13 that 'there's nowhere to go. Come hope. Come
home', statements modified in the final line of the poem: 'The
question is where you go. Come hope. Come home'.

   This conclusion prefigures the 'Hotel Esperia' of 'Meeting Aus-
terlitz', a poem we'll encounter in the next chapter. 'Hope' and

'home', as destinies of the 'journey' mapped out and related in 'Travel Book', offer reassurances of which the poem seems, at times, to despair; when, in the penultimate sonnet, 'You try the word "love", whisper "death", and make faces / at yourself', the poem expresses a discontent with itself – with poetry – that is virtually a self-repudiation: 'You are growing sick / of eloquence'. Its conclusion is, then, also a kind of consolation, a mooring of the self in 'hope' and 'home' that seeks to stabilise an autobiography mechanically rendered ('grating' and 'grinding' 'like a machine'), that will resituate itself in relation to an alternative history of self and family in the collection's concluding poem.

'Portrait of My Father in an English Landscape' focuses on the relations between image and language in constructing individual memory in words. It offers a multitude of portraits of the father-figure, from the photograph to which the poem responds and the painting *Portrait of Efim Repin, the Artist's Father* (1879) by the Russian artist Ilya Repin (who is mentioned in sonnet 7), to the narratives and anecdotes that lend the father a historical substance exceeding the intangible 'exhalation' that constitutes him early in the poem. It envisions the 'English landscape' as a contested space comprised of memories and inherited narratives, onto which it maps the contours of filial obligation encountered by the poet. It analyses how paternal authority is handed down through narratives whose recollection constitutes much of the poem, enabling it to explore different possibilities of 'escape' from a maternal history figured as 'dread', from a paternal biography couched in anecdote, and from a verbal portrait bound to paternal subjectivity and the narratives it possesses.

This desire is summarised in a phrase in the seventh sonnet, a caption to imagined scenes or chapters in the father's life: 'Escape on the March Back', implying the potential of memory as escape. Szirtes' father escaped from the Nazis in 1945 by stealing a train and driving it back to Budapest. This heroic act signifies a moment of transcendent action, a sublime historical event around which, in its constructions of the father's life, the poem circulates. In doing this, Szirtes' poem becomes what Hélène Cixous calls 'a text of evasion',[163] comprised of elusive meanings and cryptic images that evade clear definition or simple explanation, in which allusions to English Romantic traditions and to its own literariness allow the translation of the experience in which it originates into its own poetic version of events and memories.

The poem's deep project, concluding that of the collection, is to follow the father's footsteps into the English landscape that will contain and frame the future of the poet, allowing the emergence of a narrative not of the father but of the son (and thus developing the autobiographical impetus of the preceding sequences). The poem moves from a 'dread' of the real, formless experience of history (symbolised by the mother's experience), into language, the sublime, formally composed structure of the Hungarian sonnet sequence, in order to scrutinise and dissect the processes by which words seem to facilitate the apparent return of the past in symbolic form, providing a ground on which a narrative of self can be built. These processes allow reader and narrator to encounter experiences of personal and inherited emotional intensity and apparent immediacy which are yet seductive and threatening, recurrently metaphorised in the poem as 'traps' set by language – 'Best to suspect a trap', the first sonnet warns us. The father exists as a 'scattered text' susceptible to endless recomposition as a symbol of narrative transition and movement, and simultaneously as a static, image-like repository of inherited memory, residing outside of but translated into the English language and the 'English landscape'. Autobiography, the poem argues, is endlessly compromised by the burden of narratives that constitute the very ground of its possibility, the family romance against which the autobiographically constituted subject struggles to define itself.

Szirtes returns to photography to initiate this process. The 'Portrait' of the title is a photograph of the poet's father, a 'classic shot', described in the first sonnet, capturing an image of the family that excludes the mother, who, herself a photographer and presumably the creator of the image, escapes containment within it. In excluding the mother, the image, and, consequently, the poem, constructs an exclusively male familial security, and replaces one version of history with another. Like the mother, the 'landscape' of this photograph is verbally absent, a voided space filled by verbal description of an image, in which the characters simply appear, recorded in static activity ('striding', 'holding') lacking the context which is subsequently fleshed out in narrative. The narrator's childhood, imaged in the photograph, mutates, in the poem, into a post-memorial construction of the father's childhood, a Proustian lost time (complete with 'a small gâteau') reconstructed in words. The poem's concern turns from image to word, and from image in words, to words constructing images, in order to interrogate the forms of memory in writing. It finds inspiration in the paternal exhalation ('He exhales / his own monument'), a creative force like Wordsworth's 'gentle breeze', 'blessing' the poet's creativity. This counteracts the image of destructive, historical imprisonment and loss suggested by 'the cells of wind that whistle through him / and could destroy his body at a whim' (an image echoing the 'wind' blowing through the mother's body in 'Metro'). The destructive, mobile temporality of the modern world, embodied in the photograph, contrasts with the seductive, static Romantic nostalgia implicit in the image's silent exhalation that inaugurates the poem, a movement outwards into the world of words that the poem takes as its creative impulse: the poet declares in the opening sonnet that '…there is something solid and spherical / about the figure I feel I have to build / into and out of language'.

This opening sonnet offers a series of mobile oppositions – image and word, falling and rising, exhaling and inhaling – initially coalescing into the central narrative relation between son and father, itself a specific variant of that between present and past, which becomes in turn a movement into and out of pictorial and historical space. Each offers a version of a conflict between progress and stasis that the poem enacts in its formal structure, and which the narrator experiences as demand and obligation. Its demand is the compulsion to write, to create in words 'something I feel I have to build', a verbal compulsion demanding a tactile form, 'something solid and spherical' (like the sonnet sequence itself) which becomes the rhythmic counterpoint and circularity of the poem itself, 'language doing its rounds'. These tensions develop later in the poem into a grounding opposition between interiority (of the self) and exteriority (of the other), exemplified in 'that interior shelter' and 'the high street' of the twelfth sonnet. In terms of these oppositions, the whole poem enacts what we can read as the movement of exile, a movement from inside (belonging) to outside (exclusion).

This moving 'into and out of language' and that which language constructs – the image in the landscape and the landscape represented in the poem – is the source of the poem's relation of the experience of displacement. It situates the in-between condition of exile as a foundation, the horizontal movement of the self out of or away from its self-sourcing, from its own narratives of origin, into vertical, inherited, displaced versions of becoming. This is implicit in the poem's title, with its evocation of image, object and landscape, all contained in prepositional phrases that enact grammatical displacement, movement from one noun to the next, a folding from the vertical axis of 'Portrait' to the horizontal axis of 'Landscape' via the refracting lens of the father's (historical/personal) experience. 'Landscape' here signifies territory (the territory encountered in the father's and the family's exile from Hungary, and the *tájkép* or 'picture of a region' evoked by the Hungarian word for 'landscape'), the arena of memory and experience constructed in the poem, within which sits the inaugural image-in-words of the photograph. The 'classic shot' is thus, in the double logic of the poem's repetitious structure, both a tangible, durable space, a 'frozen ground' upon which to 'build / into and out of language' a poetic analysis of the poet's past, and, in the final sonnet, 'the one / most easy to destroy', a flimsy façade, a representation as susceptible as reality to the 'whims' and vicissitudes of historical decay.

Despite its titular emphasis on the visual forms of 'Portrait' and 'Landscape', the entire poem is clearly structured around narrative as the medium of the transmission of memory, and its narrative voice assumes a role reminiscent of Walter Benjamin's 'storyteller'.[164] 'Anecdote' sits centrally in three of its fifteen sonnets (8, 9 and 11) and at the end of the fourteenth; other sonnets mention story-telling and various forms and genres of narrative: 'Parables' (2), 'telling stories' (3), 'Ghost stories, gothic tales' (4), 'a true tale', 'the truth of every story' (7) and so on, up to the final sonnet's retelling (in its repetition of the concluding lines) of the preceding narratives. One 'escape' that the poem performs through such insistence is its own evasion of the symbolic import of the image. It evokes pictorial memory only in order to replace it with language as a less 'authoritative', and therefore more flexible, mode of remembering. Marking a crucial development in Szirtes' comprehension of the relations between word and image, the poem asserts that the father's memories reside in narratives, while the mother's are contained in images. The second sonnet, effecting this necessary switch from photograph as stimulus to narrative as vehicle of memory, establishes the childhood of paternity as a space into which the father 'drops', a space inheriting its own verbal traditions, as the father-child (father of the man) is 'entranced by old men's words...tales and jokes'. 'Entranced' implies magical seduction (alluding forward to paternal Prospero's appearances in the fifth and sixth sonnets) as well as the entry into the space of the father's childhood, the poet's entrance into the accommodating space of narrative as tradition.

Such paternal 'parables', offerings of narratives encoding knowledge, are momentarily balanced by 'feminine', grandmotherly and avuncular familial offerings of 'sweets', constructing a nostalgic past of textual and confectionary consumption where loan words assume the significance of exotic edibles ('gâteau', 'éclairs') imported from another language, redolent of (linguistic and national) difference and, of course, existing themselves in a kind of verbal exile. The poem insistently locates itself within a tradition of experience inherited as narrative, summarised as 'world as anecdote'. The closing lines of sonnet 7 articulate this anecdotal world in power-fully historical terms, offering in epigrammatic form a condensed narrative of a violent, specifically European history. 'Escape' and 'mad Flight, sane Flight' lead inexorably into new westward dis-placements further figured in the allusion to the painter Ilya Repin, and in the Czech loan words '*Malenky robot*' (entering English, unlike Szirtes and his father, from literary sources – the Čapek brothers' *Rossum's Universal Robots* and Anthony Burgess' *A Clock-work Orange*).

The second sonnet's central question, uttered by the italicised voice of the child-father, addresses the function of paternal author-ity in religion: '*How did Jesus get to be God?*' It calls faith, father-hood and filial accession into complex relationship, and confirms narratives in their Biblical forms ('parables') as clues to the read-ing of the poem. These narratives elaborate through subsequent sonnets into the poem's meditation on its own poetic status, encoded in fractured, awkward invocations of religious and secular mys-tique, further parables of arcane yet familiar pasts: 'Short words. God's scattered text. The scholar's passim', 'Ghost stories, gothic tales'. The father himself becomes this metaphor: 'His surface / is a broken narrative' 'which', the next sonnet asserts, 'must be inter-preted'. The demand of the hermeneutic task of interpreting this 'broken narrative' implies both the gleaning of meaning and the performance of reparation, the repairing of semi-apocryphal narra-tives through their restoration into the canon of poetic subjects, their movement into and out of forms of mediation, from forget-ting into memory. The Marxist literary critic Fredric Jameson argues that 'History is what hurts':[165] Szirtes' poem asserts that 'What hurts is the truth of every story, things being just / as they are'. The 'truth' resides in history, but only in the sense that his-tory, too, is comprised of anecdote and story.

The poem works towards a formal, if not ideological, closure via the central caption noted earlier: 'Escape on the March Back'. The language of the last seven sonnets becomes increasingly, self-consciously difficult and unstable as anecdotes, rather than facts, accumulate, and paternal authority over English words is compro-mised by the mother's proximity to the real history ('things being just / as they are', the irony of 'just' emphasised by its placement at the end of the line) that remains implicit in the poem: 'He knows she has touched dread / with her bare fingers'. In the face of this 'dread' of historical truth, language 'slips, words slide / and take pratfalls' as 'ghosts' and 'photographs' are replaced by 'presences', figures of the 'dread' history that exceeds the linguistic world of the poem: 'I cannot quite conjure / this robust presence', the poem asserts; 'Anecdotes hide / the very thing they describe in their pure / linear fashion'. 'Portrait of My Father in an English Landscape' thus constructs its argument within a contradictory situation. It attempts to escape the 'linear' confines of representation, be they narrative, photographic or poetic, to achieve a pure historical-aesthetic presence that escapes words, even as it seeks in words an escape from the pure presence of a history that 'hurts', into a 'centre' or 'core' which, in the ninth and tenth sonnets, 'remains unknown'.

The poem increasingly emphasises its own contradictory movements into and out of language, and its own formal circularity, as repetitions accumulate and structural demands develop. Landscape, like the father's experience of which it is a figure, becomes a space structured by its own repetition in language, both containing an elusive 'presence, like the ghost in a photograph'; and, in turn, it becomes something central to and yet excessive to the poem itself, 'a surfeit, a core that can't be truly known'. This unknowable 'core' figures the poem's abiding concern with escape in language via 'anecdote', into a textual reality reiterating history in the form of paternal memory. Like the tales told by Walter Benjamin's 'Storyteller', the narratives that constitute the verbal construction of the 'Portrait' offer a 'chaste compactness'[166] in which history, anecdote, memory and poetry circulate in a complex economy of linguistic exchange. The poem's narratives condense the 'dread' history associated with the mother, and the anecdotal biography of the father, into a poetic form that closes with a further anecdote of the interchange between self and other as a final territory upon which memory and history struggle, within a domesticity polarised 'at opposite ends of the table'. The penultimate sonnet shifts pronouns from 'I', via the third person of 'My Father', to the concluding 'You', a movement encrypted in a narrated dialogue of gesture:

It's getting late,
I look at my watch. He makes that worried gesture
with his hands which moves me. His eyes
are a warm cave swimming in faint moisture...

Here subjectivity becomes a 'scattered text' enacted in a language of eyes and bodies, and in the movement between 'I' and 'he', 'my' and 'his', 'my watch', 'his hands' and 'his eyes', momentarily blurring (as by 'faint moisture' in the eyes) the distinction between poet and father.

The concluding sonnet, confirming Benjamin's assertion that

'storytelling is always the art of repeating stories',[167] insists on rep-
etition as the necessary mode for relating histories. Its versions of
the preceding fourteen concluding lines offer formal closure through
yet more condensation, lines as summary motifs repeated to evoke
the memories and anecdotes that comprise the sequence. In its
conclusion the poem re-reads itself, gathering up into its own for-
mal edifice the 'scattered texts' that comprise the various poems in
the collection itself, its narratives of the father's life, tales whose
'edges [are] neither straight nor true', within which the poem seeks
out its relationship to the language into and out of which it escapes
the Father, the past, and the English landscape. In doing so, it
refigures and redefines that landscape as viable territory for poetic
enquiry, which becomes the terrain of Szirtes' next collection, *An
English Apocalypse*.

7

'Imposing order':
An English Apocalypse and Reel

It's a problem of identity.

EVA HOFFMAN

In 1996, Oxford published Szirtes' *Selected Poems 1976–1996*, which sampled every collection from *Poetry Introduction 4* onwards. After Oxford closed its poetry list in 1999, Szirtes moved to Bloodaxe, who quickly published two volumes of his work – a retrospective selection of poems dealing with Hungarian memories and experiences, *The Budapest File* (2000), and a second compilation of poems addressing England and Englishness, *An English Apocalypse* (2001). This double publication confirmed, and to an extent formalised, a division latent in the previous organisation of Szirtes' work, and reinforced 'in-between-ness' as the defining element of his poetic identity. The latter volume also included over 80 pages of new poems, thereby combining retrospection with a substantial new collection. Szirtes' shift of focus towards his adopted country had begun earlier, in *Portrait of My Father in an English Landscape*. *An English Apocalypse* confirms this movement, offering an extended engagement with the double estrangement between the poet's 'foreign heart' (in *Metro*'s 'Preludes') and the 'foreign commotion' of England (in *An English Apocalypse*'s 'All In'). The key concerns of these collections extend motifs and concerns prevalent in Szirtes' earlier work; they centre on relations between the strange and the familiar, the senses of belonging and of alienation, and the construction of notions of 'home' and 'hope' as origins and conclusions of human life and its journeys within and through the domestic spaces and landscapes into which history deposits those it chooses to displace.

An English Apocalypse

The new poems in *An English Apocalypse* are remarkably consistent in form, comprising thirty-three sonnets or sonnet-sequences of various lengths, followed by 'An English Apocalypse', a *terza rima*

sequence of twenty-five poems and a prologue, sub-divided into
five sections, culminating in the apparent destruction (and then
miraculous salvation) of England by four apocalypses. Two other
uncollected poems – 'Acclimatisation', which would fit in theme
and tone into the 'Appropriations' sequence in *Bridge Passages*,
and 'A Prayer for my Daughter', in homage to the famous poem
by Yeats – are included in the retrospective section of the book.
The eye cast on England in these poems is by turns involved and
dispassionate, observing from the perspective of the 'foreigner' the
'foreignness' of the home country: as it's put in 'English Words',
'You say a word until it loses meaning'. 'England' begins to 'lose
its meaning' under Szirtes' poetic scrutiny, becoming a new kind
of place, which, in the major poem 'Backwaters: Norfolk Fields'
(discussed below), is both 'years behind' and 'at the end' of some-
thing indeterminate. Szirtes' major concern here, and in the sub-
sequent *Reel*, is to analyse his relation to his adopted country through
an examination of its culture and history.

Belatedness and an accompanying sense of cultural exhaustion
permeate the poems in *An English Apocalypse*. The first of them,
'History', begins: 'It was all so long ago', and continues into its
second sonnet, 'It was once upon a time, it was history, / it was
the day before, the day that never happened'; in 'VDU', 'it was
all too late and slow / to make much difference to anyone'; and in
the small revenge narrative 'The boys who beat up my brother',
'It's late in the day, too late and much too late'. 'It' in these poems
is the past, an obsession of the conservative modern and contem-
porary ideologies of Englishness examined here – both the 'fairy-
tale' world of 'once upon a time' and a proximal moment in the
seemingly immediate past, tangible but elusive, present but outside
the grasp even of language, an object instead of repeated, despairing
laments. In 'Pearl Grey', 'Time' itself becomes 'simply the product /
of flight and language'; underlying Szirtes' versions of English past-
oral (again a key concern) is England as a place of arrival, the des-
tiny of a narrative of displacement through time and space of which
his poetry repeatedly tries to make sense. 'The end of something', in
this context, becomes the 'end' of a history of 'flight', of migration,
exile, displacement, and the concern with terminal spaces explored
here, into which the exiled, migrant, displaced subject is deposited
to begin life anew, echoes the formal concern of *Portrait of My
Father in an English Landscape* with origins and conclusions.

England, then, is a destiny that is also an ideological condition,
a complex of moods and emotions. The poems repeatedly diag-
nose these national character-traits (referring with some linguistic

irony, in the fourth 'Apocalypse', 'Death by Suicide', to 'the national *folie / de grandeur*'), relating them to climate, geography, landscape, culture and tradition. One poem, 'History', declares the project: 'I want a voice to speak this'. Another, 'All In', later glosses this desire: 'There is a language for this and I am trying / to speak it'. In searching for a 'voice' in which to 'speak' the 'language' that may symbolise and comprehend, or at least express an understanding of, contemporary England, Szirtes' poetry confirms its authoritative marginality, its awareness of exclusion as a potential strength. 'History', in trying to deal with the world 'as it is', acknowledges the intervention of the available voice: 'And as it is my dear, / I can't tell it straight, I don't think I would believe me'. This honest assertion of the 'slant' over the 'straight' – exploiting what Eva Hoffman calls 'the advantages of an oblique vision'[168] – returns us to the surreal, indirect angle of approach to reality established in his earliest poetry.

The re-engaging with English themes and observations confirms *An English Apocalypse* as a kind of 'return', offering the poet as 'the semi-transparent spectre that you see' (later the 'visitor, a ghost', 'almost transparent' in 'VDU'), a figure of a subjectivity laden with conflicting but productive pasts that offer either 'consolations' or 'death-traps'. The imagery of 'History', deriving from the Audenesque (the 'hum heard down telegraph wires', the 'train that is only a rumour'), suggests the echo of crisis, the 'vague presentiment' to which the poem alludes. Its act of ventriloquism, substituting the 'too straight' voice of the (English-speaking) poet for the 'singing' of the radio, is a symbolic transference from the authentic but unstable subject position of a self which has to qualify 'The thing I am' with 'or think I am', to the 'ghost music', the 'evanescent trick' of the radio, which offers new recordings of 'that noise we made / ... still humming in the wires'.

The poem opts for the mediated voice of experience; its 'History' (gesturing forward to *Reel*) is 'reeled off', 'a frozen frame / in a film made of frames'. It offers a voluntary 'loss' of voice, a renunciation of the poetic voice that contrasts with the forced silencing experienced in 'The boys who beat up my brother': 'To be kicked in the ribs and lose your power of speech / is to be tied to someone else's bed / of pain.' 'History', in opting for the radio's 'singing', offers, in contrast, an act of empowerment, of liberating distancing, a separation of the familiar self (not the anonymous self of *Bridge Passages*' 'Recording') from its recorded utterances, allowing those utterances authority to speak for and of history. This version of the modernist persona, the distancing of the poet from his utterance

and the achievement, through this, of pseudo-objectivity, charac-
terises the poems in *An English Apocalypse*, which return repeatedly
to this division and its effects.

'VDU' presents the poet's position as divided, appearing to
himself 'as if across an immense gulf, / between two worlds, one
inside one out'. 'I speak as a witness', asserts 'History' (and in
'Dusty Springfield: My Brother's Wedding', 'Everything points to
the presence of a witness'); the self is both divided and yet called
into self-presence by its role as witness of its own historical involve-
ment, offering testimony for or proof of the 'truth' of things as it
experiences them. Even the voice is fractured: 'White Hart Lane'
self-reflexively comments that 'Time is fracture and compression, /
like this line'. The 'you' in this poem is an object of self-address,
the man's awareness of his difference from the child that he was:
'The hours you spent by a suburban brick wall / in north-west
London! You were already a man / without a future...'.

The pastoral mode in these poems is now 'unfrozen', affording
a self-conscious discourse through which Englishness (convention-
ally constructed in pastoral terms) is analysed. 'Spring Green',
subtitled (in deference to the coming 'English Apocalypse') 'Three
Apocalyptic Grotesques', offers its colour as a metonymy of the
pastoral itself: 'Think of it at the feet of a young dandy / in emblem-
atic Tudor costume, part / nature, part intellect...'. The notoriously
ambivalent ideology of pastoral, its reification of the natural world
as an expression of "timeless" but politically coded values and of
nature as an object to be "read" and "decoded" for ideological
purposes, affords Szirtes much ammunition in the collection's
deconstruction of Englishness. 'Spring Green' is both natural,
'common as grass', and constructed, a pseudo-innocence 'painted
by a child / in her first school'; it is both 'innocuous' and 'wild', a
marker of the ideological contradictions that divide national iden-
tities. Its constituent elements – 'White rabbits, mushrooms, snails,
blackberrying, / the sherbet dip with liquorice stick, pence / in
purses' – develop the now familiar form of the list into a summary
of the popular-cultural baggage of a particular post-War mythology
of England in the second sonnet: 'It is *Brighton Rock*, Sid James,
Diana Dors, / Brylcreem and Phyllosan[169] and Lucozade'. These
lists, metonymies of desire and loss, are also markers of genera-
tional identity and difference, the narrator of 'History' carrying his
experience into the present as a kind of inheritance of memory.

The Marvellian 'perfect greenness' of 'Spring Green' 'over-
whelm[s] / desire', transcending the symbolic attributes of the
English landscape; but, like the lawn in David Lynch's *Blue Velvet*

(1986), it masks a seething horror of literal nature, a dark world of 'earthworms' and 'beetles' that lies beneath the surface colour, while above, 'Birds are singing serenades / to the great chain of being for the last / time.' The poem offers little respite from this momentary insight into the 'skull beneath the skin' – 'It is, I think, the end / of the world'. Apocalypse thus lurks within the 'green thought in a green shade' of Szirtes' Edenic England, staining with its shadowy presence 'the space between things' and offering (in a faint echo of Prague, 1968, as well as of the Aprils of English poetic tradition) 'a spring to cap and end all other springs'. Later, in the first 'English Apocalypse' poem, 'Jerusalem', the 'green and pleasant land', is 'a country of eternal regret', 'a forsaken garden', and the 'meaning' of pastoral is laid bare:

> ...the sun is always about to set
>
> on an empire laying down its burden.
> Which is what pastoral means: life in a field
> of death, natural activity as boredom,
>
> the air crowded with unreconciled
> facts...

Historical transition, mutability and the conflicting demands of ideology constitute the 'field' of Englishness. In 'Victoriana', pastoral England is by turns aristocratic and surreal, the world of Victorian fantasy: 'Pastoral is a voice in the shrubbery, / the sound of a tennis ball, a lawn where croquet / is being played by flamingos with rubbery / elegance...' (although in *Through the Looking-Glass* it's played with flamingos as mallets). 'Survivor' echoes Empson in describing its protagonist as 'away in your own / version of pastoral which is compressed / into such moments'.

The compression, and the consequent symbolic force, of the versions of 'pastoral' in these poems, resides in part in their connection to the landscape of melancholic nostalgia that comprises Szirtes' England. The 'Apocalypse' poems are frequently set in northern places ('Keighley', 'Orgreave', the 'Harehills' of 'Night Out'; 'The Deluge' moves southwards and westwards from 'The Wash' to 'Land's End'), contrasting with the London- or southern-based pastorals of other poems like 'Backwaters: Norfolk Fields'. Each poem contributes to the construction of an England outmoded in historical terms, disconnected from the contemporary world in which the poems are written, semiotically coded instead in the garb and the concerns of the 1960s and 1970s. This prevailing sense of temporal dislocation is powerfully exploited in the longest of these poems, 'Backwaters: Norfolk Fields', the centrepiece of the new poems in *An English Apocalypse*, a sequence of twelve sonnets that maps the landscape of Szirtes' adopted East Anglia onto the psychological territory of an English identity perceived to be in terminal decline.

Dedicated to the German writer W.G. Sebald (who, like Szirtes, taught in East Anglia), and written before his death in a car crash in 2001, 'Backwaters' initiates a coded dialogue between Szirtes' own work and that of Sebald, just as the later 'Meeting Austerlitz' (in *Reel*), which elegises Sebald, seeks a different dialogue, or rather to extend the dialogue into a different set of relations. From the opening line's sequence of paired words – 'Backwaters. Long grass. Slow Speech. Far off' – Szirtes establishes a compressed sense of territory, disuse, language and distance, the interconnected parameters of his exploration of the landscapes and histories of place that constitute the 'Norfolk Fields'. This environment is encountered by both Sebald and Szirtes in radically different but formally analogous circumstances, and ultimately experienced by both, despite the poem's initial use of the inclusive 'We', from the point of view of the 'outsider':

> We're years behind. Even our vowels sag
> in the cold wind. We have our beauty spots
> that people visit and leave alone, down main
> arterials and side roads. A paper bag
> floats along the beach. Clouds drift in clots
> of grey and eventually down comes the rain.

Here the assertion of historical persistence (echoing in its tone the rhetorical flourishes and broad historical sweep of another contemporary elegy to East Anglia, Graham Swift's *Waterland* [1983]) breaks down into a shared present of isolated images. 'Sagging' vowels decline into silent, disconnected images of desolation, and solitude and isolation (the word 'alone' seemingly central spatially and thematically to the passage) initially overwhelm the traces of a social world already implicitly sick ('spots' and 'clots' rhyming external and internal signs of malaise, 'beauty spots' eliding the bodily and the topographical). 'We're at the end,' the poem continues contradictorily – not behind, but too far advanced, beyond even decline: 'It might simply be of weather / or empire or of something else altogether'.

While this final clause establishes an initially indeterminate but radical otherness as central to the poem's analysis, its deliberately unspecific historical diagnosis rests uncomfortably with the poem's construction of a detailed and highly imagistic visual rhetoric through which to encode the emotional resonances embedded within a landscape. Such tension, between the deliberately vague and the meticulously specific, extends the tendency in Szirtes' poetry for the reliably visual to override perceptual and interpretative uncertainties to provide at least some sureness, the visual precision of the artist offering something to rely upon in a contemporary world of increasing uncertainty. 'Backwaters' hovers within this tension, exploiting it to generate its initial sensation of frustrated stasis, its sense of teetering on the brink of the impending 'English Apocalypse'.

The second sonnet switches from 'We' and 'I' to 'You', the familiar indeterminate second person address involving self, narrator and reader as compound, ambiguous addressees in a new level of uncertain complicity. 'You cannot wipe the face / of the clock or restore a vanished kingdom', we are warned; historical processes are irreversible, the poem argues, as the emptiness of the landscape begins to take on allegorical significance, much as it does in Sebald's novel-memoir *The Rings of Saturn*, a travelogue of a walk around Suffolk (the county bordering Szirtes' Norfolk), with its opening descriptions of the 'thinly populated countryside' and 'the traces of destruction' 'that were evident even in that remote place'.[170] Szirtes notes the seeming significance of natural forces in 'The wind at its eternal droning harangue'; nature itself is an active contributor to the social desolation, 'the empty houses' in 'the back of beyond'.

Natural and social desolation are, the poem suggests, comparable figures of historical abandonment, and summarise the poem's representation of the experience of dislocation to the margins (the end) of time and space, exclusion from the centres of agency to the ends of the earth (a rhetorical implication developed intertextually in the poem's later allusion, in sonnet 7, to Conrad's *Heart of Darkness*). With this allegorical import established, the poem turns towards the social world in order to ground it in contemporary observation. Figures in the landscape reply to the construction of landscape as figure by assuming parabolic significance (the man in the third sonnet is 'biblical'; social roles metonymically replace people in sonnet 4, allowing the poem's meditative shift towards the significance of naming as the determining function of identity). Again, recorded visual detail provides a shorthand for the underlying themes; 'War memorials' appear suddenly amid the names, bearers of names themselves as well as markers of the traces of history towards which the poem ceaselessly strives.

But the poem refuses the simple surface meanings presented by the world it observes and records – 'Too easy all this' – and seeks instead to reintegrate the initial theme of natural isolation into an elaboration of the observation of contemporary social decay and transience, metonymically indicated in 'Broken windows' and 'The police presence'. The sense of an ending is self-reflexively encoded in the contradictorily non-terminal enjambment of 'End / of a line', and the central insight of the poem (and, by extension, of all Szirtes' poems about England) is asserted just before the central poem of the sonnet sequence:

> This is your otherness where the exotic
> Appears by a kind of homely conjuring trick.

These lines summarise the contradictory, complex concerns of this poem and of *An English Apocalypse*. The 'otherness' here is ambiguous, as 'your' exemplifies (as in sonnet 2 and throughout Szirtes' work) the narrator's self-address (and thus refers to his own sense of otherness from himself) as well as, implicitly, referring to the addressee of the poem – the reader. The abrupt collocation in the same line of 'otherness' and 'the exotic' suggests Szirtes' experience as an immigrant writer, resident within but not wholly belonging to the landscapes indicated in the poem, as well as his own sense of the otherness of England; the appearance of these landscapes within the poem, metonymically summarised into condensed images, constitutes the 'conjuring trick' of writing which is 'homely' precisely because it affords, within the familiar confines of language and literary traditions, kinds of accommodation for both Szirtes and the dedicatee of the poem, Sebald.

This assertion of writing as a space offering symbolic accommodation (which, as we shall see, is later elaborated as the closing assertion of 'Meeting Austerlitz'), establishes the affinity of the word as the underlying territory of the poem; names, sagging vowels, the narrator's desire to 'mouth the word that fits the case' and 'History's human noises' retrospectively assume deeper significance in the light of the poem's central assertion. The 'exotic', the outside of the familiar, located in significant end-focus, emphasises the embedded concern of the poem with the anomalous existence of the unfamiliar within the familiar, and expresses cogently the poem's sense of alienation from itself, its performance of the verbal 'conjuring trick' that constructs the landscape it analyses as a space from which poetry can be written. The poem itself becomes, in this reading, like the whole of *An English Apocalypse*, 'exotic' like the 'exotic' words in 'English Words', an 'outside' rendering of English mores and views, its carefully aesthetic formalism rubbing against the crumbling, eroded formlessness of the natural and social worlds it observes, a delicate poetic construction superimposed upon the exposed flat territories of decaying East Anglia.

The second half of the poem initially develops this 'exotic' dimension by focussing in sonnet 6 on 'A 1580s mural' (a figure of 'the writing on the wall', signifying the impending ending that preoccupies the whole sequence). Here Europe, in the form of 'a trace of Rubens', and wider histories in 'a touch, even, of Chinese / in the calligraphic lines', assert the possibility of re-reading the revealed, ancient, hybridity of a landscape and a culture that has, until now, appeared symbolically but irreducibly English. New forms of expression are encountered in the old, 'something far flung in the code / of a different language', but the significance is the same – the restoration of the mural is balanced by its depiction of 'Devastation'. As this modulates into the poem's extended critique of Conradian figures of empire ('New explorers come / out of the light to exploit the heart of darkness'), we return, as if on the homeward bound leg of a slow voyage, past the 'biblical' 'man with welded wings' (now more reminiscent of Icarus, and therefore of Greek rather than Biblical myth) in sonnet 8, into a cinematic image of 'The slow unravelling / of a long reel where everyone is travelling', an image that again foreshadows Szirtes' next collection, *Reel*.

Return thus becomes unravelling, the homeward journey also a decline into old age (and home is, implicitly, impending death and dissolution in 'the sea' of sonnet 11), as the next two sonnets summarise 'The old in their gerontopolis' and 'The dead fields in their last-gasp fantasy'. The poem works towards its conclusion through an insistent invocation of the word 'End!', a marking of England as the terminus of journeys (historical as well as geographical) from distant places that is also a question recognising the place shared by Szirtes and Sebald as one circumscribed, in the contemporary, by the possibility, in sonnet 11, of the (British) empire writing back:

> And what
> are you doing here, yes, you and your friend
> from Morocco, Uganda, St Kitts or Pakistan?
> Whatever has brought you to this far, flat
>
> kingdom with its glum farmers?

The answer to the question asked of the 'You' with its strange 'friends' is provided at the end of this sonnet: 'Homing. We are homing to the sea. Back / where we never were, at the end of the track', a return, the poem suggests, to non-existent, imagined origins implicitly located somewhere in history rather than geography, and an echo of the concluding 'Come hope. Come home' of 'Travel Book'. The concluding sonnet offers a lyrical summary of the persistent destructive forces of nature, of distance and proximity, of the confusion of sea and sky ('you could drown in sky / round here' it asserts, suggesting an illusory death by water) characteristic of flat, featureless landscapes that connotes the non-difference of death. 'Homing' is thus returning, a figure of the voyage towards death that ultimately grounds the allegory of 'Backwaters: Norfolk Fields' on a complex concluding figure of historical closure.

Home, then, is a territory made unfamiliar by historical processes that corrode a past seemingly traceable only in the meticulous observation of the residues of the past they leave surviving in the present, an illusory origin towards which the death drive, rendered as the force of historical movement, unconsciously pushes us. 'Backwaters' meditates on the relations between migration, belonging and death within a specific, poetically rendered geography, and on the potential of language and of the literary text to afford a symbolic version of residency within this geography – a posthumous, post-historical literary existence in the comforting space seemingly available in literature to writers like Szirtes and Sebald. If literature itself becomes, in this reading, a shared territory, criss-crossed by thematic repetitions and doubled concerns, then the asserted affinity between the two migrant writers serves to reinforce the potential of writing to respond to and, potentially, to alleviate, the experiential hostility of loneliness.

If 'Backwaters: Norfolk Fields' elegises an England in terminal decline, the title sequence of *An English Apocalypse* symbolises the causes of that decline, imagining apocalyptic destruction as the vehicle transporting England from its supposedly glorious past into its ignominious present. The sequence re-imagines the 'homeliness' of England, offering, in 'Preston North End', a crucial statement of identity and belonging that draws on earlier poems like 'Soil':

> I'm being bedded in –
> to what kind of soil remains a mystery,
>
> but I sense it in my marrow like a thin
> drift of salt blown off the strand. I am
> an Englishman, wanting England to win.
>
> I pass the Tebbitt test. I am Allan Lamb,
> Greg Rusedski, Viv Anderson, the boy
> from the cornershop, Solskjaer and Jaap Stam.

The 'Tebbitt test' (or 'cricket test') was a measure of national identification (if not identity) proposed by the Conservative MP and former minister Norman Tebbitt in 1990 to examine the allegiances of immigrant communities by asking them which national team they support. Allan Lamb and Greg Rusedski both qualified to represent England in their respective sports of cricket and tennis, despite being born abroad – Lamb in South Africa (a country banned, from 1970 to 1991, from participating in international sport due to its apartheid political system) and Rusedski in Canada. Viv Anderson was (in 1978) the first black footballer to play for the English national team. Solskjaer (Norwegian) and Stam (Dutch) have been distinguished players for England's most successful football team, Manchester United (which Szirtes supports). Englishness, the poem suggests, depends in part on who you identify with rather than who you are; 'I know King Priam. I have lived in Troy', the poem concludes, ironically relocating its deconstruction of English myths within the foundational myth of Western civilisation, the Homeric war with Troy.

The 'Apocalypse' poems offer visionary accounts of grand destruction as a kind of social comedy, rooted in historical fact. 'Death by Power Cut' seems to conflate the State of Emergency declared by Edward Heath's government in 1974 with the Blitz of 1940: 'The old would grin / and bear it. It was their finest hour. It weighed / on them like history'; 'Death by Meteor' draws on imagery derived from the apocalyptic films popular at the end of the millennium (like *Armageddon* [Michael Bay, 1998] and *Deep Impact* [Mimi Leder, 1998]); while 'Death by Suicide' is grounded in sociological statistics ('It began with the young men'). 'Death by Deluge' returns to the conceit of an earlier sonnet, 'Punctuation', in which the Norfolk landscape around Sheringham (site of another long poem in the next collection *Reel*) is constructed in terms of language: 'It was a matter of language. The glottal swell / of waves as its long tongue came pitching in / lapping at land'.

'Death by Deluge' sees the 'meaning' of the world coming to an end:

I have seen roads come to a full stop in mid-
sentence as if their meaning had fallen off
the world. And this is what happened, what meaning did
that day in August.

The control of the line endings here generates the poem's force: 'mid- / sentence' is also mid-phrase, an enjambment that enacts the curtailing of the roads it describes; 'fallen off / the world' repeats the trick, as the second line falls off into the next. Szirtes' *terza rima* exploits this potential in the form, using enjambment and end-stopping to suspend or conclude phrases, while the rhyme-scheme continues motifs and themes across stanzas. The poem oscillates between disjunction and interconnection, short and long sentences, complete and incomplete phrases, generating a world that is alternately fractured or re-patched together, in which, in a contradictory image in the final poem, 'The whole country seemed to float / like a vast web, unattached'.

Reel

Disconnection and displacement, the poet's sense of alienation within the 'transplanted' belonging he self-consciously adopts in 'Preston North End', are thus the emotional signifiers that prevail in *An English Apocalypse*. They are developed in the opening poems of his next collection, *Reel*, into a condensed exploration of origins and territories, combining Szirtes' personal experiences of history as enforced displacement with new modes of formal performance and new motifs of the visible and the visual. The collection is structured by three long sequences, offering a tripartite division of the experience of the *Reel* / 'real' in bodily ('Flesh: An Early Family History'), imaginary ('The Dream Hotel') and symbolic or narrated ('Accounts') terms; these are prefaced by four lyric-dialogic poems exploring different territories and spaces of experience, in which are established the dynamics of the collection as the new instalment of the coded autobiographies of Szirtes' late poetry – as 'Noir' asserts, 'There are secrets you keep / and secrets you don't yet know'. *Reel* won the 2004 T.S. Eliot Prize, making it Szirtes' most successful collection to date. Its poems are structured around the pun *Reel*/'real', where the former term bears a variety of meanings, each of which renders problematic memory's recording of past events. Foremost is the filmic resonance; the title-poem encounters Budapest being filmed as Berlin, East standing for West in a visual substitution that the poem offers as 'the Theatre of the Absurd'. *Reel* also explores the stunned consciousness rebounding (reeling) from contact with the real, and the wild dance of perceptions and signs that open the collection: 'You wake to car sounds, radios, the cold sunlight...'. Its key early poem is 'Meeting Austerlitz', an elegy for W.G. Sebald, which offers by contrast a slowed-down meditation on death through which to explore again the experience of the exile's accommodation in an adopted land.

'Meeting Austerlitz' enacts a familiar, symbolically Dantesque encounter, a descent into the underworld of the poet's memory in order to perform a work of mourning through the Odysseus-like consultation with a ghost. The poem's concerns extend from its own specific circumstances, its elegising of an individual death, through words and themes explored in many of Szirtes' other poems, and into the English poetic tradition, even as it memorialises a writer and memories largely separate from or 'grafted onto' that tradition, and only tangentially connected to its own movement. Where 'Backwaters: Norfolk Fields' contained its own rendering of (literary) history, displaced only momentarily into allusions to or echoes of displaced writers like the Polish Joseph Conrad and Sebald himself, in the later poem Szirtes asserts his own Hungarian origins and his own literary concerns as suitable analogies for the situation of Sebald's writing and his memory. The poem becomes an elegy for both self and 'other', a simultaneous exploration of a literary friendship and a shared series of encounters with the weight of literary tradition that transcends each individual writer. The poem's self-consciousness mourns its own past as well as the personal pasts of which it writes, where the representational media of writing and photography have offered, as they do throughout Szirtes' *œuvre*, analogous and often complementary, if distinct, technologies of remembrance. In 'Meeting Austerlitz' Sebald's death offers a figurative space in which Szirtes' memories are reworked through the remembered mediation of the other writer; a double dialogue is established, between the writers and between poem and tradition.

The poem was first published in the Norfolk-based poetry magazine *The Rialto*,[171] and subsequently appeared, in 2004, as the opening text in a major volume of critical essays on Sebald's works, where it functions as a poetic and critical meditation on Sebald, a text to introduce and accompany the more formally literary-critical and theoretical essays which follow. The editors of *W.G. Sebald: A Critical Companion* offer the following introductory comment on 'Meeting Austerlitz':

> This volume begins, rather unconventionally, with a poem... In the light of Sebald's untimely and shocking death, it offers a meditation on friendship, loss and memory. But it is also a lyrical engagement with Sebald's work; Szirtes takes up and develops the themes of walking and travel, employing similar techniques of allusion and quotation, and, like Sebald, embedding his philosophical speculations within a precisely delineated object-world.[172]

'Meeting Austerlitz' appears between this introductory chapter and the following critical discussions – it is, ultimately, neither introduction to nor commentary on Sebald's work, but instead both offers and occupies an in-between space in which that work is encountered by the work of another writer. The poem meditates on questions of culture and identity and their relations to difference and sameness; death figures the ultimate transformation from the possession of an identity to its loss, but also invests the dead with a different kind of identity, marking them as 'strange'.

'Meeting Austerlitz' opens in the solitary lyric world of the observer which is also the solitude of writing, the alienation of the writer, commenting on but seemingly excluded from the social world he observes. It works that social reality into a form in which his own solitude can be interrupted by the 'Meeting' which gives the poem its title, and which takes place in Section 1 'some way off the road', 'in the nearby fields', immediately linking this poem's geographical situation with the 'Norfolk Fields' of the earlier poem. This meeting-as-interruption opens up the poem's process of mourning, and leads to a series of remembered and imagined dramatic scenarios in which an extended conversation takes place between the two writers, where the voice of the dead writer, and the words of other texts he cites or alludes to, come to be heard and read within the written poem, transforming its lyric into a variety of narrated dialogue. These meetings and conversations construct, out of the poem's initial solitude, a writerly experience of imagined 'being-together', a connectedness in which the specificity of the self is momentarily compromised in acknowledgement of the other, a moment in which one aspect of identity, 'writer', with its sharing of literary traditions and forms, overrides other potential aspects of difference (nation, language, age). Solitude is thus the paradoxical condition of being accompanied, in writing, by that which is absent, which allows in turn the possibility of colloquy within and across texts; it is the shared experience of the exotic (again echoing the central theme of 'Backwaters: Norfolk Fields'), modulated into the experience of exclusion and exile, experiences simultaneously unique and common to both writers. Their imagined 'being-together' constructs a space outside of the social reality of the poem's opening section, a space 'both day and night,' as Austerlitz describes it in Section 1.

Sebald, an imagined figure renamed 'Austerlitz' after the eponymous figure who narrates the bulk of his final novel, provides a voice in the poem offering a commentary on the circumstances of the two writers' meeting, on the poet's work, on history (*'You can't explain / history to itself'*), and on names: *'But names are like dreams we disappear into / where all things seem to fit into the frame / of their narrative. It is names we journey through...'*. These themes of writing, history and names constitute the literary territory explored by Szirtes' poem, a territory whose specific features and contours he shares with Sebald, and which have already been mapped out in different ways in 'Backwaters: Norfolk Fields,' in particular in that poem's assertion of names (in sonnet 4) as traces of historical presence. Both writers have been displaced out of country, even out of language; both take the centrality of memory to the construction of imagined identities as a central concern, and both offer, in different ways, extended meditations on the experience of solitude that seems to characterise a particular configuration of recent European history and European literary modernity. Through Austerlitz's voice, we encounter parables of what the poem calls, in Section 2, 'the homeless / intellect', found here, in East Anglia, 'a long way from his birthplace' on a 'speculative journey / into melancholy'.

'Meeting Austerlitz' also locates itself within an English literary tradition of modern elegies, echoing in its title Wilfred Owen's 'Strange Meeting' (1918) and alluding, in its opening lines, to another familiar source-text for Szirtes' poetry, the opening of W.H. Auden's 'In Memory of W. B. Yeats' (1939), both poems by English writers addressing figures of other nationalities – the Irish poet Yeats, and Owen's 'one' who 'sprang up,' who, like Sebald, is German.[173] A comparison between Szirtes' poem and these significant precursors allows the complexities of 'Meeting Austerlitz' to become apparent, and establishes the extent of his poem's dialogue with its chosen tradition. Auden's poem famously opens 'in the dead of winter: / The brooks were frozen, the airports almost deserted,' lines echoed in Szirtes' opening lines: 'The cold sat down with frozen fingers. Cars / were iced up, the pavements were treacherous'; Auden's 'Snow disfigured the public statues' is revised and reversed by Szirtes' 'Perhaps we were statues and time would pass / leaving us unaltered'.

In a more complex way, Auden provides in his lines 'And the seas of pity lie / Locked and frozen in each eye,' a lexical and thematic link between Szirtes' work and Owen's famous assertion of 'The pity of war, the pity war distilled'. Auden's lines comment on human refusal and impotence in the face of the impending history which is the wider theme of his elegy for Yeats (and which retain a subtle ambiguity in the potential of 'lie' to connote 'untruthfulness' as well as reluctant or enforced passivity). The 'freezing' of 'pity' offers a condensed metaphor for the modernist mood of frustrated empathy or paralysed suffering – for Auden, the impotence of poetry in the face of history – that characterises the tradition to which Szirtes' poem belongs. This line of descent connects his own poetry and the writings of Sebald to the melancholy characteristic of modernist pessimism as experienced, in different ways, by Auden and Owen, in which frozenness usually connotes impotence and inability to act. In 'Meeting Austerlitz', reversing the sequence familiar from earlier poems, the present is iced up and the past, in those moments where it intrudes into the present as memory, is mobile, symbolised in the movement of Austerlitz's voice, defrosting the present. The metaphor for this is the image, a product of the 'Frozen motion. Blind field' Austerlitz relates in Section 5, quoting Szirtes quoting Barthes to himself. This 'frozen motion' melts, in the final section, into erotic images of silky fluidity, the movement of the image in the reels of cinema.

In contrast to this mobile conclusion, the poem's opening offers a world of illusory stasis, of repetitive activity expressed in clichéd language and actions, the annual repetition of Christmas as consumer festival in which 'The shops were a chorus / of seasonal favourites, every one the same,' and the same shops all stock 'the latest must-have toy / (each one expensive, every one alike)'. The narrator meets Austerlitz, with his 'droll / melancholy expression', on a terrain in which 'everything had a double or existed / in some version of itself wrapped in a winter cloak'. Against this backdrop of sameness and doubling, which offers a series of figures for the banality of contemporary consumer reality, occurs the specific event of difference which defies belief, the death of Austerlitz: 'I could not believe that Austerlitz was dead'. The stasis of death is thus, in an act of symbolic transference, translated into the repetition of existence; death becomes unique, an event outside of repetition, a frozen moment of specific inaction jarring with the debased, repetitive celebration of a birth that preoccupies the wider culture. Its unbelievable status is contrasted with other repetitive events, other deaths; Austerlitz is an other to the narrating self in this poem, but not, the poem argues, an 'other' the same as the relentless sameness of 'others': 'Though others had died that year', the poem states, 'his death was strange' (an ethically curious assertion, in the year of 9/11).

It is the 'strangeness' of this particular event, this specific death, which is the theme of Szirtes' meditation. Just as the meeting with Austerlitz is different, an encounter out of the ordinary, so his death marks this difference as significant, 'strange' in the initial sense that combines 'unfamiliar' and 'foreign'. The *Shorter Oxford English Dictionary* indicates the semantic richness and complexity, resonant in the context of Szirtes' usage, of this word by listing ten distinct but overlapping meanings for 'strange,' the first of which is 'Of or belonging to another country; foreign, alien'. Others significant in this context include 'Belonging to some other place or neighbour-hood', 'Belonging to others', 'Added or introduced from outside', 'Unknown, unfamiliar', and 'Distant or cold in demeanour'. Szirtes offers Sebald's death as multiply 'strange' in its conflation of all these different meanings, as being 'other' than the 'others' to which, in its strangeness, it would seem to belong. Like the poet's life in the shared historical and geographical spaces of 'Backwaters: Norfolk Fields,' death is 'exotic', introducing into 'Meeting Austerlitz' the absent presence of the exotic other as dead; death is 'distant or cold' in its frozenness, its strange difference from the otherness of the poem's alienating social reality.

These meanings of the 'distant', the 'belonging to others', ulti-mately extend, of course, to account also for Sebald and Szirtes and the shared experience that they have carried into England as 'strangers' themselves, writers living in England but nevertheless 'Belonging to some other place or neighbourhood', 'Added or introduced from outside' to the geographical-historical matrix that constitutes England and its language and literature. Sebald's 'strange' death thus affords space for a literary meditation on 'strangeness' that takes up the multiple implications of 'strange,' established already in the poem's allusion to Owen's 'Strange Meeting', itself an imagined encounter with the foreign and the dead – 'Strange friend', as Owen's narrator addresses his counterpart, oxymoroni-cally confusing familiar and unfamiliar in precisely the way Szirtes' poem seems to address Sebald. In 'In Memory of W.B. Yeats' Auden also uses the word 'strange', with the sense of 'unfamiliar' or 'out-of-place': 'Time that with this strange excuse / Pardoned Kipling for his views'. Strangeness is also the defining feature of the day of Yeats' death, and is present in synonymic form in Auden's poem: 'a day when one did something slightly unusual', Auden writes, a day on which the dead poet becomes 'wholly given over to unfamiliar affections'.

In the tradition of elegies into which Szirtes' poem inserts itself, death is an event intrinsically connected with strangeness, with being or becoming estranged from the familiar, and with the dis-tance pertinent to that which has become unfamiliar – to die is to become strange, to be strangely estranged. At the same time, death, 'Meeting Austerlitz' insists, is canonically and traditionally familiar, an event and theme repeated across generations of elegies, recur-rent yet unique in its specificity, immediate to each poet as an ele-ment of individual, unique experience, and at the same time con-stituting a shift in reality that challenges 'belief'. Szirtes' meditation on Sebald's death explores these connections and contradictions through the juxtaposition of images of stasis with those of movement, the familiar with the unfamiliar, and ultimately in the opposition between loss and hope which, 'Meeting Austerlitz' implies, characterises the poetic space in which such a 'Meeting' can take place.

Contrasting its dominant mood of frozenness, Szirtes' poem offers movement in recurring clouds of breath, smoke and ash, ambivalent signifiers of both life and death. Sebald's writing is remembered in these terms:

> A puff of dust from the library,
> swirling like ashes, had settled across his prose,
> its flavour tart, magical and scholarly.

The collocation of 'dust' and 'ashes' implies burial and death even as its 'swirling' re-establishes motion in writing, in the movement between 'library' and 'prose.' If this is balanced by the stasis of 'settled', the ambiguity of the word re-introduces migration and settling as embedded themes of Szirtes' meditation, opening again the space of writing as offering a potential accommodation to the migrant writer. Further echoes and allusions reinforce the literary tradition as homely territory. '*We can distil / our terrors and make them hang like a grey mist / beyond the garden*', Austerlitz notes in Section 3, echoing Owen's 'pity war distilled'; at the end of Section 3, 'He breathed out and the air stood still / before it vanished slowly like a ghost'. In the first section,

> The air was frosty, oddly tobacco-scented,
> thick grey clouds rose from his mouth as he spoke.
> I could not be certain whether the wisps that entered
> my mouth were frozen breath or cigarette smoke.

The strange figure of the transience of exterior intimacy offered by shared breath, 'frozen' but balanced by the implicit heat of 'cigarette smoke', momentarily connects the two writers, as does the expression of hope in poem's concluding section. 'Whatever hope is yours', writes Owen in 'Strange Meeting', 'was my life also': 'Meeting Austerlitz', following this declaration of shared aspiration, ends in 'the Esperia Hotel in Athens', returning to a similar mode of second person address through which we are informed of 'The name / of the hotel, which, as you know, means hope'. The poem refers in its conclusion to a photograph of a girl with a doll and a dog, an image discussed (and asserted as being from the drowned Welsh village of Llanwddyn) and reprinted in Sebald's *Austerlitz* as one symbol (among many others in that narrative) of how lost things persist in images and writing, becoming, the narrator asserts, 'as familiar to me as if I were living with them down at the bottom of the lake'.[174] The metaphor of the 'Esperia Hotel', along with the extended ekphrastic description of this photograph of 'the young girl in the garden', close Szirtes' elegy, establishing the literary dialogue between himself and Sebald that constitutes the poem itself as an attempt to transcend death through art. These metaphors also rework, in relation to Szirtes' familiar imagery of the frozen and the fluid, the drowned and the saved, the tropes of hope and home that preoccupy the poems in *Reel*.

The closing assertion of 'Meeting Austerlitz', then, is borrowed from Sebald and cements the dialogic relation between Szirtes' poem and the narrative from which Sebald's poetic persona is taken. This dialogic relation constitutes the shared experiences of the strange becoming familiar and of identity within difference encountered by the two writers, establishing the shared, estranging but familiar territory of memory and its resurrections in various forms of representation as a common theme, as the space within which each writer can potentially find a self. Szirtes' closing section makes use of poetry in ways analogous to *Austerlitz*'s use of photography, to 'unfreeze' the frozen or fixed memory and to explore its resonances in relation to experiences of exile and displacement. Where 'Backwaters: Norfolk Fields' establishes English spaces and histories as territories of contradictory, shared experiences of inclusion and exclusion, 'Meeting Austerlitz' shifts its focus onto the elements of English poetic tradition in order to seek out a space within which Szirtes can poetically express these experiences. Both constitute major poems in Szirtes' œuvre, offering long, complex poetic meditations on its central themes of identity, belonging, displacement and alienation. Both poems work to reconcile the themes of memory and hope, word and image, living and dying within the space of literature, offering, in the final lines of 'Meeting Austerlitz', the metaphorical hotel of hope as a temporary accommodation for the estranged, migrant writer, a momentary residing in a strange, foreign tongue and in its literary traditions.

This symbolic accommodation, a residency in language and literary traditions, structures the poems in *Reel*. The collection's central sequence extends the metaphor of the 'Hotel Esperia' into 'The Dream Hotel', and offers a series of metaphors for the experience of exile, its relations to the writing of poetry, and its traces in and influences on memory, history and autobiography. Szirtes finds, in what in the sequence's concluding poem 'Shoulder' is anxiously defined as 'the space of the word', an accommodation that can, in its non-fixity, its fluid, linguistic instability, effectively mimic the experiences of displacement and exile that constitute the poet's past, and account for his present. Szirtes' figurations of exile and theorisations of migration and diaspora in these poems explore a historically specific, European experience of displacement as a foundational encounter with the loss of foundations, as a displacement which both erases and prioritises place and placelessness, and as the enforced undergoing of a movement which finds its expression in the 'static' forms of poetry and in the voided space of the word, in which, as it's put in 'Dead Sea Sonnets', 'The dead / sing'.

'Shoulder', a complex and despairing appeal to the muse, offers a way into *Reel*'s exploration of the eccentric experience of mid-century Hungarian displacement. The poem's palpable angst, its howl of anguish, is also its initiation of a movement out of the world of 'The Dream Hotel' towards the ordered sequence of language, which the poet despairs of attaining: 'Am I capable of writing / or thinking or feeling the space of the word?' The poem's response to this alienated anxiety is to offer impersonation and imitation, its own version of the desire to enter into and find a home within the poetic tradition. It performs the 'singing' of 'the language of life', which is also, and ambiguously, both 'not my language' and yet the language of poetry, 'uninterpreted / And therefore incomprehensible and yet singing'. The poem (echoing *An English Apocalypse*) is aware of its historical belatedness, its displacement in time, and of the simultaneous persistence of historical traumas in the present: 'It is late', we are told, and yet, 'it is still the same'. 'It' here refers to language itself, and part of the problem, the poem implies, is language's constant struggle to represent historical difference, the present tense engaging with the past.

'Shoulder' shares with 'Meeting Austerlitz' the territory of the literary tradition, appropriating a Romantic rhetoric of lyrical creation. It marks the closure of 'The Dream Hotel' sequence as an entry into symbolic (rather than imaginary or 'dream') space – the world of the collection's final sequence, 'Accounts', a world of reckoning and of narrating histories. In this world, we're informed in 'Shoulder', the poet 'can hear people speaking'. The reciprocal relation established by speech (like the imagined conversation in 'Meeting Austerlitz') cements entry into the social world, a movement from the mythical time of the 'Goddess' into the ordered sequence of everyday temporality, 'the days of my life'. As we shall see, this symbolic arrival, expressing a desired closure to the experience of migrancy, is re-enacted from the perspective of childhood in 'My father carries me across a field'. In 'Shoulder', the poet's exile from 'the space of the word' seems absolute, and embodies the experience of exile itself as a fundamental exclusion from the familiarity of language – 'my language, this language' – that would afford appropriate symbolic accommodation in what is called, in the next poem, 'Retro-Futuristic', 'a space among illusions'.

Like the symbolic awakenings that structure *Reel* from the collection's opening line ('You wake to car sounds...'), the recurrent symbolic deferral-as-arrival signifies the marginal, dispersed centrality to the movement of exile of a dislocated experience of subjectivity. The poet's Whitmanesque desire in 'Shoulder' is to 'sing the body' and, in doing so, to resist such a dispersal, by locating poeticised experience at the level of the physical. It is also a compromised poetic urge towards aesthetic purity (a Romantic urge to lyrical beauty), fatally tempered by history ('The usual business of war' which goes on 'uninterrupted', echoing 'uninterpreted' language) and by the relentlessly mundane, in which 'the weather goes on'. The body, in turn, resists appropriation for such a pure aesthetic purpose: elsewhere it provides the collection's recurrent metaphors of the brutality of historical truth, in the opening sequence 'Flesh: An Early Family History', or 'the shit, blood, semen smell of mortality' in 'Rough Guide'. More menacingly, these are the body's remaindered accoutrements, laden with historical import, remaining as traces of bodies and peoples which have themselves been violently and tragically dispersed: in the fifth poem of 'Decades', we encounter again such a list of residual items signifying the horror of the Holocaust – 'folded spectacles, shoes, gold teeth'.

In concluding 'The Dream Hotel' sequence, 'Shoulder' offers a summary allegory of the sequence's specific concern with the historical burden of the expression of exile in poetry. This concern is central to the collection as a whole. It reiterates what the sequence's opening poem, also called 'The Dream Hotel', calls 'the form of the dream' and its re-awakening of the past as 'Some vague, dim recollection', as alluring to the exiled poet as 'The song of the sirens'. In 'Siren Voices', a poem published in *Metro*, Szirtes wrote of 'the old song / of Europe and the philanderer', which 'The sirens sang and held the world together'. The poet's desire, in 'Shoulder', to emulate the sirens and to 'sing' what the French critic Maurice Blanchot calls 'a song still to come', is also the urge to repeat the sirens' song that, Blanchot writes, 'guides the sailor towards that space where singing would really begin'.[175] It offers poetry and its traditions as the space of the 'dream hotel' itself, a symbolisation of memory and history in which every guest-poet is an exiled subject, seeking a song and a language that would offer a means of escape from the experience of displacement that characterises exile. The 'song still to come' that would comprise Szirtes' poetic analysis of the unanswerable questions posed to the migrant by history is also, of course, the collection itself, *Reel* as the 'Real' of historical trauma inscribed upon the 'stage' or 'page' of historical experience. The sequence of Decades that comprises part of the concluding section of *Reel* expresses in condensed, semi-cryptic form this traumatic 'real' that constitutes the barely-contained historical material of Szirtes' analysis, the horror of the Jewish diasporas of the first half of the twentieth century.

Szirtes has written of his sense of a shared identity of Eastern-European-ness:

> As exiles (to employ the romantic term) we are not particularly nostal-gic about places or historical circumstances, though nostalgia for a certain spontaneous intimacy flickers in us and at times even singes us a little.[176]

Exile, in this pseudo-'romantic' formulation, is a shared experience of separation and of the loss of intimacy, a sharing of the burden of division. Its encoding within poetry affords a double alleviation, allowing it to be expressed and shared anew. Such expression and sharing, in turn, offers poetry up to the forces of historical exigency. The 'spontaneous intimacy' remembered here is akin to what Szirtes describes, in the 'Preface' to *The Budapest File*, as 'the intimate spaces arising from the no-man's-land of childhood memory'.[177] The expression of such 'intimate spaces' in poetry, an aim essential to Szirtes' extended project, repositions them outside of the subjective space of memory, documented in 'the space of the word' which is simultaneously within and without, the essential, in-between experience of solitude that embodies exile.

Exile and escape – the escape afforded by poetry from the alienation of homelessness, and poetry's offering, within the exile symbolised by residency in the 'dream hotel', 'the sense of home as a distant speck' – configure Szirtes' poetic ambiguities in particular ways. Such configuration allows the expression of tensions between memory and desire which are reified, ultimately, in the identification, in *Reel*'s title poem, of the space of exile as 'the heart of the exotic / Which is only a transferred idea of home'. Szirtes' concern is with what, in 'Meeting Austerlitz', he calls 'the home-less / intellect', an intellectual condition of 'émigré consciousness' shared with Sebald and other post-memorial writers of twentieth-century European histories. Edward Said refers to the contemporary relocation of the creative forces of Western culture in what he calls 'its unhoused, decentred and exilic energies whose incarnation today is the migrant'.[178]

The diagnoses of this exilic relocation produced by Szirtes, Sebald and others in their writings share many characteristics with Paul Gilroy's analysis of Black diasporas. In Gilroy's formulation, the process of reification of the space of exile is also a process of re-definition and reaffirmation of historical experience that takes place in and through history:

> What was initially felt to be a curse – the curse of homelessness or the curse of enforced exile – gets repossessed. It becomes affirmed and is reconstructed as the basis of a privileged standpoint from which certain useful and critical perceptions about the modern world become more likely.[179]

The experience of the translation from home into exile, and exile's repossession' and 'affirmation' as a new configuration of 'homeliness', constitutes a central element of *An English Apocalypse* and *Reel*. The strategic and contradictory conflation in 'Reel' of the 'exotic' with 'home' is, for Szirtes, the exile's response to what the title-poem calls the 'peculiar imperative' of the experience of displacement, its determination by uncontrollable historical forces; it also offers a figure for the surreal domesticity that has been the territory of much of his poetry. The 'English holiday town' of 'Reel', the 'fishing port' 'time blew me to' (the force of history here symbolised as a natural agency, like the storm of 'Drawing the Curtain' in *Bridge Passages*), is both home and destination, the exile's temporary residence, from which other symbolic movements – 'bits of flotsam' – can be monitored, fuelling the progress of the poem. In the filmic reality of 'Reel', present and past mingle inseparably: just as exile is a form of home, so 'Today', the poem asserts in homage to Auden's Spain, 'is history'. Movement and migration between geographical and historical spaces continually clash with conflicting desires for stasis (embodied in Szirtes' recurrent metaphor of the 'frozen') and for 'home', whether that home be geographical or, more likely, metaphorical, in language, say, or in the coded intimacies afforded by familiarity with literary traditions.

Szirtes is acutely aware in these poems of temporality as the burden of the (post) modern poet, and of the poet's responsibility to render it in words. In the four interlinked sonnets of 'Silver Age', a poem expressly concerned (as are so many of the poems in *Reel*) with the subject's awakening from the romanticised childlike unreality of the dream into a debased reality which permits only the dream's memory, form allows the expression of the alarming sense that poetry (here the dream itself, housed in the 'hotel' of language) momentarily reduces the entirety of the past to 'images and nothing more'. The spatialisation of remembered experience in the image and its 'nothing more' is, however, repudiated in the poem's closing assertion of writing itself as a redemptive act, resisting the 'nothing more' with the apparently immediate, Heaney-esque presence of the written word: 'And so time passed, down to the very minute / I write these thoughts down with my adult pen'. However, this immediacy, the inexorable flow of temporality, is immediately pinned down by the fixity of writing, by the poem itself; the dialectic of past and present constructs the future that is only the poem's existence. 'Silver Age' enacts the agon of past and present through such shifts of focus, drawing the world of events back to the poet's self-possession within self-reflexivity, and offering, in compensation for the disappearance of the past, the space of writing as the territory upon which exiled, transient identities can find some illusory mooring.

Reel combines familiar and insistent motifs, including childhood experience, migration, and parental authority, within the 'field' of poetic mediation, which, for Szirtes, performs in its linguistic and ideological indeterminacy a double function. It constructs a specific, intermediate space of exile, a marginal linguistic, historical and ideological 'field'. For the Hungarian and English Szirtes it offers a position of 'double-consciousness' which allows the poet to perform, through such objectifying, extrinsic aesthetic devices as montage, fragmentation and juxtaposition, the internal, intrinsic 'movements' of meaning that delineate memories and histories within the conditions of belonging and exile.

The 'no-man's-land of childhood memory', the specific memorial 'field' that motivates so much of Szirtes' poetry, finds powerful expression in a short but important poem in *Reel*, 'My father carries me across a field'. Here Szirtes revisits, through the recollection of memories, dreams, and imaginings, the enforced migration of the eight-year-old boy and his family from Hungary in 1956, in order to explore the remembered experience of border crossing in terms of a narrative of displacement. It allegorises the experience of exile as, in its foundation, the experience of passive movement, of being carried by forces beyond the child's comprehension but embodied in the figure of the father. Exile, in the poet's memory of movement, is as inexorable as paternal Law and the law of historical demand: 'we go where we have to go'.

The imperative of history is, simultaneously, history's erasure, its replacement by the limitless 'field' of the 'present' of memory.

Edward Said quotes Adorno's assertion that 'the past life of émigrés is annulled',[180] an erasure Szirtes figures in a snowy field and 'a blank page', awaiting the inscription of 'the song to come', the poem of the future towards which the child-poet moves. The past reclaimed by the poem – its enactment in the poem's movement from the security of connection with the father to the 'dread' of displacement – encounters a historical limit in the absence of a space that pre-exists the 'field' of the poem itself. The time that 'passed' in 'Silver Age' is here again spatialised, reified as the 'field' across and within which the drama of subjectivity – the poet's coming-into-being – is repeated. Exile is thus a repeated experience of multiple, re-enacted migrations, displacements, separations, and dislocations from one's past, one's family and one's self, as well as a movement towards an unknown future, 'something frightening I don't yet know'.

The 'field' of this poem is simultaneously geographical, historical, linguistic, ideological, cultural and national. It is the field of non-identity, the space (the 'no-man's-land) between nations (on the Austro-Hungarian border); the field of the present as a battle between past and future ('There are trenches filled with snow') and therefore of social conflict and discord; a field empty and yet 'filled', 'field' and 'filled' offering near anagrams of each other to signify doubly the voided emptiness of the remembered experience and its momentary plenitude in the act of symbolising it. The 'field' is constructed and defined by the process of distancing and spacing ('And then there is space between /...us'), a process of differentiation allowing the emergence of the poet's subject position, mapped out on the fields of language, memory and familial relations. The poem's territory is a deformed space, neither Real nor *Reel*, encoded only in its existence as the subject of the exile's movement across, neither towards nor from. It is the neutral, 'in-between' field of memory, a 'no-man's-land of childhood memory' paradoxically populated by 'the four of us' and always susceptible to simplifying narratives, the child's versions of the past, that seek to account for its uncanniness by rendering it as a 'fairytale' space 'where the owl blinked / and the ass spoke'.

It is, ultimately, a space of death, across which the subject moves 'towards my own extinction', inaugurating the movement from the 'dread' it inspires, to the possibility of a writerly response that would produce 'images and nothing more' within 'the space of the word'. 'Dread' is central to the poem, and central to its experience, as is the 'following' that the poet performs 'in dread'. This 'following' produces, at the simplest level, the poem itself. The 'dread' of Szirtes' poem (which resurrects the 'dread' of the mother's historical experience in 'Portrait of My Father in an English Landscape', investing it with a new dimension of personal significance) is intimately connected to 'the space of the word' of the poem itself, in which exile's condition comes to expression; it is also, implicitly, the dread of writing itself, the writer's obligation to fill 'the blank page' of the exile's history.

The poem offers an account of Szirtes' dispersed subjectivity, emerging and embodied in narratives of movement that leave behind their own groundings and find only new displacements in symbol and metaphor, the 'field' of poetry. This 'ghostly scene', working within the extended rhetorical conceits of the collection, offers spectrality and self-spectatorship as conditions and actions that render the poet's entry into the symbolic as performed, like exile itself, upon the 'stage' of history. The ghostly presences of the Real in the reels of *Reel*, of the child-self within the adult self (*Reel* is dedicated 'To the ghost of childhood and the body of the adult'), of 'true' history within the uncertain memories and narratives of the past, indicate the complex, unstable status of Szirtes' experiences of exile in relation to their subsequent remembering in poetry. The poem insists on the uncertain present and the unknown future, erasing the drama of its historical grounding to leave only 'a blank page' and 'a stage', the performativity of representation awaited, at the end of the poem, as a promised redemption. 'My father carries me across a field' is *Reel*'s most explicit assertion of the centrality of exile to Szirtes' experience of writing. The poems in *Reel* circulate around this poem's themes, and are documents of the nomadic demands of the space of the word, articulating in their movement between different 'migrant metaphors'[181] the poet's experience of exile.

Reel extends powerfully Szirtes' exploration of the double poetic function of constructing the field of writing and (re-)enacting his own subjective trajectory across it. It confirms as central to his poetic project the establishment of a consolidated 'émigré consciousness', a 'frozen' condition of exile specific to his own historical displacement. Szirtes' work exemplifies the exiled writer's production of what Said calls 'hybrid counter-energies, at work in many fields',[182] including, perhaps, the 'field', the 'dark and frozen ground' Szirtes crossed as a child, carried by his father, fifty years ago. For Szirtes, family, language and identity merge within the 'field' of poetry, which is traversed by the traces of exilic histories, 'lost figures who leave only a blank page / Behind them'.

8

New poems

> Words are inanimate blocks full of sound and fury,
> signifying nothing; blocks and stones and worse than
> senseless things.
>
> GEORGE SZIRTES,
> T.S. Eliot Lecture, 23 November 2005

An English Apocalypse and *Reel* summarise the concerns of a poetic career that now spans four decades. Their central themes – poetry's basis in detailed observation of the world, the exploration of memory and perception and of the connections between the written and the visual, the relations between contemporary and historical experience, the traces of history in the landscapes and cultural features of the modern world – embody the self-conscious calling to 'account' of a career that has conducted, within clear and progressive formal and stylistic parameters, a sustained enquiry into some of the fundamental questions and defining events of modern European experience. The importance of Szirtes' poetry resides, ultimately, in this dimension of his work, in that it adds to the English traditions with which it engages a distinctly European slant, a "take" on an experience of modern European history to which conventional English poetry can only ultimately respond indirectly. Szirtes is rightly circumspect about his status as an 'English' poet, but his contribution to 'English' traditions (which, subject to critical scrutiny, reveal themselves, in poems like 'Backwaters: Norfolk Fields', increasingly to be hybridical products of 'external', imported influences) needs to be stressed; his poetry adds a crucial European dimension to the inflections, language, and formal range of contemporary English poetry, enriching it in ways that suggest potential lines of development in the future.

Szirtes' poetry ultimately addresses the possibility of transcending the 'in-between-ness' of historical and cultural circumstances that has to a greater or lesser extent determined his identity, through the discovery, imposition or revelation of interconnections between moments, things, people and perceptions. The discovery of interconnections is the reward for the intense verbal and intellectual engagement with the visible world that preoccupies the

entire *œuvre*; their imposition is achieved through the strict adher-
ence to formal constraints that effect interconnection through struc-
tures that pattern perceptions and events, and through repetition
that allows consistencies to emerge; and their revelation arrives in
the form of sublime moments of perception, sometimes religious
in impulse, often profoundly aesthetic in effect, that punctuate the
drives to documentary and verisimilitude that are the demands to
which a poet of historical responsibility must inevitably respond.
'In-between-ness' becomes, in the most powerful moments of
achieved interconnection, simply a positional effect, an instinctive
self-definition; elsewhere, of course, it determines the positions
from which Szirtes' poetic analyses can be pitched.

   The consistencies and repetitions of the *œuvre* make it possible to
identify and summarise the key features of a typically "Szirtesian"
mode or "style" of poetic production, a set of characteristic features
which embodies all the styles and mannerisms of his work. This
might be summarised as follows: a sometimes aloof but hesitant,
often implicated, narratorial position, viewing or otherwise experi-
encing events and perceptions that require constant decoding or
translating, utilising the structures offered by poetic form to impose
a kind of order upon the threatening chaos of the world, and find-
ing within that chaos moments of profound beauty as evidence of
another, ultimately divine, order in the real, and employing recur-
rent motifs, tensions or positions to negotiate, elucidate and sym-
bolise that order. These latter include the 'frozen' and the fluid,
the in-between, the compromised pastoral mode in tension with
an awareness of the symbolic significance of the city to modern
cultural experience, the struggle with the evasiveness of historical
truths and memories, the difficulties of explaining or otherwise
representing images in words, and the difficulties presented by
words themselves in their double functions of communication and
representation. Further recurrent aspects would include a relent-
less scrutiny of the nature and truth of personal and family mem-
ories in relation to the wider narratives that comprise national and
international histories, and in the context of the major events
affecting Hungarians and Jews in the mid-twentieth century. Add
to this a tendency to use a defamiliarising continuous present tense
and, by contrast, a habit of addressing reader and self simultane-
ously by a familiarising 'you', and a modernist proclivity for func-
tional allusiveness to a wide cultural range encompassing the arts
of photography and painting, music and film, as well as literature,
and the broad parameters of a "typical" Szirtes poem begin to
emerge.

As his lattermost collections indicate, Szirtes' work is increasingly concerned with making poetry (defined, in the first of 'Three Pieces for Puppetry' in *Reel*, in terms alluding to Cézanne, Matisse and Pound, as 'the formal dance of the wild, / news which stays news') a medium in which to explore issues and experiences impinging on notions of belonging and identity, and in which to express and analyse a persistent longing for identity that in turn inflects all the other themes noted above with meanings that are pointed and poignant. Szirtes' location between nations and languages, his archaeological exploration of his origins in pasts and histories that no longer 'belong', in any simple sense, to him, even his artistic development as a trained artist shifting to poetry, place particular burdens of significance on the trope of the 'in-between' in his poetry and critical writings and relate it closely (as will be discussed below) to issues of translation. His tendency, as his career develops, towards the long poem or the sequence, rather than the short lyric, implies a formal reliance on aesthetic volume as a symbolic corollary of 'in-between-ness', a situating of the poem somewhere between the immensity of historical sequence and process and the sublime aesthetic experience of the present moment; the long poem attempts to encompass history and narratives of self and becoming within frames that announce the lyric mode, with its localised intensities of perception and representation, as the bearer of such narratives.

'In-between-ness' suggests, furthermore, a problematic form of presence-in-absence, a sense of being and yet not being present to the world one inhabits, a dislocation that produces ambivalence, ambiguity and uncertainty as its defining conditions. Szirtes' poetry resides, in this non-positioning, somewhere in the middle of the superficially competing traditions (which are further historical narratives) of English Romantic and modernist verse. It recurrently constructs the natural world as surrealistically charged with oddities that demand careful scrutiny and reward it with bizarre, poetically effective juxtapositions and images; and it envisions human history and, in particular, the city as infernal spaces characterised by depths into which the poet-narrator descends, like a troubled hero of ancient myth, in search of insight and comprehension, drawing on modernist perceptions of history and the city as interconnected spaces, repositories (as we have seen in *Metro* and *The Photographer in Winter*) of memories accrued through time.

Time, encountered in the experience of temporal processes, and the desire for the poetic moment of beauty to transcend these processes, underpins the "situatedness" of Szirtes' poetry. In 'My father, crawling across the floor' (in *Reel*) the location of the child in time is presented as 'forever in an endless Now, / Except in dreams, anxieties, and school', a figuring of temporality (echoing the repeated 'nows' that punctuate the poems in *Bridge Passages*) that allows its permanence to co-reside within its transience, and emphasises psychological elements of human perception as registers of temporal change. Underneath his insistent concern with images and words lurks this anxiety about time: the insistent motif of the 'frozen' or 'fixed', like the rigidity of poetic form, always only appears intransigent, masking and barely containing the endless and potentially uncontainable flux of historical (temporal) change that pre-occupies the unconscious of the poems. Szirtes' interest in the 'ghosts of form' reveals this underlying concern; form is potentially intangible, a residual trace of an order sought continually in the present moment of perception, and equally continually confronted and compromised by the movement implicit in that moment.

'Desire', the 'undersong' of 'Metro', drives Szirtes' poetry. *Reel*'s dedication 'To the ghost of childhood and the body of the adult' (that 'ghost' again evoking temporality, mortality and the trace of the past in the present) grounds that collection's poems on the terrain of personal experience and family narratives, inscribed upon 'the body of the adult' as narratives and remembered events (transformed and transforming) from the past. Melding together time, the traces left by historical events, and their inscription on the adult body, his work offers poetry as a sounding of the desire to know and to understand. Desire is also an expression of the experience of lack – a desire to return to a condition of completeness or unity that, the poetry sometimes speculates, may have been available in a semi-mythic, semi-historical time that predates the eruption of 'real' history in 1956, or, more problematically, the 'discovery' that that 'real' history was already, in a sense, a repetition, of even more traumatic historical events – the War, the Holocaust – pre-dating the poet's birth, and utterly resistant to adequate poetic responses or assimilations. But, at the same time, the desire to 'return' to such moments in the imaginary effort performed by the poem is also an expression of the fear of the horror of history; to return is also to re-awaken this horror, and Szirtes' poetry harnesses formal disciplines and aesthetic intensities in its attempts to negotiate these contradictory impulses.

These potential mythic pasts seem only available in the form of excavated fragments, further traces of the past to be pieced together by the aesthetic imperatives of poetic form. At its most urgent, in the fraught, sinister and menacing poems responding to European and personal events of the late 1980s and early 1990s, Szirtes' work finds in its forms and its syntax a mode of expressing this sense of the impossibility of full expression. His poetry becomes in these moments a kind of testimony, a post-memorial marker of the duty of the poet to witness and to offer reparation. Clair Wills, summarising her discussion of Paul Muldoon's poetry, suggests that it can be read as concerned with 'breaking things';[183] Szirtes, in contrast, is almost always concerned with building and repairing things that have already been broken by the violence of history, and with making poetic form a container in which the possibility of repairing of damaged pasts might be explored.

A major dimension of this conception of poetry as constructive in the face of a destructive vision of history involves the assessment, and sometimes the assimilation, of lessons learned by other poets. Szirtes' reviews and introductions provide a significant forum in which his own ideas about this possibility of poetry are explored through responses to and evaluations of the work of other poets. As with all poets who write criticism, his readings and evaluations of other writers often offer insights into his own poetic practices and intentions. When he writes, for example, of Ágnes Nemes Nagy's prose poems, that 'their mystical, surreal, intellectual dis-locations are nevertheless an attempt to discover a valid structure, the principle that holds things together',[184] the description surely reflects also on what Szirtes sees as common territory between Nemes Nagy's poetry and his own. The 'regimentally disciplined freedoms' he finds in Nemes Nagy's work contrast with what he calls, discussing Ottó Orbán's poetry, 'the delights of pure form',[185] suggesting ways of thinking about Szirtes' own reliance on form as a means to a disciplined freedom that simultaneously affords a kind of 'delight', a meticulous completion of a given aesthetic pro-ject. Similarly, in discussing the work of Zsuzsa Rakovszky, he writes of 'the formal structure' which 'serves to discipline the strong waves of feeling that roll through her poetry'. Summarising the kind of modal and stylistic counterpointing of formal struc-tures with loose, fractured or informal language that characterises his own poetry, he notes a similar tension in Rakovszky: 'despite the elaborate forms, she is essentially informal'.[186]

These critical descriptions of the works of other modern Hun-garian writers suggest that Szirtes develops through his career an increasing awareness of the proximity of his own themes and styles to those of writers in Hungary, a proximity that subtly alters the initial connections (explored in Chapter 2 above) between his work

and that of writers working in English. This double inheritance
makes Szirtes' position virtually unique in contemporary British
poetry, an Eastern European poet writing in English, melding
together the apparently inherent but discrete, complementary sur-
realisms that comprise English cultural life, the vestiges of memo-
ries of a Budapest childhood and the sense of 'in-between-ness'
that has characterised and dynamised his adult career. Writing of
the Russian poet Andrei Voznesensky, Szirtes identifies 'touches of
surrealism and a broad emotional (sometimes sentimental) sweep'
that 'suggest a more politicised version of early Marc Chagall'.[187]
We recall that Szirtes described his own early paintings to John
Tusa as the works of a 'Chagallian painter', and find again that note
of identification, carefully positioning the reviewing self between
the body of work of the reviewer and the text under review, in
order to allow each momentarily to refract off the other.

Szirtes' offers the most cogent and penetrating self-commentary
on his work in an interview given in 2001 to the Romanian critic
Lidia Vianu (which has been alluded to elsewhere in this book).
Vianu, too, relates Szirtes' work to that of Chagall ('I have often
thought of Chagall when reading your verse'), but the main drive
of her questions is to interrogate the position of the poetry in
relation to the histories that make up the poet. She describes
Szirtes' work as 'a gentle dystopia', containing a 'secret' of 'past
death' (an important insight that will be addressed further below);
she asks direct and sharp questions: 'Where exactly do you belong,
where do you feel at home?'; 'How come your poetry never flares
against...injustice, just registers it in whispers?' Szirtes' responses
articulate and flesh out many of the positions expressed in his
poetry. His comments on England reveal a deep ambivalence tra-
versed by conflicting experiences of tolerance and exclusion:

> I feel the typical patriotism of the immigrant. I am fiercely defensive of
> England. At the same time I recognise I am not of it nor will ever en-
> tirely be so. I want to love the people and the land and the history and
> the culture and I am partially successful in this. At the same time there
> is much that I do not like and feel limited by. I regret its caution, its em-
> piricism, its insularity, its class system, its leadenness, its general middle
> greyness. But it is also the country of eccentric, of mad heroic projects,
> of extraordinary inventions, or remarkable tolerance. And it offers and
> continues to offer safe harbour and stability to many, including myself.

The 'partial success' barely compensates for the prevailing sense
of not fully belonging, a position of which Szirtes' poetry is some-
times perhaps painfully aware in its recourse to Hungarian and
other European identifications.

The desire ('I want to love') presses against a forbidding reality that there is much not to love; Szirtes' late poetry, dealing as it does with an England belated, almost posthumous in its historical situation, seeks European forms (*terza rima*, sonnets, sestinas) that point it in a new, continental, direction. Earlier in the interview with Vianu, Szirtes comments that 'I cannot write the songs of the tribe. I feel excluded from it'; he extends this exclusion from the English 'tribe' to a declaration of identification with poets like 'Brodsky and Hecht and Fenton in England' because 'They were also Europeans, and I am, I think, above all, a European. All that is good and all that is evil reside for me in the heart of Europe.' Such a careful, modulated identification, positioning the self in relation to the traditions of displaced writing (Brodsky and Hecht are not English; Fenton's Englishness incorporates his own experiences of travel in the far east in the 1970s) that would constitute an alternative, partly-submerged but increasingly visible narrative of a Europe of migrant identities and harbourings (evident in the phrase 'heart of Europe', with its careful Conradian echo), suggests a deep-seated awareness of the loss of a past, a language and a culture that can only ever be partially regained, in the fragmentary lists of historical and cultural detritus that punctuate poems like 'Metro'.

At the same time these poems display an increasing willingness to exploit the contemporary dialects or 'songs' of the tribe, in their recourse to the clichés and hackneyed phraseology of modern English idiom – for example (and most persistently), in the opening stanzas of 'Meeting Austerlitz', where we find 'iced up', 'the pavements were treacherous', 'every one the same', 'jollying ourselves up', 'no sense of shame', 'all good intentions', and so on, a list of conventionalised utterances that mark out in extreme terms the recurrent banality of the time of year – Christmas – against which, as we've seen, the 'strangeness' of Sebald's death registers its effect. Szirtes shares with other contemporary poets like Geoffrey Hill and Tony Harrison an urge to reclaim the language from the cosy rhetorical conventions characteristic of its frequent contemporary abuse. Hill is fond of quoting Ezra Pound: 'The poet's job is to define and yet again define until the detail of surface is in accord with the root in justice';[188] while Harrison's poetry conspicuously exploits the vocabulary and rhythms of popular and dialect speech in order to fulfil the poet's desire 'to be the poet my father reads!'[189] Szirtes likewise recognises that in words reside the meanings that are the keys to comprehending the histories and identities his poetry examines and seeks in some manner to reclaim or at least alleviate.

Poetry as reparation in and of itself is, he tells Vianu, undesirable: '…it would take a monster, a fool, or an egomaniac to think that he or she was actually succeeding in healing the world or even to consider the healing of the world as the project of their verse'. 'The great healing act of poetry', he argues, 'is to bridge the gap between language and what happens'. The 'bridging of gaps' is a recurrent concern of Szirtes' poetry, from the overt project signalled in *Bridge Passages* to the explorations of relations between writing and visual arts, or the act of literary translation that has come increasingly to pre-occupy him. A sonnet-stanza from 'Pompeian Red', in *Reel*, harnesses a sequence of images into a stately syntactic progression through key Szirtesian images and tropes to present to the reader precisely the fixity, the moment of sublime stillness, that is achieved in the successful moment of the gap's bridging:

> Imagine the whole world under glass. The ash
> in the ashtray. The dust in the urn. The face
> at the bottom of the cup, the empty space
> between more emptiness, glass one longs to smash
> simply because it's glass. And yet it's lovely,
> this sunlight trapped in the purring moment:
> nothing will ever be better than the present,
> it says, and you believe it as it moves gravely
> past you. This is the mystery. This is the house
> that guards it. This is the town by the volcano
> which is silent as if for ever but not for ever,
> the house of omelettes and wine and fraises
> where everyone is free to come and go
> down concrete steps into the subway river.

The 'world under glass' is the static, frozen world of the poem, which is also 'the mystery', 'the house' (now a familiar architectural image) that houses meaning in the stillness its form contains. The present moment (the moment of transition of *Bridge Passages*, the fixity of the image in *Blind Field*, the frozen past trapped in the images of *The Photographer in Winter* and the illusory movement of film frames in *Reel*) is also the 'movement' of the sentences across the lines, the endless movement of the moment of the present 'gravely / past you' – an enjambment, repeated from 'Wild Garden', that rhymes 'gravely' with 'lovely', suggesting that Szirtes, like Keats, can be 'half in love with easeful death'. It is the moment of the perception of inexorable transience that constitutes mortality, the 'ash' and 'dust in the urn'. The Keatsian stillness associated with the 'urn' and the echo of Keats' poem in the embedded rhymes of 'ever', 'for ever', 'not for ever' and 'everyone' point towards the aesthetic intensity of this moment of perception, its compression of Szirtes' style and image-repertoire into a moving, structured articulation of the simultaneity of beauty and death in the present moment of poetic perception. Grammar, rhyme and enjambment construct a delicate counterpoint, so that the poem's sense flows, sometimes disconcertingly, across its rhymes. The recurrent verb 'is', initially present in contracted form in 'it's' in line 5, insists on the presence of the present tense, charging the stanza with an inherent immediacy. In such a stanza Szirtes harnesses all his poetic skills to produce work of deep power and beauty, reflecting on its own processes as well as on human concerns.

The stanza from 'Pompeian Red' summarises many of Szirtes' central concerns, and epitomises the style and mood of his later poetry. It attempts to find a series of images that correspond (in the manner of objective correlatives) to deep emotional perceptions, and offers, in doing so, an illustration of the way in which the primary effects of the poetry revolve around the meanings and applications of the key word in Szirtes' life and work, translation. The poem constantly translates and re-translates its emotional register into images that present the emotion; it converts the force of the emotion into words, each image extending and offering an alternative vision of 'the mystery', which is both named and exceeds that naming, remaining simply 'the mystery' at the centre of the world constructed in the stanza. The translations effected by the poem find their source in no original text or point of meaning, but ramify out instead from this indeterminate centre, generating in turn new images, displacing resolution onto syntactic movement, an ascent (in the first half of the stanza) mirrored by a terminal decline 'down concrete steps into the subway river'.

As poet and translator Szirtes is constantly engaged in the kinds of reading demanded by translation. His recent literary output has included translations of major novels by significant (and, in the case of Sándor Márai, whose novels *Vendégjáték Bolzanóban* and *A zendülök* Szirtes has translated as *Conversations in Bolzano* [2004] and The Rebels [2007], surprisingly popular) Hungarian novels; he has translated Dezső Kostolányi's *Anna Edes* and László Krasznahorkai's *The Melancholy of Resistance* (a novel recently filmed to great critical acclaim by Béla Tarr as *The Werckmeister Harmonies* [2000]). He has translated Imre Madách's *The Tragedy of Man*, a monumental mid-nineteenth century drama of similar stature in Hungarian literature to that of Milton's *Paradise Lost* in English. The translation of Hungarian texts into English effects a kind of reverse 'appropriation' (to use the word Szirtes deploys in *Bridge Passages*); it imports into the English language elements of a new resource, a new repository of narratives and forms, shifting (in Eliot's terms) the 'ideal order' of the tradition in new, unpredictable ways. It also performs the function of offering new freedoms to the translated text or writer; Szirtes comments, in an essay on Georges Braque (addressed in more detail below) in which he discusses translation in terms of the ekphrastic rendering of visual art in language, on 'the voice of the writer-who-might-be-translated who, most of the time, very much wants to be translated... , especially if the language into which he or she is locked is as obscure as Hungarian'.[190]

Translation offers a powerful metaphor for the central dynamic processes that organise and direct Szirtes' work. Translation, as George Steiner has powerfully argued, is 'fully implicit in the most rudimentary communication';[191] in poetry it is absolutely fundamental. All Szirtes' poetry involves translation as a process of conversion, of perception into words, of experience into narratives, of memories into forms, of vision into argument. His prose writings include two extended statements concerning these functions, which will be discussed here. Firstly, in the essay 'Translating Zsuzsa Rakovszky' (published in *The Hungarian Review*), he comments (as we have seen earlier) on form and its relations to the process of translation. This essay provides a series of important insights into Szirtes' engagement with Hungarian writers and texts; he notes, for example, that 'Before 1984 I hadn't spoken Hungarian in twenty-eight years and even in 1990 the evaluation of a Hungarian poem in itself was a little beyond me – I had in fact to translate a poem into English before I could appreciate it'). He notes that 'form, too, changes meaning as it is transferred into another language and literary tradition' – an ambiguous statement, in that form's meaning may change, or form may alter meaning, in the transference. Both these meanings apply; Szirtes offers what he implies is a typically English 'compromise' with deeper literary-theoretical arguments, suggesting that the translator must seek a balance between the expectations engendered by the familiarity of certain forms ('the sonnet, the ballad, the terza rima') and the 'ingenuity' of a different or innovative kind of form, in which 'a complex rhyme scheme or metrical structure...is strictly and ostentatiously adhered to'. The translator, Szirtes argues, 'must do something similar' to the creator of the original text; the translator must strive 'to understand the condition of the poem and what makes it work'. Translation is here conceived as an act of correspondence, the translated text corresponding to the original in terms of 'similarity' of form.

Furthermore, Szirtes returns to the notional expectations that
form may engender in a given reader, to emphasise the act of
reading as integral to the generation of meaning from a given
poem. 'The power of the poem', he argues, 'resides outside the
intentions of its writer or of this or that specific reader. Nevertheless,
each specific reader assumes the pleasures and responsibilities of
reading'. His argument drives home its point: 'A translation of a
poem is in effect a reading of the poem' – a reiteration of the
assertion by W.H. Auden that provided the epigraph at the open-
ing of this book: 'To read is to translate'. Translation, as Szirtes
comprehends it, is reading 'in effect', in the effect that it has on
the poem in terms of the production of meaning and the possibili-
ties of interpretation and transformation that the translation opens
up. Translations, furthermore, 'are interventions in the public
arena too' – they democratise both poetry and the processes of its
reading, making available to other readers a version (the transla-
tion) of the reading that forms the basis of the translator's version
of the original; 'Reading', in turn, 'is, or should be, a matter of
excitement'.[192]

'The Late Flight of Georges Braque' considers translation in
relation to a different fundamental concern of Szirtes' poetry, the
relation – the transference of meanings – between words and images.
The essay focuses on *ekphrasis* and comments on the current aca-
demic interest in its mechanisms and possibilities (particularly
W.J.T. Mitchell's identification of indifference, hope and fear as
the three modes or moods in which *ekphrasis* operates) as a model
for the conception of these relations. 'The practical question in
ekphrasis now', Szirtes feels, 'is not so much whether one art can
be replaced by another and mean the same thing, but whether
there can be useful communication between them at all'.[193] Szirtes'
poetry, and his own 'translation' from painter to poet early in his
career, suggests that the question is of academic rather than prac-
tical interest. His essay turns instead to 'another fertile site for
theoretical anxiety', the question of translation from one literary
text to another. After a brief discussion of the academic territory
and its (non-) relation to issues of practicality, Szirtes switches
attention to translation as he comprehends it:

> Translation is a complex act and encompasses a range of activities,
> among which is the kind of semi-conscious exegesis involved in the
> reading of any text in its original language by a native speaker of that
> language. It depends who is reading, where, when, under what cir-
> cumstances, and...there is room for productive disagreement.[194]

He goes on to cite Walter Benjamin's argument that 'the "true" poem is in some sense "under" this or that language', like 'the reality under its façade and its interpretations'. Alternatively, 'there are moments when feel that we, instinctively but perfectly "really", understand the poem or picture'. Somewhere between these two extremes, Szirtes suggests (with more of that English compromise), lies the apprehensible, sensible medium in which the processes and effects of translation can adequately be felt: 'the work you are facing is more than the sum of its parts and agendas, including your own, including even this one'.[195]

Translation is to be understood in this negotiated, compromised way as the finding, by way of reading, of equivalences of form and content between texts produced in different languages. The poem exceeds any single reading or translation of it; it contains within it the potential for limitless readings, each of which may be a kind of translation. Each poem, in turn, translates the perceptions or experiences of the poet into words. Szirtes suggests that Braque's cubist paintings, responded to by a range of modern French poets, offered a particular freedom to poets, 'an appropriate kind of non-binding, not-wholly-defined creative space' akin to what he calls 'free translation'. These 'freedoms' constitute, ultimately, a definition of the relation between image and text that may summarise the modes of operation to be found in Szirtes' own poetry: 'What begins as looking or listening, slowly moves to the condition of dialogue, and eventually becomes a new object'.[196] 'Looking or listening' are the primary activities; 'the condition of dialogue' corresponds to the poem's construction out of self-critique, the *agon* of poetic production described by Yeats: 'Good poems come from arguments with others; great poems come from arguments with ourselves'. The 'new object' is the poem itself, the aesthetic object produced by this process. Translation and reading, versions of each other, reside at the heart of the process, suggesting that poetry is endlessly engaged in a process of self-redefinition.

New Poems

Szirtes' new poems demonstrate new directions in his refinement of the balance between formal consistency and a more experimental tendency towards variation. One group comprises the concluding section of his *New & Collected Poems* (2008); the second, mainly longer poems and sequences, make up a new collection, *The Burning of the Books and other poems* (2009). ([BB] denotes poems from the latter discussed here.)

Sharing with much of his previous work a series of concerns with contemplating art and its varieties and functions, these poems evince also a new level of assuredness of voice, an authorial certitude balanced, in turn, by an increasingly complex and grave, at times angry, awareness of the ontological uncertainties surrounding, and even defining, human existence, and by an increasing reluctance to yield to the superficial clarities of understanding seemingly afforded by language. Mortality, encoded in an adult awareness of and concentration on childhood memories, is the recurrent figure of this new level of awareness, alongside an increasingly critical attitude towards conventional discursive constructions of history as comprising narratives of progress. These developments are evident in momentary turns of phrase and in deeper, more structural themes, that surface at key moments in poems otherwise addressing different, more transitory concerns. Mortality, imagined in general and social terms as well as in relation to individual destinies and to the poet's own self-awareness, is also often presented in these poems as a counter-balance to, as well as a necessary corollary to, the creative potentials offered by the work of art, mobilising a series of critiques of different ideologies of art and their effects in practice.

This balancing structure and consequent critique is evident in 'Horse Painter', which imagines a monologue by the English painter George Stubbs (1724-1806) in which the artist's construction of his 'elegiac / landscape' is also a reduction of the world to neo-Classical inanimacy (a version of Szirtes' familiar frozen landscapes, seen also in 'the barbarity of cold' of 'Six Airs for William Diaper'), producing images of animals that seem 'more furniture than horses'. This dissecting function, his 'privilege / to lay them bare with a scalpel's edge', deploys a familiar truism of modern aesthetic theory – that art 'lays bare' reality – which Szirtes' poems interrogate, and link to a Wordsworthian protest against artists who 'murder to dissect'. 'Horse Painter' notes how Stubbs records, in his paintings, 'a minor event in England' that has, in its very recording by the artist, political implications: 'Earth is nature but landscape is property'. Szirtes offers Stubbs as a paradigm of the assured artist, confident and powerful within his limited aestheticised landscape, asserting through the mapping of English repression ('under the skin...blood runs') offered by his monologue that he is 'sane' (the poem's final word). This is a particular style or mode of art envisaged as a form of death, the absolute imposition, rather than the revelation, of an order that is repressive, paralleling the social order 'maintained by stewards with guns'. Szirtes' poems characteristically resist, divert, or circumnavigate such subscriptions of the aesthetic to the 'machines' of social regulation and seek other ways in which form can liberate experience.

'A Poster of Marlene, 1937: After Brassaï' offers the aestheticised image of woman as object of desire, responding to a Brassaï photograph in the critical, excavatory manner seen elsewhere in collections like *Blind Field*. Art, here, is doubled, the image and the image in the image; its 'monstrous' position, overlooking Paris, situates it firmly in the collective unconscious as an epitome of the power of film and photography – 'Everyone dreams / Of laughing Marlene'. But, at the same time, the image offers a graphic, artificial perfection implicitly critiqued in the poem: Marlene, with 'her high-arched brows' / Absolute precision' and 'her white teeth', offers a kind of image that distorts desire, supplementing a more 'authentic' vision of beauty in her 'beatitude'. The 'Unknown future' towards which history and the poem move is, of course, the core of this sonnet. The image, unlike 'life', is static (the poem notes, with Auden-like resignation, that 'Life moves forward, as it must'); images, the poem suggests, offer both a vision of stasis and (the image doubled again) the potential critique of that stasis. This is, after all, a poem about a photograph by a Hungarian photographer, not a film poster; but it's also a poem about that inexorable historical progress into a future both unknown, to those enthralled by Marlene's image in Paris in 1937, and, to the 21st century reader, known.

In 'The Child as Metaphor' we're offered the experiential experimentation characteristic of childhood as a nascent version of the adult poet's desire, the child's 'voice' figuring the voice of the poet (a 'deep-voiced child'), 'pushed out' in order 'To see how far it would go'. In a threateningly frozen allegorical world familiar to readers of Szirtes, and redolent also of Coleridge, Melville and Poe or of the opening pages of *Frankenstein* as much as of earlier Szirtes poems, the voice takes its bearings from a geography of alienation. 'An indifferent sea' and an 'Arctic' terrain, marked by echoes of poems like *Blind Field*'s 'Inuit' ('newly drowned / Babies'), establish a hostile environment guarding over which stands the figure of the mother, so often for Szirtes a symbol of aesthetic reassurance but also of the despair that history lends to art. The poem ends with self-reference and warning: 'The metaphor / That is your son is crying out. Beware', admonitions that are both corrective and explanatory – the 'Mothers' addressed are putative authorial symbols, figures of the creative force attenuated by but resistant to the polar climate of reality.

The poem's central vision imagines the world as a space in which 'all chances are slim / And everything, even love, freezes and disappears / Or snaps in two as the long night draws in'. This hellish vision (the poem is written, again, in terza rima) could stand as a register of Szirtes at his most pessimistic. 'The long night' (reiterated in the 'first darkness' of the next poem, 'Plunge') is death itself, radical in its contrast with the child's exploratory 'voice'. What price the adventures of this poetic voice in the face of the 'long night' of death, the poem's allegory wonders: the 'voice' as 'boat', in the opening stanza, with its cargo of meaning, detaches itself from authorial control ('It floated free / Of him'), becoming just another voice amid the noises of the world, a 'metaphor' 'crying out' amid other 'metaphors' of natural creative power.

Voices recur in these late poems, the vocal cacophony of the social world and of literary traditions, registered in the poems' struggle to be heard over what 'Beckmann's Carnival' refers to as 'the peculiar noise'. 'Esprit d'Escalier' ponders how to distinguish one's own voice from the voices of the crowd:

> The air was packed solid with voices we had once known
> or were ours, it was hard to tell which, for how do
> you tell the inner from the outer, or distinguish the I
> from the not-quite-I?

These voices signify life: they oppose the (silent) space of mortality, figured in 'Song' as the place where 'there is neither voice nor pulse', where self dissolves into the silence of death. This theme of the dissolution of self is elaborated further in 'Plunge', via childhood memory and specifically the memory that belongs to childhood, not the 'voice' of the child but his recall of other 'voices', menacing like 'fins suddenly plunging upwards / from the walled garden'.

Condensing several allusions to T.S. Eliot's *Four Quartets*, notably the voices in the garden of *Burnt Norton* and the 'deep lane' of *East Coker* (which becomes Szirtes' 'dead / lane with its berries'),

'Plunge' resolves itself from metonymic elements of a primal nature ('the rewards / of childhood and first darkness') into an adult anecdote, simply the aftermath of a drunken revel. Its deictic assertions construct a proximate world both physical and externalised, and internally psychological – 'Here is the bark / of the tree', 'Here is the step, the boiling and the loss / of memory'. Time and movement (further echoes of Eliot) are central to this construction: 'Most noises are lost in the pitch / of the moment', the poem asserts, seeking its central metaphor of the darkness that ends and follows life. It finds this in another metaphor of motion harnessed to exploration, in 'the yawl of light an ordinary switch / plunges to oblivion'. The Woolfian 'plunge' ('What a lark! What a plunge!' thinks Clarissa Dalloway, remembering her own adventures in the garden at Bourton)[197] is, in Szirtes' poem, another figure of the death of the author. The 'yawl' and 'pitch' remind us of the floating movement of the child's voice, a 'boat' 'floated free' of his control. 'Plunge' thus elaborates the symbolic potential of the preceding poem's opening image into new directions, linking childhood, memory, literary allusion and a prevailing system of metaphors into an increasingly complex analysis of the place and destiny of the poet's voice in the world.

The recurrent images in these new poems concern memory, desire, the natural world and its problematic rendering in poetry and art, and, amid this, the poet himself engaged in creative acts of writing, imagining and remembering. Perceptions and moments of experience trigger deep-seated emotional responses which poetic form harnesses into meaningful, symbolically effective expression. 'Fire', a pair of sonnets, addresses desire itself as struggle, adult 'agony', imagining and remembering again 'an eight-year-old child' positioned both as an object of the adult's nostalgic desire (the 'spring / of longing' inculcated by seeing, in an echo of 'Meeting Austerlitz', 'a distant fire across a field', the fire itself symbolising the distance of childhood and of childish things) and as a symbol of the potential adult, the man who will be product of this child 'without desires that he would call desires'. Desire, the poem suggests, is a province of adult experience, excessively so in its potentially destructive effects and its ever-presence: 'You know too much of fires, / their terror, rage, impatience, agony'. Furthermore, the poem implies that desire is defining and constitutive of the adult, the elemental force that makes the man: 'Sometimes you think you might be made of fire, a shape / leaping and dancing, shrunk over or blowing / through dry grass'. This metaphorical potential is extended in the poem's relation of fire-as-desire to fire-as-memory, a connection that leads, paradoxically, to another version of the MacNeice 'Snow' image familiar from earlier collections: 'it is like anything in memory: / nowhere, yet fixed, an image of escape, / the windows wide, the whole room glowing'.

The opening sonnet of 'Fire' offers an allegory of the ways in which the adult's nostalgia for childhood is distorted, or at least transformed, into other kinds of desire, more destructive, less controllable. In its reworking of older Szirtesian motifs (and of Eliotesque echoes like the 'dry grass' of 'The Hollow Men') the poem stands as a thematic résumé, a summary of key concerns structured into cogent, condensed symbolic patterns. The poem's second sonnet echoes the linkages of Szirtes' Hungarian sonnet sequences by opening with a rewriting of the concluding line of the first. It then turns to a revised version of the scenario that opens 'Reel', where that poem's 'traffic' is replaced by 'pre-traffic silence' in which time and memory atrophy into attenuated versions of themselves: 'Time, it seems, is slowing / to a bare passage of moments' (in 'Apology for a Broken Glass', we are advised to 'Keep order between objects and allow / Each thing clear passage'). The 'pitch of the moment' in 'Plunge' is now reduced further, a 'bare passage' indicating mere transition rather than development, a slowing returned to in the later poem 'Cards in the Garden' as 'Not so much slow motion as stillness'. In the seclusion of intimate privacy, where existence is reduced to the bare activity implied in 'We wait', history too (in the private and public forms of 'solid grief', 'parades' and 'bands' and a 'cannonade') is held at bay, excluded from the 'glowing' room, and rendered external to the experience which concerns the poem. Fire is reduced to the habitual passions of others, symbolised in their lighting cigarettes. The natural world of 'Plunge', the 'branch' and the 'wind at the pane', is relegated to an external space in counter-balance to the internal emptiness of the room 'possessed by light'. A sublime image of momentary stasis, the glowing 'room' is thus another version of the space of the poem itself, a refined, sublimated version of the anxious 'space of the word' of 'Shoulder'.

These poetic spaces are also, potentially, spaces of fixity and death. 'Geneva', following 'Horse Painter', imagines the depths concealed within another superficially ordered social reality, a 'proper civilisation'. The poem's 'prim' formality mocks its subject, and opens up a rift between social ideas of order and their necessary psychological and aesthetic effects. The poem's diagnostic dissection of Genevan society is deadly: within 'the slim / volume of hope death is the blank spaces of poems', both the relegation of the aesthetic to ritualised functionality (poems to be read at funerals) and the symbolic annulment of aesthetic creativity, the poem itself as 'blank space'. Deixis, here, indicates ownership (like the owned 'landscape' painted by Stubbs): 'These are our terraces and gardens', we are told by the possessive, collective narrating voice. The social effects, however, are palpable: 'These unheard screams / are our glassiness. We are not asleep but awake'. 'Geneva' resembles Huxley's *Brave New World* in its vision of a nightmare social order offering no adequate balance to the horrors of history remembered elsewhere by Szirtes.

In 'Clear', a meditative and deeply sceptical poem that takes its epigraph from William Empson's villanelle 'Missing Dates', clarity (the intellectual function of illumination) is both desired and obscured by the poem's insistence on the difficulty of being clear in words. After all, 'To be clear is to be convinced / about things like death' or (Auden-like) 'the necessity of certain actions', which surely in actuality lack any clarity at all. Light, in this poem, does not illuminate: 'day brings / no solutions nor does devoted practice / make perfect.' 'Perfection', the poem insists, resides in the mechanical or natural world of 'the light / in its socket' or 'the burst and flight / of the swift overhead' or 'the ever distant star'. It resides in the physical efficiency of the natural world, the movement and constancy of natural cycles that transcend human actions and anxieties. Mortality and human creativity accompany each other in a tragic, inexorable progress:

> So says the child to the hole in the ceiling
> if it could but say it, to the tongue
> that bursts into light, to the lost feeling
> in its limbs, to the debris in the lung.

The poem's closing assertions present Szirtes' most pessimistic conclusions about the reality of human existence (a 'reality' which, in 'Station', becomes Eliot's 'more reality than most of us can bear'):

> The only clear thing in history is pain.
> The only clear thing in history is silence.
> In suffering there is no equality. In the hot rain
> of silence there is no balance.

'Pain' and 'silence', inscribed in history on human bodies and, sometimes, on entire populations, double each other in history's 'clear' lesson. The poem's meditation on Empson's 'consequence a life requires' leads to this grim conclusion, art's efficacy dwindling in the face what it is forced to comprehend as the onslaught of historical repetition. 'Clear' offers an extended argument over the

moral implications of meaning and slack usage of a word (just as
'Checkout' searches for 'the right word' to define life, and opts in
the end for 'vertigo'). It decries the 'virtue' of clarity as 'a disgrace',
an opting for the easy and simple in the face of the manifestly,
challengingly complex. Ease defines the present, 'here where I
hear no bombs fall' (reversing conventional nostalgia; in the his-
torical past things were immeasurably worse than they are now);
the past of 'lost feeling' and 'debris', of 'the tongue / that bursts
into light' (an image borrowed from Tony Harrison's 'Marked with
D', in which Harrison imagines his dead father's 'cold tongue burst
into flame' in the cremating oven)[198] is also the history of 'pain' and
'silence', where, the poem bleakly concludes in a condemnation
that resonates through Szirtes' works, 'there is no balance'.

'Clear', in condemning clarity, is itself paradoxically clear in its
message, simple and direct in its concluding assertions. It offers
little scope for ambiguity (that most Empsonian of literary qualities)
and saddles the aesthetic instead with the burden of total perspic-
uity, a declarative frankness that unsettles the reader expecting
poetic indirection and subtlety of effect. In focussing on a single
word and its apparently passing usage by another poet, Szirtes
redefines the lexical 'space of the word' in momentarily literal
terms and, inserting his own poem into the tradition that exploits
that word, claims his own jurisdiction over the parameters of its
meanings within that space. 'Clear' thus becomes a contested term,
laden with imputations of slackness and indeterminacy, reinvested
by Szirtes with momentary force. But 'clear' is a quality of things
as well as of language ('Apology for a Broken Glass', we remem-
ber, asks us to 'allow / Each thing clear passage': clarity belongs to
the passage and, by association, to the things as well). The poem
implies, in its deliberate blurring of the distinction between words
and things, the extent of the intermingling of the two in habitu-
alised engagements with the effects of history. In effect, the poem
attacks cliché, insisting instead on the poet's duty of linguistic
rigour and honesty.

The sequence of slightly longer poems at the centre of this new
series of works explores the tension between memory and human
transience. 'Flight' and 'Snowfield' are miniature sonnet-sequences
that offer profound meditations on human existence, and stand as
defining poems of Szirtes' late period. Their insights are elaborated
in 'The Street in Movement', which develops Szirtes' mode of
accumulating observational detail into a philosophical meditation
on existential agency. 'Flight', in particular, returns to the terrain
of the pastoral in order to construct across its triple-sonnet form a

love poem that originates in the movement from the infinitely
transient 'one brief frame of time', to 'The terrible moment' and
'the long game' (the poem's metaphor for life), and finally to 'eter-
nity', a temporal expansion that develops as the poem expands its
range of reference and address. 'Flight' thus allegorises human life
in its apparent inscrutability and insignificance, 'the long game /
Of no discernible message or set text'. The poem concludes with a
declaration of existential faith, an assertion of contemporary surety:
'I think we are here just once, that here is where / All hereness lies'.
Its final lines, with their interwoven imagery of water, sky, light,
air and eternity, echo Henry Vaughan and George Herbert, meta-
physical poets evoked elsewhere by Szirtes in poems like 'Winter
Wings'. They return the reader to the 'moments in full flight' which,
it seems, Szirtes' late poems undertake to analyse and comprehend.

'Snowfield' elaborates this central concern, developing the clos-
ing sequence of images of 'Flight', via the image of snow, into a
sequence of metaphors of poetic form. While ice and the frozen
are symbols of apparently static permanence, snow is altogether
more ephemeral. It 'takes form' (like words, like the poem itself)
from the world to which it moulds itself, and can be shaped by
human hands. But, in doing so, it also creates form anew: 'the
shapes it makes mount up / and vanish against sky'. This dialectic
of forming and being formed leads to the central word of the first
sonnet, 'Stillness', isolated as a complete sentence amid the packing,
forming and fitting of the rest of the sonnet. The effect of the snow-
field is to dampen down the noise of the world into 'whispers and
sighs', a soundscape that is 'little enough' after the cacophonous
voices of earlier poems. Snow's effect, ultimately, is wholly super-
ficial: 'it doesn't change the state / of the world or even Norfolk
very much, / only appearances and the curious stuff / of illusion'.
Snow, in effect, lays bare the 'illusion' by imposing another layer
over it. In doing so it exposes the illusion of 'things that we thought
were clear and ours to touch', a revelation that links this poem to
'Clear' and to the issues of ownership addressed in earlier poems.

The first sonnet of 'Snowfield' addresses the simplicity and self-
evidence of the real and of the world of property and possessions
through the conceit of superficial transformation, a variety of the
'surreal' or 'slant' vision that characterises Szirtes' poetry. The
world that seems 'clear and ours to touch' is, in the second sonnet,
dismantled into its component elements, the features and activities
of a social world defined by consuming – 'The One Stop Shop',
'The stationer / and gift shop' – the social spaces in which, the
poem passively asserts, 'Commerce happens'. This is the world

defamiliarised and laid bare by the snow, and in that defamiliari-
sation is revealed the transitoriness of human affairs – 'Our brevity /
is startling. We're outlived by trees and stones'. The central word
of this sonnet is 'properties', a plural vision of commerce as a pas-
sive, recurrent occupation, in which human life becomes (in homage
to Brueghel) 'a scene / from a Dutch painting moving against a
screen'.

In the third sonnet, the snow assumes a new metaphorical weight,
as figure of writing itself. The poem thus effects a now-familiar
series of tropisms, from the literal descriptive signification of the
dominant motif or 'field' of the poem, to an allegorical dimension
relating to social activity, to a symbolic correspondence between
these levels of meaning and the roles and functions of the art work
and the artist. The snow, seemingly 'permanent in its grave weird-
ness', becomes a kind of writing: 'There are reams / of it to be read
in invisible ink'. It offers (in an echo of 'Portrait of My Father in
an English Landscape') a 'history / of anecdotes' or 'an elaborate
joke that is told / over and over again'. Its narrative function,
repetitive and elaborate, is also its symbolic function, a portent of
the 'stillness' of death (the 'hand that is raised / sooner rather than
later'). It figures both the 'space of the word' and the text, and
that space of mortality 'that we can sink / into…as into a frozen
bath'. The world covered by snow is deformed, reformed into a
space 'lethal and perfectly phrased'. 'Snowfield' thus thematises
the movement characteristic of Szirtes' later poetry, developing an
initial detailed observation into an extended meditation on the
symbolic potential of natural phenomena to figure the writerly
preoccupation with art and death, sustained always by the recog-
nition that (as it's put in another late poem, 'Song'), 'Some depths
there are you cannot plumb'.

This network of concerns develops in a variety of directions in
these new poems, centring on the relation between movement and
stasis, transformation and consistency, and the poetic project of
pinpointing the perception of moments of transition as compres-
sions of momentum or movement in the world. 'Exhortation'
imagines life's transience as a speedy journey towards death, 'the
meeting point of slim day and huge night', scaled by the immensity
of the universe 'where dim stars flicker waiting to ignite'. This
'meeting point' (a new version of the 'in-between' moment or
place) is transformed, in 'Lilac in the rain', into the point where
'dreams fade / into objects so we can't tell which is which'. These
are figures of the transformation of self accompanying the event of
death, the imagined horizon of all these poems. Furthermore, as

meditations on ageing they offer a variety of transitory moments
and movements as expressions of temporality. In 'Dust skin glove
bowl' this process is figured as 'becoming':

> Here dust becomes you. Gloves become your skin.
> You wear your body as you might a gown:
> Dust skin glove bowl, median brown,
>
> Like washing clothes, like a good scrubbing down
> With the colours you live and die in.

Here, the burial service collocation of body and dust is refracted
through a painterly awareness of the potential of still life ('nature
morte', the theme of the earlier poem 'Golden Bream', in *Portrait
of My Father in an English Landscape*) to signify human life. In
'Dust skin glove bowl' awareness of mortality is grounded in a
comprehension of the body's proximity to its own artistic repre-
sentations; it becomes a space in which 'all art / Is lexicon or colour
chart', a written or pictorial guide to the meanings of existence.

If awareness of mortality underpins these poems, their enquiry
is also mobilised in the direction of art's relation to the divine.
'The Street in Movement' draws together the various strands of
meaning an analysis traced above through other late poems, in
order to express through this matrix of images and metaphors a
sustained enquiry into the relations between reality, art and the
divine order of creation. The poem responds to the reply of Stephen
Dedalus, in Joyce's *Ulysses*, to Mr Deasy's announcement of human
destiny as 'the manifestation of God'. Stephen's reply is to define
God in the word providing the epigraph to Szirtes' poem: 'A shout
in the street, Stephen answered, shrugging his shoulders'.[199] Szirtes
addresses the dismissal explicit in Stephen's rejection of Catholic
piety by making the 'shout in the street' the manifest subject of
its analysis. 'Movement', noise, and the tension between the
'orchestrated' and the 'chance', provide the symbolic framework
within which this analysis is performed. The poem offers a famil-
iar dynamic of urban activity, rendered through iconic 'cars' and
'houses' that embody a world seemingly inarticulate, producing
the 'orchestrated, chance cry' in terms understood as 'More sound
effects than words'. The 'effects' of these 'sounds' are the poem's
concern.

Across its seven stanzas the poem's description elaborates a world
of routine, 'the business of streets' reiterating the 'commerce hap-
pens' of 'Snowfield'. But this passive world of trade and 'business'
modulates into an emotionally rendered space, 'the tenderness / of
districts, the small patient words of houses' inviting into the poem

the sensitivities of an aesthetic sensibility, as the poem turns its
attention to the private, domestic realities in which 'lives write
themselves out'. These realities depend upon the qualities of 'clarity,
hope and routine'; 'clarity' returns us to the questionable simplicity
attacked in 'Clear', while 'hope' and 'routine' evoke sentiments
examined in earlier poems like 'Meeting Austerlitz'. The poem's
'tiny precisions' (echoing, in their following the 'subterranean sea'
and 'Storms in a teacup', Prufrock's 'indecisions' and 'visions and
revisions': Szirtes' 'precisions' is rhymed, later, by 'visions') are the
hinge on which it turns from descriptive to interrogative engage-
ment. 'The long drowned voices of the vanished' summarise the
status of the dead and of history in the poem's immediate reality.
Its rhetoric strives, through 'precisions' and the 'delicate whorls of
the ear', to convey a sense of the infinite intricacy of 'orchestrated'
creation, an orchestration that incorporates and therefore in some
sense predicts the possibility of 'chance'. Its crucial question occurs
in the fourth stanza: 'Where do such voices come from?' The
question interrogates source rather than meaning. Later, it's re-
phrased – 'Where are we?' – insisting on uncertainties of location
('The Street') as the ground of human questions. Finally, these
questions resolve into a direct enquiry about God – 'Is God / Still
shouting in the rain?' – but this interrogates activity rather than
existence. The poem's scrutiny of the divine is couched in terms
that deflect attention onto space and action as indirect evidence of
the presence of the divine in the real, away from deeper epistemo-
logical or ontological uncertainties.

Its answers to these questions express a religious sensibility seek-
ing a means of defining, in its own terms and through the lexical
resources available, a contemporary notion of faith comprehended
in relation to poetry. 'God is the rain', the poem asserts;

The noise the rain makes that seems
A voice, not quite a language but a flood
Of inchoate music in which we recognise the refrain
Of something that gathers and streams.

Szirtes' preference for images of fluidity over the frozen, of move-
ment over stillness and of noise over silence, expressed in a variety
of ways throughout these new poems, is made manifest in these
lines. The 'voices' that have echoed throughout his works, and
which clamour in these later poems, here condense into 'A voice'
that is also 'inchoate music', a sound both 'orchestrated' and
'chance', with an indeterminate 'refrain'. This is as close as his
poetry may come to a simple declaration of faith in 'something' –

any simple clarity, after all, is also an evasion of the complexity
that the interwoven strands of imagery (noise, rain, voice, language,
flood, music, refrain, streams) attempt to express.

Szirtes' most recent longer poems further refine and elaborate
these themes and the continual processes of formal and moral
redefinition characteristic of this period of productivity in ways
that both extend and consolidate them as key features of the *œuvre*.
They demonstrate, in poems like 'The Man Who Wove Grass' [BB]
and 'In the Face of History: In Time of War' [BB] (alluding to
Auden's sonnet sequence 'In Time of War'), a new level of assured-
ness in the handling of sequential forms, and a new conviction that
the long poem affords a particular kind of aesthetic space that brings
its own demands and rewards. The critic W. S. Milne, discussing
Geoffrey Hill's *The Mystery of the Charity of Charles Péguy*, cites
Basil Bunting in making the following observation:

> ...it is only in the long poem that the alienated, specialised activities of
> modern communities can be brought together to form some sort of
> cultural cohesion; that it is only there that the fluency of craft can be
> rescued, renewed or redeemed.[200]

Throughout his career, Szirtes' long poems and sequences have
offered 'cultural cohesion' at different levels, in the struggle for
reconciliation between competing experiences of and accounts of
historical events, and between the different consequences of move-
ments and displacements of people across history and geography.
His interest in the 'fluency of craft' is palpable; craft, and its product,
formal unity, constitute a principal concern throughout Szirtes'
career. This concern is alluded to, in 'The Penig Film' [BB], by an
injunction from the subjects of the film to 'Speak the speeches
trippingly, / without tripping'. The rolling rhyme-scheme of the
poem 'trips' along and demands a kind of 'tight-rope' virtuoso
performance from the poet which some critics have seen as dis-
tracting from other concerns; Sean O'Brien, for instance, observes
of the poems in *Reel* that 'there are passages which seem hobbled
by the formal obligation he has undertaken', 'problems produced
by the pursuit of scale'.[201]

'The Penig Film', a sequence of five varied-length sections of
terza rima verse, is a major example of the necessity of the strict
controls afforded by Szirtes' choices of form. It demonstrates the
combination of concerns outlined above within a now-familiar for-
mal framework, and returns equally to a specific concern familiar
from much of Szirtes' earlier work. The poem is based on Szirtes'
discovery of a film of the liberation of Penig concentration camp, in

which his mother was imprisoned in 1945; like Sebald's Austerlitz, who finds in footage of a performance at Terézin the ghost of an image (shade more than shadow) that may represent his mother, who died in the camp, Szirtes performs a horrified scrutiny of the film, seeking in the image a trace of his mother's historical existence. The film is both a persistent trace of the past and 'the scene / of one of a million crimes that are over / in a blink of Clio's eyes'. Clio, muse of history, is invoked for her Auden-like dispassion – 'She does not believe / in getting involved', a prerogative, perhaps, of the gods, but also a choice that many people, unfortunately, have been denied. The poem imagines the film – translating it – as a reverse-resurrection ('we can resurrect the voice of woman and man', it asserts in part 5) of the people it represents, a version of the conceit of temporal reversal used by Martin Amis in *Time's Arrow* and Philip K. Dick in *Counter-Clock World*:

> emerging from your cot
> of earth, mud, lime and bone, to rise, or be carried
> to a hospital from the place Clio forgot
>
> to visit, deloused, unstarved, and unburied,
> wrapped in your flimsy nightmare of memory
> drifting into consciousness, into the unhurried
>
> pace of a life that is other, into this shimmery
> surface where light is diffused across a rectangle...

These 'translated' figures, seemingly miraculously resurrected by the 'shimmery / surface' of the recorded image, offer the most graphic of Szirtes' representations of and responses to the Holocaust, suggesting that poetry's directness needs refinement in the light of a filmic representation of such personal proximity: 'What we see on screen / is what remains of it', the poem asserts, resorting to the comparative safety of a shared, plural experience that remains, like the event itself, significant in incomprehensible ways.

The film's visual rhetoric repeats, in the poem's rendering of it, its content – 'everything cropped' – allowing it to represent a curtailed historical moment in a perpetual, abbreviated present: 'All we see of the film is present tense'. The difficulty the poem addresses (a difficulty explored, in different ways, in the poems of *Blind Field*) resides in this question of representation that 'makes present' in the moment of its viewing that which is historically distant, and the repetition or reconstruction – even the re-enactment in cinematic terms – of which, is impossible (and profoundly undesirable). The poem both represents and resists the illusory resurrection and life that the film's image accords to historical death. 'Wrong movie

here', we're told, in a curt, syntactically compressed interjection in
part 4 that carefully undercuts the stately progression of the en-
chained lines of the *terza rima*, disrupting the flowing extended
sentences and enjambments that characterise the poem, and re-
introducing the 'awkward poetics' that have previously charac-
terised Szirtes' engagements with such material. 'You seek that
which is always hard to seek', the poem admonishes itself at the
end of the second section, burdening itself with a task that returns
relentlessly to the quest for understanding of the mother's life that
has preoccupied most of Szirtes' poetry, and that here encounters
a kind of limit-experience, a momentary threshold of the tolerable:

> And so in Penig, in the unexpected sighting
> of a moment that she, who is at the centre
> of this poem yet not there, lost in its low lighting,
>
> would have known as hers.... .

The (impossible) imagining of Magdalena Szirtes' experience of
suffering assumes its position in these lines as the absent centre of
Szirtes' poetry, around which his excavations of history and human
trauma constantly revolve. The 'moment', endlessly repeated in
the film, is again the 'movement' of film and of history, the his-
torical *Reel* progressing down until the present 'moment' of its re-
experiencing as visual record by the poet; its 'sighting' is also, in
an implicit pun, its 'siting', the 'placing' of the 'moment' within
the panorama of historical suffering, as well as its 'citing', its
recording by the documentary functions of film and words. The
key words of this stanza – 'sighting', 'moment', 'centre', 'poem',
'lighting' – are laden with excess meaning, punctuating the poem's
syntax, offering the 'ghosts of form' as measures of a progress that
is infinitely laboured but which grapples with its content, ensuring
some kind of witnessing out of the 'unexpected sighting'.

The poem proceeds from this deep confessional 'moment' to
represent the mortal human figures in the film in verbal terms
that evoke the iconography of Hans Holbein's *The Body of the
Dead Christ in the Tomb* (1521-22), a painting described by Julia
Kristeva in her meditation on images of divine loss and mourning
as 'the unadorned representation of human death, the well-nigh
anatomical stripping of the corpse'.[202] Szirtes writes, at the start of
the third section:

> The stone-cold body that is dressed to lie
> along the couch. The stone-cold body dressed
> for flames. The stone-cold body in its dry
>
> pod lowered into the ground. The still chest.

The flat hair. The calm statement made
at last.

These flat, uninflected declarative sentences offer a vision that is
plain, devoid of emotion or comment, the bare fact of mortality
reduced to a simple descriptive syntax. The 'stone-cold body' is
the poem's recording of a material trace of a suffering beyond his-
torical comprehension, literally de-moralised, figured in the man-
ner of a devotional icon further to suggest a religious dimension
implicit in the linguistic simplicity of the description. When, in
the poem's final section, 'the auditorium light / dips and sinks as if
into bone and blood', we encounter in the metaphorical movement
the centre of the force that Szirtes' poetry can generate. 'Bone and
blood', the metaphorical inks into which 'light dips and sinks', are
the media of the inscription of historical pain that the poem imi-
tates (we hear again in these lines the 'ordnance, bone and glass'
of the archaeological lists of 'Metro'). The poem's force resides in
its negotiation of the conflicting tensions of desire and horror in
relation to seeing the film, its refusal to allow the film simply to
represent its traumatic action, or that action simply to present
itself.

If 'The Penig Film' demonstrates a new kind of direct, or at
least less indirect, confrontation with historical truth, its formal
design still effects a displacement away from the brutality of that
truth. Szirtes' use of *terza rima* again both alludes to and eschews
the ornate patterning of Dante; it invites religious parallels only to
locate them elsewhere than in the unified formalism of a fantastic
poetic edifice, in an essentially Romantic conception of sublime
beauty (such as that encountered in 'Pompeian Red', or 'The
romantic sublime' named in the first section of another new poem,
'The Birds' [BB]), both more familiar to the modern reader (in
terms of the conventional rhetoric of aesthetic beauty) and more
containable within the frames of modern linguistic usage. Form
thus exercises emotional containment; the power of the poem
resides elsewhere, in the emotion contained. 'Trippingly', form
constitutes a means of avoiding the 'traps, pitfalls' (in 'Portrait of
My Father in an English Landscape') of conventionality, and of
imposing a notional, temporary order upon experience with which
words struggle to deal. The image, in 'The Penig Film', of the
mother's figure, 'at the centre / of this poem and yet not there', is
also a version of the centreless structure typical of modernist poetry,
the formal construction that contains Wallace Stevens' 'Nothing
that is not there and the nothing that is'.[203]

The 'low lighting' of 'The Penig Film', its focus on a 'sad square of pale / grey', an in-between figure of the horrific imbalance between 'The light / of day and the absence of light', exemplifies one facet of the concern of Szirtes' most recent poetry with the sublime potentiality of the perception and effects of light and, often, its effects on architectural formations, an impressionistically modulated set of responses to a perceived fragility of perception that comes to pre-occupy these poems with an extraordinary regularity and intensity. 'The Birds' describes 'the delicate thin / light of the room, the frail shell of the voice / within which it moves'; in 'At the Baths' (a belated companion to 'The Lukács Baths' and 'The Swimmers'), 'The Classical columns wear the light / with a knowing patience'; in 'A Budapest Wedding', 'Light dances / all by itself as if the building were untenanted'. 'One Summer Night' offers images of a house permeated by evening light, 'gold, a pool / of precious metal, and the windows spilled / warmth'; 'Who had left the light / billowing and burning like that?' the poem asks. In 'The Fish', 'My eyes are full of light, little swimming dots / of crystalline wonder'. 'On Dover Pond' returns to Matthew Arnold's 'Dover Beach': 'The dizzying light, those naked trees! Somewhere, / a hand seizes language.' And in 'Full Flight, July 2005', 'swimming' and 'light' are again conjoined: 'Our eyes are different. They absorb and shine / In the same sunlight that breaks on glass or flint / Year round, in every season'.

Light is a recurrent pre-occupation of these new poems, a register of the illuminating sublimity of the visual linking Szirtes' familiar concern with the poetic rendering of visual art to a more deeply imbedded religious instinct, and responding ultimately to the impending 'darkness' of age and death. The prevalence of the luminous is connected to an increasing awareness of the ageing body. 'Station' recounts a hospital operation; hospitals, the poem ominously suggests, are like 'railway stations somewhere abroad', 'passing buildings way off the marked road'. The whiff of mortality troubles the narrating self in this poem: the operation is revealed to have taken place in adolescence, but the poem negotiates its contemporary reference by implied contrasts ('the National Health must have been robust', it speculates, implying that nowadays it may not be – it too has aged, as have social and political commitments to it). The hospital's faint evocation of those deeper European anxieties about trains and deportations that preoccupy earlier poems makes 'Station' a troubling meditation on a mortality both escaped and, inevitably, impending, 'the train throbbing faintly in the wings' figuring death that lurks in the past and the future and investing life itself with an ultimate kind of 'in-between-ness'.

The underlying drive of these poems is towards some kind of reconciliation with death. 'Say' presents death as something to be imagined: 'Try to imagine death as a phone call.' The poem's clichés offer a survey of how language provides a vast array of mechanisms enabling us to avoid (in a literal sense, negating the 'void' that is death) the impossible actuality of death: 'before you went away', 'the perfect end / of a perfect life', 'a benign pearly joy that should portend / more joy', 'it takes a moment to destroy / a life', and so on, an un-tripping course through the familiar language of evasion towards an inevitable ending. The poem's long second sentence stretches over 36 lines, leading to a questioning final clause – 'would that be at all consoling?' – that is replied to by a kind of calm acceptance of 'the waves rolling / towards your feet in the darkness, to the fear of falling'. 'Say' is the utterance of the human voice resisting the dying of the light; its vision of death as 'swimming in the immense / indivisible particularity of a compact universe' is informed by the language of contemporary science, but, the poem suggests, no more 'consoling' for all that.

These later poems mark continuities and new directions in Szirtes' explorations of his situation between languages, cultures and histories. His poetry continually enacts his own version of the 'intolerable wrestle with words and meanings', with the 'blocks and stones and worse than senseless things' of this chapter's Shakespearean epigraph, the recalcitrant and inflexible words that are nevertheless the poet's material, out of which he must construct his being in the world and find his own version of Empson's 'consequence a life requires'. Szirtes' poetry has always concerned itself with the continuities and returns that define and enable the potentials of that being. Its trajectories along different but interlinked English and Hungarian routes have been towards the foundational experiences of a sense of modern European identity that is as inclusive and expansive as the poems themselves, and that insists on its own journey as a movement towards a tenancy in what 'Meeting Austerlitz' calls 'the Hotel Esperia', a name which, the poem reminds us, 'means hope'.

Notes

CHAPTER 1: **Introduction: Reading George Szirtes** (pp. 9-36)

1. Szirtes, 'Formal Wear: Notes on Rhyme, Meter, Stanza & Pattern', *Poetry*, Vol. 187 No. 5 (February 2006), pp. 422, 423-24.

2. Peter McDonald, *Serious Poetry: Form and Authority from Yeats to Hill* (Oxford: Oxford UP, 2002), p. 6.

3. Szirtes, 'Formal Wear', p. 419.

4. Szirtes, 'Introduction' to *The Budapest File* (Tarset: Bloodaxe Books, 2000), p. 13.

5. John Greening, 'Bit Parts in the Epic', *Poetry Review*, Vol. 88 No. 3 (Autumn 1988), p. 67.

6. Sean O'Brien, 'Big Questions', *Poetry Review*, Vol. 78 No 3 (Autumn 1986), p. 56.

7. McDonald, *Serious Poetry*, p. 9.

8. Seamus Heaney, *The Government of the Tongue* (London: Faber & Faber, 1988), p. 148.

9. O'Brien, 'Big Questions', p. 56.

10. O'Brien, 'Big Questions', p. 56.

11. Sylvia Kantaris, 'Pleasuring the Pain', *Poetry Review*, Vol. 81 No. 2 (Summer 1991), p. 70

12. Antony Rowland, *Holocaust Poetry* (Manchester: Manchester UP, 2005), p. 11.

13. Seamus Heaney, interviewed by Harriet Cooke, *The Irish Times*, 28 December 1973.

14. Rowland, *Holocaust Poetry*, p.11.

15. Szirtes, *The Iron Clouds* (Hitchin: The Dodman Press, 1975), p. 1.

16. Szirtes, 'The Late Flight of Georges Braque', *Pretext*, Spring / Summer 2003, p. 111.

17. Seamus Heaney, *The Spirit Level* (London: Faber & Faber, 1996), p. 70.

18. Szirtes, 'The Muse of Absolute Zero', *Poetry Review*, Vol. 78 No. 4 (Winter 1988/89), p. 41.

19. Szirtes, *The Iron Clouds*, p. 4.

20. Szirtes, 'Formal Wear', p. 417.

21. Sean O'Brien, review of *Reel*, *Poetry London*, 50 (Spring 2005), at http://www.poetrylondon.co.uk/index.htm?reviews/issue50.html

22. Boyd Tonkin, review, *The Independent*, 30 April 2005.

23. Eva Hoffman, *Lost in Translation* (London: Minerva, 1991), p. 124.

24. Michael Murphy, *Poetry in Exile: A Study of the Poetry of W.H. Auden, Joseph Brodsky and George Szirtes* (London: Greenwich Exchange, 2004), p. xvi.

25. Szirtes, 'Fables of Home'.

26. Szirtes, *The Hungarian Quarterly*, Vol. XLII No. 164 (Winter 2001); 'Introduction' to *The Budapest File*, p. 12.

27. Szirtes, *Hungarian Quarterly*, Vol. XLII No. 164 (Winter 2001).

28. Szirtes, 'Introduction' to *The Budapest File*, p. 14.

29. Poetry reading organised by the British Council in Warsaw with George Szirtes and Moniza Alvi, 23 November 2005.

30. Szirtes, Review, *Poetry Review*, Vol. 79 No.1 (Spring 1989), p. 66.

31. Jonathan Raban, *The Society of the Poem* (London: Harrap, 1971), p. 10.

32. Szirtes, in *The Guardian*, 21 November 2005.

33. Szirtes. 'Fables of Home'.

34. Marianne Hirsch, *Family Frames: Photography, Narrative and Post-memory* (Cambridge, MA: Harvard UP, 1997), p. 243.

35. Hirsch, *Family Frames*, p. 243.

36. Szirtes, 'Losing our Identities', *The Independent on Sunday*, 28 May 2000, p. 16.

37. Murphy, *Poetry in Exile*, p. xvii.

38. Hoffman, *Lost in Translation*, p. 163.

CHAPTER 2: 'Cold Pastorals': *The Slant Door, November and May, Short Wave* (pp. 36-60)

39. Neil Corcoran, *English Poetry Since 1940* (London: Longman, 1993), pp. 269-70.

40. Szirtes, 'Preface' to *The Budapest File*, p. 12.

41. D.A.N. Jones, review of *The Slant Door* in *The Listener* cited on dustcover of *November and May*; Robert Welch, review in *Yorkshire Post*; Shirley Toulson, review in *British Book News*: both cited on dustcover of *Short Wave*.

42. Corcoran, *English Poetry Since 1940*, pp. 196-97.

43. Raphaël Ingelbien, *Misreading England: Poetry and Nationhood Since the Second World War* (Amsterdam: Rodopi, 2002), p. 4.

44. Sean O'Brien, *The Deregulated Muse: Essays on Contemporary British and Irish Poetry* (Newcastle upon Tyne: Bloodaxe Books, 1998), p. 99.

45. John Lucas, review in *The New Statesman*. Cited on dustcover of *Short Wave*.

46. Peter Porter, 'On This Day I Complete My Fortieth Year', *Collected Poems* (Oxford: Oxford UP, 1983), p. 141.

47. Anthony Thwaite, *Poetry Today: A Critical Guide to British Poetry 1960-1984* (London: Longman, 1985), p. 128. Thwaite expanded his discussion of Szirtes in the revised and updated edition of this book in 1995.

48. Rodney Pybus, 'New Poetry', *Stand*, Vol. 26 No. 3 (Summer 1985), pp. 64-5.

49. Iain Sinclair, *Edge of the Orison* (London: Hutchinson, 2005), p. 9.

50. Szirtes, 'Preface' to *The Budapest File*, p. 12.

51. Peter Porter, 'Introduction, Memoir and Critical Note', Martin Bell,

Complete Poems (Newcastle upon Tyne: Bloodaxe Books, 1988), p. 19.

52. Martin Bell, *Complete Poems* (Newcastle upon Tyne: Bloodaxe Books, 1988), p. 117. The next poem, 'With a Presentation Copy of Verses', continues the pastiche of Eliot.

53. Rowland, *Holocaust Poetry*, pp. 18-19.

54. Derek Mahon, 'Grandfather', in *Night Crossing* (Oxford: Oxford UP, 1968), p. 7.

55. Ezra Pound, *Hugh Selwyn Mauberley: Life and Contacts*, Part X, in *Selected Poems* (London: Faber & Faber, 1977), p. 104.

56. Nicholas Royle, *The Uncanny* (Manchester: Manchester UP, 2003), pp. 1, 6.

57. 'Without looking back you would grab the trowel that breasts are made of.' Jean-Pierre Cauvin and Mary Ann Caws (editors and translators), *Poems of André Breton* (Austin: University of Texas Press, 1982), pp. 66-67.

58. *Penguin Modern Poets 14* (Harmondsworth: Penguin, 1969), pp. 20-22; see also Alan Brownjohn, *Collected Poems* (London: Enitharmon, 2006), pp. 41-44.

59. John Haffenden (ed.), *Selected Letters of William Empson* (Oxford: Oxford UP, 2006), cited in Stefan Collini, 'Scraps of Empson', *The Times*, 5 July 2006; available at http://www.timesonline.co.uk/tol/incomingFeeds/article683213.ece

60. In Ted Hughes, *Lupercal* (London: Faber & Faber, 1960), pp. 21-22.

61. A. Alvarez, 'The New Poetry, or Beyond the Gentility Principle', Introduction to *The New Poetry* (Harmondsworth: Penguin, 1962), p. 27. Alvarez reprints Hughes' poem in its entirety, pp. 26-77.

62. Anthony Hecht, *Collected Earlier Poems* (Oxford: Oxford UP, 1990), p. 124. The poem was originally published in 1977.

63. Szirtes, 'Introduction' to *Leopard V: An Island of Sound* (London: Harvill, 2004), p. xvi.

64. William Shakespeare, *Twelfth Night*, I. 5. 299-300.

65. James Fenton, *The Memory of War and Children in Exile: Poems 1968-83* (Harmondsworth: Penguin, 1983), pp. 63-71; John Fuller, *Epistles to Several Persons* (London: Secker & Warburg, 1973); *Collected Poems* (London: Secker & Warburg, 1996), pp. 89-120.

66. Peter Porter, *The Cost of Seriousness* (Oxford: Oxford UP, 1978). The cover of this book features a photograph of a carved angel in Blythburgh church.

67. In 'Evolution', published in *Preaching to the Converted* (Oxford: Oxford UP, 1972). See Peter Porter, *Collected Poems* (Oxford: Oxford UP, 1983), p. 159.

68. Porter, *The Cost of Seriousness*, pp. 15-16.

69. Porter, *The Cost of Seriousness*, pp. 30-32, 18, 27.

70. In Peter Porter, *Living in a Calm Country* (Oxford: Oxford UP, 1975). See Porter, *Collected Poems*, p. 204.

CHAPTER 3: *The Photographer in Winter* and *Metro* (pp. 61-84)

71. *Martin Booth, British Poetry 1964-84: Driving Through the Barricades* (London: Routledge & Kegan Paul, 1985), pp. vii. 3, 164.

72. 'Interview' with John Tusa, *The John Tusa Interviews*, BBC Radio 3; transcript available at http://www.bbc.co.uk/radio3/johntusainterview/szirtes_transcript.shtml

73. Szirtes, 'Fables of Home'.

74. Szirtes, 'Fables of Home'.

75. 'I was a Chagallian painter. I can now say that with a clear conscience because I no longer paint. ...At the time I would have said I'd looked at Chagall and I'd understood Chagall, and I was doing something else. But now I think, looking back at it from distances, it was skating a bit too close to Chagall.' 'Interview' with John Tusa.

76. Fred Beake, 'Generations of recent poetry', *Stand*, Vol. 32 No. 2, p. 54.

77. Peter Nicholls, *Modernisms: A Literary Guide* (Basingstoke: Macmillan, 1995), p. 107.

78. 'Interview' with John Tusa.

79. Simon Critchley, *Very Little ... Almost Nothing: Death, Philosophy, Literature*, revised edition (London: Routledge, 2004), pp. 123-24.

80. Lawrence Sail, 'Recent verse', *Stand*, Vol. 28 No. 3 (Summer 1987), p. 76.

81. George Orwell, *1984* (Harmondsworth: Penguin, 1970), p. 234.

82. Szirtes, 'Introduction' to Miklós Radnóti, *Camp Notebook*, translated by Francis Jones (Todmorden: Arc Publications, 2000), p. 15.

83. In Ottó Orbán, *The Blood of the Walsungs: Selected Poems*, edited by George Szirtes (Newcastle upon Tyne: Bloodaxe Books; Budapest: Corvina, 1993), p. 32.

84. Fred Beake, 'Generations of recent poetry', p. 53.

85. Sean O'Brien, 'Big Questions', *Poetry Review*, Vol. 78 No. 3 (Autumn 1988), p. 56.

86. Szirtes, 'Preface' to *The Budapest File*, p. 13.

87. See George MacBeth, *Collected Poems 1958-1982* (London: Hutchinson, 1989), pp. 118-21.

88. Marc Augé, *In the Métro*, translated by Tom Conley (Minneapolis: University of Minnesota Press, 2002), p. 9.

89. Angela Carter, *The Infernal Desire Machines of Doctor Hoffman* (London: Rupert Hart-Davis / Granada Publishing, 1972), p. 20.

90. Geoffrey Hill, 'September Song', in *Collected Poems* (Harmondsworth: Penguin, 1985), p. 67.

91. Marianne Hirsch, *Family Frames*, p. 22.

92. 'Interview' with John Tusa.

CHAPTER 4: 'A furious year': *Bridge Passages* (pp. 85-108)

93. *At the End of the Broken Bridge: XXV Hungarian Poems 1978-2002*,

edited by István Turczi (Edinburgh: Scottish Poetry Library, 2005), un-paginated.

94. Szirtes, 'Introduction' to *Leopard V: An Island of Sound – Hungarian Poetry and Fiction Before and Beyond the Iron Curtain* (London: Harvill, 2004), p. xxiii.

95. William M. Brinton & Alan Rinzler, 'Introduction' to *Without Force or Lies: Voices from the Revolution of Central Europe in 1989-90* (San Francisco: Mercury House, 1990), p. x.

96. Hans Magnus Enzensberger, untitled essay, *Granta 30: New Europe!* (Winter 1990), p. 137.

97. Cited in Document 6, National Security Archive Declassified Material at http://www.gwu.edu/~nsarchiv/news/19991105/index.html

98. Misha Glenny, *The Rebirth of History: Eastern Europe in the Age of Democracy* (Harmondsworth: Penguin, 1990), pp. 184, 186.

99. Stephen Brook, *The Double Eagle: Vienna, Budapest, Prague* (London: Picador, 1989), p. 186.

100. 'Interview' with John Tusa.

101. http://thedublinreview.com/archive/five/szirtes.html

102. George Szirtes, 'Introduction' to *Leopard V: An Island of Sound*, p. xxi.

103. Szirtes, 'Preface', *The Budapest File*, p. 14.

104. Szirtes, 'The Underground in the Underground', BBC Radio 4, broadcast November 28th 1989.

105. Szirtes, 'The March Marches: A Progress Report from Budapest', *Poetry Review*, Vol. 79 No. 3 (Autumn 1989), p. 15.

106. Szirtes, 'Learning from Brezhnev', *Poetry Review* Vol. 81 No. 3 (Autumn 1989), pp. 22, 21.

107. George Szirtes & George Gömöri, editors, *The Colonnade of Teeth: Modern Hungarian Poetry* (Newcastle upon Tyne: Bloodaxe Books, 1996), p. 16.

108. Szirtes, 'Introduction' to Ágnes Nemes Nagy, *The Night of Akhenaton: Selected Poems* (Tarset: Bloodaxe Books, 2004), p. 10.

109. Seamus Heaney, 'Punishment', in *North* (London: Faber & Faber, 1975), pp. 37-8; p. 38.

110. Orbán, *The Blood of the Walsungs*, p. 37.

111. Martin Heidegger, 'Building, Dwelling, Thinking', in *Basic Writings*, edited by David Farrell Krell (London: Routledge, 1993), p. 354.

112. 'The March Marches', p. 14

113. Geoffrey Hill, 'Of Diligence and Jeopardy', *The Times Literary Supplement*, 17 November 1989; reprinted in *Style and Faith* (New York: Counterpoint, 2003), p. 27.

114. Szirtes, 'Letter to Brezhnev', p. 22.

115. Willi Apel, Harvard Dictionary of Music (London: Heinemann, 1970), p. 112.

116. Simon Critchley, *Things Merely Are: Philosophy in the Poetry of Wallace Stevens* (London: Routledge, 2005), p. 60.

117. Tadeusz Rózewicz, 'Humanity's Footprint', translated by Adam Czerniawski, *Granta 30: New Europe!* (Winter 1990), p. 63.
118. George Szirtes, 'Learning from Brezhnev', p. 20.
119. George Steiner, untitled essay, *Granta 30: New Europe!* (Winter 1990), p. 129.
120. Szirtes, 'The Underground in the Underground'.
121. Angela Carter, *Wise Children* (London: Chatto & Windus, 1991), p. 1.
122. George Szirtes, 'Introduction' to *The Budapest File*, p. 14.
123. Hecht, *Collected Earlier Poems*, p. 237.
124. Hoffman, *Lost in Translation*, p. 209.
125. Julia Kristeva, *Strangers to Ourselves*, translated by Leon Roudiez (New York: Columbia University Press, 1999), pp. 32, 16.
126. Ted Hughes, 'The Thought-Fox', in *The Hawk in the Rain* (London: Faber & Faber, 1957), p. 14.
127. Miroslav Holub, *The Dimension of the Present Moment*, edited by David Young (London: Faber & Faber, 1990), pp. 2-3.
128. Holub, *The Dimension of the Present Moment*, p. 3.
129. Christopher Isherwood, *The Berlin Novels: Mr Norris Changes Trains & Goodbye to Berlin* (London: Vintage, 2004), p. 453.
130. Holub, *The Dimension of the Present Moment*, p. 5.
131. Walter Benjamin, 'The Task of the Translator', in *Illuminations*, edited by Hannah Arendt (London: Fontana, 1992), pp. 71-72; p. 82.
132. Szirtes, 'Translating Zsuzsa Rakovszky'.
133. Szirtes, 'Introduction' to Orbán, *The Blood of the Walsungs*, p. 15.
134. Szirtes, 'Introduction' to Orbán, *The Blood of the Walsungs*, p. 11.
135. Orbán, *The Blood of the Walsungs*, pp. 60, 74.
136. Nemes Nagy, *The Night of Akhenaton*, p. 88.
137. Nemes Nagy, *The Night of Akhenaton*, p. 89.
138. Nemes Nagy, *The Night of Akhenaton*, p. 8.
139. Szirtes, 'Introduction' to *Leopard V: An Island of Sound*, p. xxiv.
140. Heaney, *North*, pp. 57-61.

CHAPTER 5: **'A whole life external':** *Blind Field* (pp. 109-33)

141. Szirtes' poems addressing Arbus' photographs have been reproduced in a recent undergraduate textbook on photography and critical theory. See Ashley la Grange, *Basic Critical Theory for Photographers* (London: Focal Press, 2005), pp. 189-92.
142. Martha Rosler, 'In, Around and Afterthoughts (On Documentary Photography)', in Richard Bolton (editor), *The Contest of Meaning* (Cambridge, MA: MIT Press, 1990), p. 307.
143. Szirtes, 'Preface' to *The Budapest File*, p. 14.
144. Anne Marsh, *The Darkroom: Photography and the Theatre of Desire* (Basingstoke: Macmillan, 2003), p. 218.
145. Murphy, *Poetry in Exile*, p. 175.
146. See Murphy, *Poetry in Exile*, p. 162 ff; Sontag is cited on p. 174.

147. Roland Barthes, *Camera Lucida*, translated by Richard Howard (London: Flamingo, 1984), pp. 45-57.

148. Roland Barthes, *S/Z*, translated by Richard Miller (London: Jonathan Cape, 1975), p. 5.

149. Roland Barthes, *S/Z*, pp. 26, 27.

150. James Heffernan, 'Ekphrasis and Representation', *New Literary History*, 22, No. 2 (Spring 1991), pp. 297-316; p. 299.

151. Szirtes, 'Preface' to *The Budapest File*, p. 14.

152. Szirtes, 'Preface' to *The Budapest File*, p. 14.

153. W. H. Auden, *Collected Poems*, edited by Edward Mendelson (London: Faber & Faber, 1976), p. 427.

154. Paul Dermée, 'Brother Seeing-Eye', *André Kertész: Sixty Years of Photography* (London: Thames & Hudson, 1972), p. 5.

CHAPTER 6: **'Ghost in a photograph'**: *Portrait of My Father in an English Landscape* (pp. 134-60)

155. Szirtes, 'Preface' to *The Budapest File*, pp. 14.

156. Szirtes, 'Preface' to *The Budapest File*, p. 13.

157. Michael Glover, *New Statesman*, 24 April 1998.

158. Szirtes, 'Preface' to *The Budapest File*, p. 15.

159. www.georgeszirtes.co.uk/dynamic/articles/IntroductionPortrait.doc

160. The poem was published in *Poetry Review*, Vol. 81 No. 3 (Autumn 1991), p. 34.

161. Wallace Stevens, *The Collected Poems of Wallace Stevens* (London: Faber & Faber, 1984), pp. 128-30.

162. Murphy, *Poetry in Exile*, p. 193.

163. Hélène Cixous, *Readings: The Poetics of Blanchot, Joyce, Kafka, Kleist, Lispector and Tsvetayeva*, translated by Andermatt Conley (Minneapolis: University of Minnesota Press, 1991), p. 95. Cixous is discussing Maurice Blanchot's *The Madness of the Day*.

164. Walter Benjamin, 'The Storyteller', in *Illuminations*, pp. 83-107, especially part XIII, pp. 96-97.

165. Fredric Jameson, *The Political Unconscious: Narrative as Socially Symbolic Act* (Ithaca: Cornell University Press, 1981), p. 102.

166. Benjamin, 'The Storyteller', p. 90.

167. Benjamin, 'The Storyteller', p. 90.

CHAPTER 7: **'Imposing order'**: *An English Apocalypse* and *Reel* (pp. 161-86)

168. Hoffman, *Lost in Translation*, p. 134.

169. A health supplement popular in England in the 1950s, which 'fortifies the over-40s'.

170. W.G. Sebald, *The Rings of Saturn*, translated by Michael Hulse (London: The Harvill Press 1998), p. 3.

171. Michael Mackmin (ed.), *The Rialto*, 51 (Norwich: Rialto, 2002).

172. J.J. Long and Anne Whitehead (editors), *W.G. Sebald: A Critical Companion* (Edinburgh: Edinburgh UP, 2004), p. 9. The poem is reproduced on pp. 16-22.

173. Jon Stallworthy (editor), *The Poems of Wilfred Owen* (London: The Hogarth Press, 1985), p. 125. The editor cites Keats' 'The Fall of Hyperion' as a source for Owen's description.

174. W.G. Sebald, *Austerlitz* (London: Penguin, 2002), pp. 73-74.

175. Maurice Blanchot, 'The Song of the Sirens', in *The Station Hill Blanchot Reader* (Barrytown: Station Hill, 1999), p. 443.

176. http://www.georgeszirtes.co.uk/index.php?page=newsarchive

177. Szirtes, 'Preface' to *The Budapest File*, p. 12.

178. Edward Said, *Culture and Imperialism* (London: Vintage, 1994), p. 403.

179. Paul Gilroy, *The Black Atlantic: Modernity and Double Consciousness* (London: Verso, 1993), p. 111.

180. Said, *Culture and Imperialism*, p. 403.

181. Elleke Boehmer, *Colonial and Post-Colonial Literature: Migrant Metaphors* (Oxford: Oxford UP, 2005).

182. Said, *Culture and Imperialism*, p. 406.

CHAPTER 8: **New poems** (pp. 187-215)

183. Clair Wills, *Reading Paul Muldoon* (Newcastle upon Tyne: Bloodaxe Books, 1998), p. 216.

184. Szirtes, 'Introduction' to Nemes Nagy, *The Night of Akhenaton*, p. 14.

185. Szirtes, 'Introduction' to Orbán, *The Blood of the Walsungs*, p. 13.

186. Szirtes, 'Introduction' to Zsuzsa Rakovszky, *New Life* (Oxford: Oxford UP, 1994), p. viii.

187. Szirtes, 'Russian Beats', *Poetry Review*, Vol. 78 No. 1 (Spring 1988), p. 24.

188. Geoffrey Hill, 'Poetry as "Menace" and "Atonement"', in *The Lords of Limit: Essays on Literature and Ideas* (London: André Deutsch, 1984), p. 3.

189. Tony Harrison, 'The Rhubarbarians' II, in *Selected Poems* (Harmondsworth: Penguin, 1987), p. 114.

190. Szirtes, 'The Late Flight of Georges Braque', *Pretext* (Spring / Summer 2003), p. 116.

191. George Steiner, *After Babel: Aspects of Language and Translation* (Oxford: Oxford UP, 1975), p. 471.

192. Szirtes, 'Translating Zsuzsa Rakovszky'.

193. Szirtes, 'The Last Flight of Georges Braque', pp. 111-19; p. 115.

194. Szirtes, 'The Last Flight of Georges Braque', p. 116.

195. Szirtes, 'The Last Flight of Georges Braque', pp. 116-17.

196. Szirtes, 'The Last Flight of Georges Braque', p. 119.

197. Virginia Woolf, Mrs Dalloway (Harmondsworth: Penguin 1974), p. 5.

198. Tony Harrison, *Selected Poems* (London: Penguin 2006), p. 155.

199. James Joyce, *Ulysses* (Harmondsworth: Penguin 1986), p. 28.

200. W.S. Milne, *An Introduction to Geoffrey Hill* (London: Agenda/ Bellew, 1998), p. 148.

201. Sean O'Brien, review of *Reel* in *Poetry London*, 50 (Spring 2005).

202. Julia Kristeva, 'Holbein's Dead Christ', in *Black Sun: Depression and Melancholia*, translated by Leon S. Roudiez (New York: Columbia UP, 1989), p. 110.

203. Wallace Stevens, 'The Snow Man', in *The Collected Poems of Wallace Stevens*, p. 9.

Selected Bibliography

Works by George Szirtes

POETRY VOLUMES AND SELECTED PAMPHLETS

The Iron Clouds (Hitchin: The Dodman Press, 1975).
The Slant Door (London: Secker & Warburg, 1977).
November and May (London: Secker & Warburg, 1981).
Short Wave (London: Secker & Warburg, 1983).
The Photographer in Winter (London: Secker & Warburg, 1986).
Metro (Oxford: Oxford University Press, 1988).
Bridge Passages (Oxford: Oxford University Press, 1991).
Blind Field (Oxford: Oxford University Press, 1994).
Selected Poems 1976–1996 (Oxford: Oxford University Press, 1996).
Portrait of My Father in an English Landscape (Oxford: Oxford University Press, 1998).
The Budapest File (Tarset: Bloodaxe Books, 2000).
An English Apocalypse (Tarset: Bloodaxe Books, 2001).
Reel (Tarset: Bloodaxe Books, 2004).
New & Collected Poems (Tarset: Bloodaxe Books, 2008).
The Burning of the Books (Chichester: Circle Press, 2008)
The Burning of the Books and other poems (Tarset: Bloodaxe Books, 2009)

RECORDINGS

The Poetry Quartets 6: Exiles (with Moniza Alvi, Michael Donaghy and Anne Stevenson), audio cassette recording (Tarset: Bloodaxe Books/ The British Council, 2000).
George Szirtes reading from his poems, audio CD recording (Stroud, Gloucestershire: The Poetry Archive, 2006)
In Person: 30 Poets, filmed by Pamela Robertson-Pearce, edited by Neil Astley, filmed reading by George Szirtes (with other poets) on DVD (Tarset: Bloodaxe Books, 2008).

AS EDITOR AND TRANSLATOR

The Colonnade of Teeth: Modern Hungarian Poetry, edited by George Gömöri & George Szirtes (with some translations by George Szirtes) (Newcastle upon Tyne: Bloodaxe Books, 1996).
Leopard V: An Island of Sound: Hungarian Poetry and Fiction Before and Beyond the Iron Curtain, edited and with an introduction by George Szirtes (London: Harvill, 2004).
Dezsö Kosztolányi, *Anna Édes*, translated with an introduction by George Szirtes (Budapest: Corvina Books and London: Quartet Books, 1991).

László Krasznahorkai, *The Melancholy of Resistance*, translated by George Szirtes (New York: New Directions, 2002).

László Krasznahorkai, *War and War*, translated by George Szirtes (New York: New Directions, 2005).

Imre Madách, *The Tragedy of Man*, translated by George Szirtes (Budapest: Corvina 1988).

Sándor Márai, *Conversations in Bolzano*, translated by George Szirtes (London: Penguin 2004).

Sándor Márai, *The Rebels*, translated by George Szirtes (London: Picador 2007).

Ágnes Nemes Nagy, *The Night of Akhenaton: Selected Poems*, translated and with an introduction by George Szirtes (Tarset: Bloodaxe Books, 2004).

Ottó Orbán, *The Blood of the Walsungs: Selected Poems*, edited (and with some translations) by George Szirtes (Newcastle upon Tyne: Bloodaxe Books; Budapest: Corvina Books, 1993).

Zsuzsa Rakovsky, *New Life*, translated and with an introduction by George Szirtes (Oxford: Oxford University Press, 1994).

INTERVIEWS

'Hungarian Roots, English Traditions', interview with András Gerevich et al, *Hungarian Quarterly*, Vol. XLII No. 164 (Winter 2001).

'Wrestling with Englishness: A life in writing', interview with James Hopkins, *The Guardian*, 27 October 2001, p. 11.

John Tusa, Interview with George Szirtes, BBC Radio 3. Transcript at http://www.bbc.co.uk/radio3/johntusainterview/szirtes_transcript.shtml

Lidia Vianu, Interview with George Szirtes, available at http://www.lidiavianu.go.ro/george_szirtes.htm

ESSAYS, FOREWORDS, PREFACES, INTRODUCTIONS AND REVIEWS

'Lost in Translation' (review of Jaroslav Seifert's *Selected Poetry*), *Poetry Review*, Vol. 76 No. 3 (October 1986), p. 59.

'A Natural Elegist' (review of Douglas Dunn's *Selected Poems*), *Poetry Review*, Vol. 76 No. 4 (December 1986), pp. 50-51.

'Russian Beats', *Poetry Review*, Vol. 78 No. 1 (Spring 1988), pp. 24-25.

'The Muse of Absolute Zero' (review of Joseph Brodsky's *To Urania*), *Poetry Review*, Vol. 78 No. 4 (Winter 1988-89), pp. 40-2.

'The Leeds Lamentations' (review of Martin Bell's *Complete Poems*), *Poetry Review*, Vol. 79 No. 1 (Spring 1989), p. 41.

'The March Marches: A Progress Report from Budapest', *Poetry Review*, Vol. 79 No. 3 (Autumn 1989).

'The Underground in the Underground', BBC Radio 4, broadcast 28 November 1989.

'Learning from Brezhnev', *Poetry Review*, Vol. 81 No. 3 (Autumn 1991), pp. 20-22.

'Belgravia to Belgrade' (review of A. Alvarez [ed.], *The Faber Book of Modern European Poetry*), *Poetry Review*, Vol. 83 No. 2 (Summer 1993), p. 21.

'Paper Wars: Bosnia and Public Poetry', debate with Ken Smith, *Poetry Review*, Vol. 83 No. 4 (Winter 1993-94), pp. 44-45.

'Out for the Elements', *Poetry Review*, Vol. 86 No. 1 (Spring 1996), pp. 58-59.

'Budapest Diaries', *Hungarian Quarterly*, Vol. XXXVIII No. 146 (Summer 1997).

'Translating Zsuzsa Rakovszky', *Hungarian Quarterly*, Vol. XXXIX No. 150 (Summer 1998), available at http://www.hungarianquarterly.com/no150/031.html

'The Visible City' (review of Géza Buzinkay, *An Illustrated History of Budapest*), *Hungarian Quarterly*, Vol. XXXIX No. 152 (Winter 1998).

'Two Anecdotes of Miroslav Holub', *Poetry Review*, Vol. 88 No. 4 (Winter 1998-89), pp. 58-9.

'Outsize' (review of Ottó Orbán, *The Journey of Barbarus*), *Hungarian Quarterly*, Vol. XL No. 156 (Winter 1999).

'Delivering Dante: Literature in the Art of Sandy Sykes', *Modern Painters*, Winter 1999, pp. 94-96.

'Human Nails: Ana Maria Pacheco at the National Gallery', *Modern Painters*, Autumn 1999, pp. 41-5.

'Great Expectations' (review of translations of Attila József), *Hungarian Quarterly*, Vol. XLI No. 158 (Summer 2000).

'Preface' to Sándor Kányádi, *There is a Land: Selected Poems*, translated by Peter Zollman (Budapest: Corvina, 2000).

'Introduction' to Miklós Radnóti, *Camp Notebook*, translated by Francis R. Jones (Todmorden: Arc Publications, 2000).

'Hungary's Secrets' (review of Attila József's *The Iron-Blue Vault*), *Poetry Review*, Vol. 90 No. 4 (Winter 2000-01), pp. 83-84.

'The candle that burned right down', *The Guardian*, 15 December 2001, p. 13.

'Superb Poems Superbly Translated' (review of Attila József, *Sixty Poems*), *Hungarian Quarterly*, Vol. XLIII No. 165 Spring 2002.

'New World Lines' (review of poetry by C.K. Stead and others), *Poetry Review*, Vol. 92 No. 1 (Spring 2002), pp. 89-91.

'Within, Beyond and Under: Remembering Ottó Orbán', *Hungarian Quarterly*, Vol. XLIII No. 166 (Summer 2002).

'The Late Flight of Georges Braque', *Pretext*, Spring/Summer 2003, pp. 111-9.

'Foreword' to Sándor Petőfi, *John the Valiant*, translated by John Ridland (London: Hesperus Press, 2004).

'Tectonic Elegance', *London Magazine*, April-May 2004, pp. 105-08.

'The crystal maze', *The Guardian*, 15 May 2004, p. 37.

'The business of being', *The Guardian*, 7 May 2005, p. 25.

'The Sweet Dance', *Poetry Review*, Vol. 95 No. 3 (Autumn 2005), pp. 94–97.

'Thin Ice and The Midnight Skaters', T.S. Eliot Lecture, *The Guardian*, 23 November 2005.

'Foreign Laughter', *Hungarian Quarterly*, Vol. XLVI No. 180 (Winter 2005), available at http://www.hungarianquarterly.com/no180/15.html

Review of Jan Mladovsky, available at http://www.georgeszirtes.co.uk/index.php?page=articles

'Invisible Cities: Budapest', radio broadcast; transcript available at http://www.georgeszirtes.co.uk/index.php?page=articles

'The sweetest sound of all', *The Guardian*, 21 November 2005, p. 29.

'Book of a lifetime: A Secret and Subversive pleasure – *The Waste Land*, *The Independent*, 25 February 2005, p. 33.

'Formal Wear: Notes on Rhyme, Metre, Stanza & Pattern', *Poetry*, Vol. 187 No. 5 (February 2006), pp. 416-25.

Reviews of work by George Szirtes

Dalya Alberge, 'Hungarian-born writer wins prize that poets most covet', *The Times*, 18 January 2004, p. 14.

Fred Beake, 'Generations of recent poetry', *Stand*, Vol. 32 No. 2 (Spring 1991), pp. 49-56.

Paul Farley, 'A world of memory' (review of *Reel*), *The Guardian*, 5 February 2005, p. 25.

Tibor Fischer, 'Budapest boom' (review of *Leopard V: An Island of Sound*), The Guardian, 1 May 2004, p. 27.

Michael Glover, 'Chapter and verse – something old, something new', (review of *The Budapest File*), *Financial Times*, 16 December 2000, p. 4.

Michael Glover, review, *New Statesman*, 24 April 1998.

John Greening, 'Bit Parts in the Epic', *Poetry Review*, Vol. 88 No. 3 (Autumn 1988), p. 67.

Daniel Hoffman, 'Poetry not lost in translation' (review of Ottó Orbán, *The Blood of the Walsungs*), *Hungarian Quarterly*, Vol. XXXVII No. 142 (Summer 1996).

Sylvia Kantaris, 'Pleasuring the Pain', *Poetry Review*, Vol. 81 No. 2 (Summer 1991), p. 70.

Hugh Macpherson, 'Hungary and History' (review of *The Budapest File*), *Poetry Review*, Vol. 91 No. 2 (Summer 2001), pp. 101-02.

Alan Marshall, 'Forgive this garrulousness' (review of *The Budapest File*), Daily Telegraph, November 16th 2000.

Michael Murphy, 'Some Hope' (review of *Reel*), *Poetry Review*, Vol. 94 No. 4 (Winter 2004-05), pp. 79-80.

Sean O'Brien, 'Big Questions', *Poetry Review*, Vol. 78 No. 3 (Autumn 1986), pp. 56-8.

Sean O'Brien, 'Poems of Wintry Futility, a Chill Atmosphere and Learning about Autumn' (review of *Reel*), Poetry London 50, available at http://www.poetrylondon.co.uk/index.htm?reviews/issue50.html

Rodney Pybus, 'New Poetry', *Stand*, Vol. 26 No. 3 (Summer 1985), pp. 62-69.

Lawrence Sail, 'Recent verse', *Stand*, Vol. 28 No. 3 (Summer 1987), pp. 75-77.

William Scammell, 'Poetry in brief' (review of *Selected Poems 1976-1996*), *The Independent on Sunday*, 2 June 1996, p. 34.

Anne Stevenson, 'Grudging Lyrical Earth' (review of *Selected Poems 1976-1996*), *Poetry Review*, Vol. 86 No. 3 (Autumn 1996), p. 70.

Boyd Tonkin, review of *Leopard V: An Island of Sound*, *The Independent*, 30 April 2005.

John Whitworth, 'A Webster Among the Ruins' (review of *Blind Field*), *Poetry Review*, Vol. 85 No. 2 (Summer 1995), pp. 54-55.

Clive Wilmer, review of Zsuzsa Rakovszky's *New Life*, *Poetry Review*, Vol. 85 No. 2 (Summer 1995), pp. 58-59.

Other works cited

A. Alvarez, 'The New Poetry, or Beyond the Gentility Principle', Introduction to *The New Poetry* (Harmondsworth: Penguin, 1962).

Willi Apel, *Harvard Dictionary of Music* (London: Heinemann, 1970).

Timothy Garton Ash, *We The People: The Revolutions of '89 Witnessed in Warsaw, Budapest, Berlin & Prague* (Harmondsworth; Penguin, 1990).

W.H. Auden, *The Dyer's Hand* (London: Faber & Faber, 1963).

W.H. Auden, *Collected Poems*, edited by Edward Mendelson (London: Faber & Faber, 1976).

Marc Augé, *In the Metro*, translated by Tom Conley (Minneapolis: University of Minnesota Press 2002).

Roland Barthes, *S/Z*, translated by Richard Miller (London: Jonathan Cape, 1975).

Roland Barthes, *Camera Lucida*, translated by Richard Howard (London: Flamingo, 1984).

Martin Bell, *Complete Poems*, edited by Peter Porter (Newcastle upon Tyne: Bloodaxe Books, 1988).

Walter Benjamin, *Illuminations*, edited by Hannah Arendt (London: Fontana, 1992).

Maurice Blanchot, *The Station Hill Blanchot Reader*, edited by George Quasha et al (Barrytown: Station Hill, 1999).

Elleke Boehmer, *Colonial and Post-Colonial Literature: Migrant Metaphors* (Oxford: Oxford University Press, 2005).

Eavan Boland, *Object Lessons* (Manchester: Carcanet, 1995).

Martin Booth, *British Poetry 1964-84: Driving Through the Barricades* (London: Routledge & Kegan Paul, 1985).

William M. Brinton & Alan Rinzler, 'Introduction' to *Without Force or Lies: Voices from the Revolution of Central Europe in 1989-90* (San Francisco: Mercury House, 1990).

Stephen Brook, *The Double Eagle: Vienna, Budapest, Prague* (London: Picador, 1989).

Alan Brownjohn, *Collected Poems* (London: Enitharmon, 2006).

Anthony Burgess, *A Clockwork Orange* (Harmondsworth: Penguin, 1961).

Karel Capek, *R.U.R.: Rossum's Universal Robots* (Harmondsworth: Penguin, 2004).

Angela Carter, *The Infernal Desire Machines of Doctor Hoffman* (London: Rupert Hart-Davis / Granada Publishing, 1972).

Angela Carter, *Wise Children* (London: Chatto & Windus, 1991).

Jean-Pierre Cauvin and Mary Ann Caws (editors and translators), *Poems of André Breton* (Austin: University of Texas Press, 1982).

Anatoly Chernyaev, cited in Document 6, National Security Archive Declassified Material available at http://www.gwu.edu/~nsarchiv/news/19991105/index.html

Hélène Cixous, *Readings: The Poetics of Blanchot, Joyce, Kafka, Kleist, Lispector and Tsvetayeva*, translated by Andermatt Conley (Minneapolis: University of Minnesota Press, 1991).

Neil Corcoran, *English Poetry Since 1940* (London: Longman, 1993).

Simon Critchley, *Very Little...Almost Nothing: Death, Philosophy, Literature*, revised edition, (London: Routledge, 2004).

Simon Critchley, *Things Merely Are: Philosophy in the Poetry of Wallace Stevens* (London: Routledge, 2005).

Adam Czerniawski, 'Contained in the Order of an English Landscape', *Poetry Review*, Vol. 81 No. 3 (Autumn 1991), p. 34.

Paul Dermée, 'Brother Seeing-Eye', *André Kertész: Sixty Years of Photography* (London: Thames & Hudson, 1972).

Slavenka Drakulic, *Café Europa: Life after Communism* (London: Abacus, 1996).

Nicholas Ducrot (editor), *André Kertész: Sixty Years of Photography* (London: Thames & Hudson, 1972).

T.S. Eliot, *The Complete Poems and Plays* (London: Faber & Faber, 1984).

Hans Magnus Enzensberger, *Europe, Europe: Forays into a Continent*, translated by Martin Chalmers (New York: Random House, 1989).

Hans Magnus Enzensberger, untitled essay, *Granta 30: New Europe!* (Winter 1990), pp. 136-42.

Richard S. Esbenshade, 'Remembering to Forget: Memory, History, National Identity in Post-War East-Central Europe', *Representations*, No. 49 (Winter 1995), pp. 72-96.

James Fenton, *The Memory of War and Children in Exile: Poems 1968-83* (Harmondsworth: Penguin, 1983).

John Fuller, *Epistles to Several Persons* (London: Secker & Warburg, 1973).

John Fuller, *Collected Poems* (London: Secker & Warburg, 1996).

Paul Gilroy, *The Black Atlantic: Modernity and Double Consciousness* (London: Verso 1993).

Misha Glenny, *The Rebirth of History: Eastern Europe in the Age of Democracy* (Harmondsworth: Penguin, 1990).

Ashley la Grange, *Basic Critical Theory for Photographers* (Oxford: Focal Press, 2005).

Granta 30: New Europe! (Winter 1990).

Geoffrey Grigson, *The Private Art: A Poetry Notebook* (London: Allison & Busby, 1982).

John Haffenden (editor), *Viewpoints: Poets in Conversation with John Haffenden* (London: Faber & Faber, 1981).

John Haffenden (editor), *Selected Letters of William Empson* (Oxford: Oxford University Press, 2006).

Fred Halliday, 'The Ends of Cold War', *New Left Review*, 180 (March / April 1990), pp. 5-23.

Tony Harrison, *Selected Poems* (London: Penguin, 2006).

Seamus Heaney, interviewed by Harriet Cooke, *The Irish Times*, 28 December 1973.

Seamus Heaney, *The Government of the Tongue* (London: Faber & Faber, 1988).

Anthony Hecht, *Collected Earlier Poems* (Oxford: Oxford University Press, 1990).

James Heffernan, 'Ekphrasis and Representation', *New Literary History*, 22, No. 2 (Spring 1991), pp. 297-316.

Martin Heidegger, 'Building, Dwelling, Thinking', in *Basic Writings*, revised and expanded edition (edited by David Farrell Krell) (London: Routledge, 1993), pp. 343-64.

Geoffrey Hill, *The Lords of Limit: Essays on Literature and Ideas* (London: André Deutsch, 1984).

Geoffrey Hill, *Collected Poems* (Harmondsworth: Penguin, 1985).

Geoffrey Hill, 'Of Diligence and Jeopardy', *The Times Literary Supplement*, 17 November 1989; reprinted in *Style and Faith* (New York: Counterpoint, 2003).

Marianne Hirsch, *Family Frames: Photography, Narrative and Postmemory* (Cambridge, MA. & London: Harvard University Press, 1997).

Eva Hoffman, *Lost in Translation* (London: Minerva, 1991).

Miroslav Holub, *The Dimension of the Present Moment*, edited by David Young (London: Faber & Faber, 1990).

Ted Hughes, *The Hawk in the Rain* (London: Faber & Faber, 1957).

Ted Hughes, *Lupercal* (London: Faber & Faber, 1960).

Raphaël Ingelbien, *Misreading England: Poetry and Nationhood Since the Second World War* (Amsterdam: Rodopi, 2002).

Christopher Isherwood, *The Berlin Novels: Mr Norris Changes Trains &* *Goodbye to Berlin* (London: Vintage, 2004).

Fredric Jameson, *The Political Unconscious: Narrative as Socially Symbolic Act* (Ithaca: Cornell University Press, 1981).

James Joyce, Ulysses (Harmondsworth: Penguin 1996).

Mary Kaldor, 'After the Cold War', *New Left Review*, 180 (March/April 1990), pp. 25-37.

Julia Kristeva, *Black Sun: Depression and Melancholia*, translated by Leon S. Roudiez (New York: Columbia University Press, 1989).

Julia Kristeva, *Strangers to Ourselves*, translated by Leon Roudiez (New York: Columbia University Press, 1999).

Peter McDonald, *Serious Poetry: Form and Authority from Yeats to Hill* (Oxford: Oxford University Press, 2002).

George MacBeth, *Collected Poems 1958-1982* (London: Hutchinson, 1989).

Derek Mahon, *Night Crossing* (Oxford: Oxford University Press, 1968).

Derek Mahon, *The Snow Party* (Oxford: Oxford University Press, 1975).

Michael March (editor), *Child of Europe: A New Anthology of East European Poetry* (Harmondsworth: Penguin, 1990).

Anne Marsh, *The Darkroom: Photography and the Theatre of Desire* (Melbourne: Macmillan, 2003).

W.S. Milne, *An Introduction to Geoffrey Hill* (London: Agenda/Bellew, 1998).

Michael Murphy, *Poetry in Exile: A Study of the Poetry of W.H. Auden, Joseph Brodsky and George Szirtes* (London: Greenwich Exchange, 2004).

Peter Nicholls, *Modernisms: A Literary Guide* (Basingstoke: Macmillan, 1995).

George Orwell, *1984* (Harmondsworth: Penguin, 1970).

Peter Porter, *Preaching to the Converted* (Oxford: Oxford University Press, 1972).

Peter Porter, *Living in a Calm Country* (Oxford: Oxford University Press, 1975).

Peter Porter, *The Cost of Seriousness* (Oxford: Oxford University Press, 1978).

Peter Porter, *Collected Poems* (Oxford: Oxford University Press, 1983).

Peter Porter, 'Introduction, Memoir and Critical Note', in Martin Bell, *Complete Poems* (Newcastle upon Tyne: Bloodaxe Books, 1988).

Jonathan Raban, The Society of the Poem (London: Harrap, 1971).

Peter Robinson, *Entertaining Fates* (Manchester: Carcanet, 1992).

Nicholas Royle, *The Uncanny* (Manchester: Manchester University Press, 2003).

Penguin Modern Poets 14: Alan Brownjohn, Michael Hamburger, Charles Tomlinson (Harmondsworth: Penguin, 1969).

Ezra Pound, *Selected Poems* (London: Faber & Faber, 1933).

Miklós Radnóti, *Forced March*, edited and translated by Clive Wilmer and George Gömöri (London: Enitharmon Press 2003).

Christopher Ricks, *The Force of Poetry* (Oxford: Oxford University Press, 1987).

Christopher Ricks, *Allusion to the Poets* (Oxford: Oxford University Press, 2004).

Martha Rosler, 'In, Around and Afterthoughts (On Documentary Photography)', in Richard Bolton, editor, *The Contest of Meaning* (Cambridge, MA: MIT Press 1990).

Antony Rowland, *Holocaust Poetry* (Manchester: Manchester University Press, 2005).

Tadeusz Rózewicz, 'Humanity's Footprint', translated by Adam Czerniawski, *Granta 30: New Europe!* (Winter 1990).

Edward Said, *Culture and Imperialism* (London: Vintage, 1995).

John Sears, 'George Szirtes' Meetings with 'Austerlitz'', *The Anachronist*, 11 (2005).

John Sears, "God's Scattered Text': Wordscape and Escape in George Szirtes' *Portrait of My Father in an English Landscape*', in Paul Volsik & Abigail Lang (editors), *Scapes: Cahiers Charles V* (Paris: Université Paris Diderot, 2006).

W.G. Sebald, *Austerlitz*, translated by Anthea Bell (London: Penguin, 2002).

Jon Silkin (editor), *The Penguin Book of First World War Poetry* (Harmondsworth: Penguin 1979).

Iain Sinclair, *Edge of the Orizon* (London: Hutchinson, 2005).

Jon Stallworthy, *The Poems of Wilfred Owen* (London: The Hogarth Press, 1985).

Wallace Stevens, *The Collected Poems of Wallace Stevens* (London: Faber & Faber, 1984).

George Steiner, *After Babel: Aspects of Language and Translation* (Oxford: Oxford University Press, 1975).

George Steiner, untitled essay, *Granta 30: New Europe!* (Winter 1990), pp. 129-32.

Gale Stokes, *The Walls Came Tumbling Down: The Collapse of Communism in Eastern Europe* (Oxford: Oxford University Press, 1993).

Anthony Thwaite, *Poetry Today: A Critical Guide to British Poetry 1960–1984* (London: Longman 1985; revised edition, 1995).

István Turczi (editor), *At the End of the Broken Bridge: XXV Hungarian Poems 1978-2002* (Edinburgh: Scottish Poetry Library, 2005).

Ildiko Vasary, 'Comrades, It's over! The Election Campaign in Hungary 1990', *Anthropology Today*, Vol. 7 No 4 (August 1991), pp. 3-6.

Daniel Weissbort (editor), *Modern Poetry in Translation*, 15: 'European Voices' (London: King's College London, 2001).

Clive Wilmer, *Poets Talking: Poet of the Month Interviews from BBC Radio 3* (Manchester: Carcanet, 1994).

Virginia Woolf, *Mrs Dalloway* (London: Penguin 2000).

Websites

http://www.georgeszirtes.co.uk
http://www.hungarianquarterly.com/no150/031.html
http://www.timesonline.co.uk/tol/incomingFeeds/article683213.ece
http://thedublinreview.com/archive/five/szirtes.html
http://www.georgeszirtes.co.uk/dynamic/articles/IntroductionPortrait.doc

INDEX